D0463663

THE SENSATE CULTURE

by Harold O. J. Brown

WORD PUBLISHING
Dallas•London•Vancouver•Melbourne

All material from *The Crisis of Our Age* 2d ed. by Pitirim Sorokin is used by
permission of Oneworld Publications, Copyright 1992, all rights reserved.

All Scripture quotations in this book, except those noted otherwise,
are from the *New American Standard Bible* © 1960, 1962, 1963, 1971, 1972,
1973, 1975, and 1977 by the Lockman Foundation, and are used
by permission.

Other Scripture quotations are from the following sources:
The *New International Version* of the Bible (NIV), copyright © 1983
by the International Bible Society. Used by permission of
Zondervan Bible Publishers.
The *King James Version* of the Bible (KJV).

Project Editor: Terri Gibbs

Brown, Harold O. J., 1933–
    The sensate culture / by Harold O. J. Brown.
    p.   cm.
    Includes bibliographical references and index.
    ISBN 0-8499-1313-6 (alk. paper)
    1. Culture.   2. Civilization, Modern.   3. Sorokin, Pitirim
    Aleksandrovich, 1889–1968.   I. Title.
HM101.B777   1996   96-24595
306–dc20   CIP

Printed and bound in the United States of America

6 7 8 9 BVG 9 8 7 6 5 4 3 2 1

Uxori meae dilectissimae

CONTENTS

ACKNOWLEDGMENTS

AS AN UNDERGRADUATE AND GRADUATE STUDENT in theology, I was vaguely aware of the presence on campus of one of the great thinkers of our age; his son Sergei was a classmate and an acquaintance. Unfortunately, like many students, I failed to take advantage of the opportunity to study with the man himself, although I did hear Pitirim Sorokin lecture and preach in Harvard's Appleton Chapel and did read two of his books. During an illness in 1990, half a century after it was first published, I read *The Crisis of Our Age* again and was struck both by Sorokin's incredibly accurate judgments and prophecies and by the note of hope that distinguishes his work from that of so many futurologists and would-be prophets. The following year I was able to take part in a scholars' conference on Sorokin's work organized by the Liberty Fund of Indianapolis, and conceived the idea of attempting to redo his *Crisis* for the end of our millennium and to bring in a more consciously Christian approach both the end-phase of our present culture and to the prospects for its renewal rather than its collapse. Trinity Evangelical Divinity School, under the leadership of its then Dean, Walter C. Kaiser, Jr., offered me a sabbatical and a leave of absence to work on the project, and the Rockford Institute, directed by Allan C. Carlson, secured substantial funding for me, without which it would have been impossible to carry the task to conclusion. I am grateful to thinkers such as Professors Milton Rosenberg of the University of Chicago, Hans Millendorfer of Studia Austria, and Sergei P. Sorokin of Boston University Medical School for advice and encouragement; to my assistants Eric Carlsson, Brian Dean, Hugh Hughes, and John Lierman and my secretaries Matilda Hunsicker and Stacey Guzzardo for work, correction, and encouragement; and above all to my wife Grace, whose love, support, and patience have helped me through the task itself and through the adversity of a serious mountaineering accident that threatened to interrupt it. Any errors and omissions it contains are my own.

Harold O. J. Brown

PREFACE

AS WE TRY TO FACE what's going to be happening at the end of the second millennium, we are bombarded with all manner of predictions, prophecies, and prognostications. These inspire in some religious and other concerned leaders a future shock, in the form of cold terror. That but intensifies the angst or "past shock" that may already have accumulated in the minds of those who have seen a good bit of the twentieth century's horrors—spectacular dictatorships, world wars, the Bomb, genocide and, in the nineties, the growing normalization of abortion, euthanasia, and homosexuality. But there are others who see this past as (with a few dreadful gaps) progress. They discover that, indeed, in these new normalizations, and they manifest a kind of relentless cheer as they point to the beauties of an antiseptically secularist order that science and education will form and guide.

Enter Harold O. J. Brown, with his long and unmatched background of familiarity with the world scene. This he couples with a perspective that can meaningfully address mankind's hopes and fears with far better judgment than the popularizers of pessimism or the secularist optimists. What follows in these pages is both a survey and a testament. The survey, the reader will see, runs throughout the book. We are soon presented the full meaning of its title as Dr. Brown graphically particularizes the crisis of our "sensate culture." He shows a crisis that is both universal and systemic—in the arts, law, religion, philosophy, medicine, the media, our whole social fabric. I confess to have found this particularizing—written without appeal to sensation—breathtaking.

The crisis, we see, is nothing so simple as another Great Depression or another Cold War. In bodily terms it is not comparable to a bad fracture or other isolated injury; cancer is more like what Brown sees. But if that analogy holds, he does not see it as terminal, *necessarily*. It is here that the other great point of his book takes over—what I call his testament, or the Christian convictions he applies to the scene he surveys. Hence, in his last chapter, he asks us whether our Western civilization, in its "exhausted and degenerate state," is not at an end, "'one with Nineveh and Tyre,' those vanished cities of history and legend." With wit and welcome asperity he denigrates the nostrums now being promoted as helpful to our society (e.g., enforced cultural diversity).

Yet our author does not leave things at that. Instead he asks whether, out of our present depths, we can find any reason for hope. Here he finds inspiration in Pitirim Sorokin, the eminent Russian expatriate sociologist who in 1941 addressed the crisis of Sorokin's own tormented time. As one whom we may properly call our age's successor to Sorokin, Brown turns to the same well-spring from which Sorokin drank hope: the "grace of understanding." God's grace, our understanding of his purposes for his creatures as taught by Christ, our comprehension also of the world in light of that understanding, in these must be our hope and in this is the only certainty. The author convincingly leads us to this.

William Bentley Ball
April 1996

| INTRODUCTION

THE DESIRE TO KNOW THE FUTURE is as old as the human race itself. But how can we possibly know what the future holds? Some believe the study of history tells us what we can expect of the future. As we observe the development of societies in the past, if we detect similar trends in our own day, we may expect similar consequences. Others contend that history is not a useful guide because our *modern* or *postmodern* culture is so different from past cultures that the regularities and causalities that we see in the past have little relevance for us today. Many believe that only an understanding of what technology has accomplished and where it is headed will enable us to make accurate predictions of what lies before us.

Some writers of fiction have tried to imagine what the future will be like, usually by extrapolating from trends that are already visible in society. The more scholarly and scientific members of this tribe are called "futurologists," and some of them are so convincing that businesses and governments base important decisions on their predictions.

What most of these attempts to predict the future have in common is a pronounced pessimism. Among the writers in the genre of future prediction, two of the most famous—Aldous Huxley, *Brave New World,* and George Orwell, *Nineteen Eighty-Four*—predict a bleak and dismal future for mankind. There are some futurologists who are more hopeful—such as Alvin Toffler, *Future Shock* and *The Third Wave,* and Charles Reich, *The Greening of America*—but futurologists as a whole are a melancholy lot and do not see much that is encouraging or hope-inspiring in the future of this earth. Paul Ehrlich, *The Population Bomb,* and the Club of Rome, *The Limits of Growth,* predict an increasingly crowded world with growing poverty, loss of freedom, and hopelessness. Demographer Pierre Chaunu predicts exactly the opposite of Paul Ehrlich, namely that the world's population will go into decline and the entire human race will die out sometime around the year 2500—a different line of reasoning but the same sense of impending disaster. As Austrian sociologist Hans Millendorfer observes, what all of the futurologists think is needed is a different kind of human from the kind we seem to be. Futurologists differ widely with respect to the reasons, but they are remarkably uniform in agreeing that catastrophe lies ahead.

These bleak and hopeless visions are also spread by some of the great philosophers of history such as Arnold Toynbee, *A Study of History,* and the most famous of all (although not many have actually read his complex and difficult work) Oswald Spengler, *The Decline of the West.* Spengler, and to some extent Toynbee as well, looked on societies as living organisms and believed that each human society passes through stages from birth through growth, youth, maturity, old age, decrepitude, and ultimately death. Both of these writers see our society, especially Western Christendom, as either totally decrepit or nearly so.

Religious people often seek answers in the prophetic books of the Bible, such as the Revelation of St. John and the prophecies of Daniel. Yet both scholars and dabblers in biblical prophecy usually focus on visions of the horrors of the Great Tribulation that is to precede the End of the Age rather than on the attractive features of the Kingdom of God that is to be inaugurated. In other words, pessimism and lack of hope for the future of the planet have become the rule when people speculate about the future today, whether they do so on the basis of secular data or biblical prophecies.

It was not always so. From Plato's *Republic* to *Men Like Gods* by H. G. Wells, many writers in the past have thought that mankind could and probably would learn how to become healthy, wealthy, and wise. There are a few optimistic visions among recent writers, such as B. F. Skinner's *Walden 2,* usually based on a superior group of humans taking charge and wisely but firmly directing the destiny of everyone else, by means of control so sophisticated they are hardly resented. The optimists remain the exceptions however. From science fiction writers to excited Christian interpreters of the Revelation of St. John, the general attitude is to predict growing trouble and disaster.

There seems to be a mentality that enjoys predicting the worst. The bleak and dismal vision of the future evoked by writers such as Huxley, Toynbee, and Spengler is the secular counterpart to the biblical prophecies that predict a time of troubles. Coming from vastly different perspectives, futurologists and Bible scholars have different reasons for thinking that we are headed for a bleak and dismal future, but pessimism is common to them all.

There is something paradoxical about this widespread pessimism. The nations of the West are awash in material benefits. Medical care and welfare programs have expanded enormously. Extended vacations and luxurious cruises are within the reach of larger and larger numbers of people. Where distant regions of the world were once the target of imperialists and colonizers, today they are overrun by swarms of tourists with expensive cameras. Entertainment is available virtually everywhere at the touch of a remote-control button. Those who are not satisfied with the pleasures and fascinations that this material world offers have a broad smorgasbord of religions from which to choose.

The peoples of the West no longer fear a major war; the danger of an economic collapse like the Great Depression is supposedly prevented by highly refined government economic policies. While disease has not been eliminated and everyone must expect to die, many previously deadly maladies have been checked, and medicine and society have discovered ways of alleviating some of the most serious disabilities, making it possible for countless handicapped people to live productive lives. Never have so many young people enjoyed the advantages of higher education. Increasing affluence and the availability of schooling make it possible and popular for people to begin or return to college in middle age or even later to study to change occupations.

Yet in spite of all these advancements, a dramatic loss of confidence and hope for the future is typical of the kind of culture that prevails across most of the world today. For our contemporary society, there is a danger that these bleak prophecies will prove self-fulfilling. People who are convinced that their prospects are hopeless will not be inclined to make much of an effort.

In order to break out of the pessimistic mold, it is necessary to understand the current phase of our culture and to see where it is situated on the great canvas of human history. Just as people suffering from severe depression cannot remember a time when they were not depressed and cannot imagine a time in the future when they will no longer be depressed, people immersed in our culture cannot imagine that other viewpoints are possible and so cannot see any way to avoid the predicted catastrophes. Even many devoutly religious people, who cherish religious and spiritual values and put their hope in God and in the ultimate transformation of the present world and the establishment of Christ's kingdom, predict only decline and doom for the world that we know. For this reason, many of the people who want to think positively and to work for a better world ignore the futurologists and eschatologists and think only in terms of the immediate future. Unfortunately, this short-sighted attitude is not adequate to deal with the problems of our age, for many of them require long-term solutions.

With regard to the future, we seem to be faced with two undesirable alternatives: Either we take our problems so seriously that we despair of finding a way out, or we ignore the big picture and work to improve things here and there, with the likelihood that such short-term improvements will eventually prove meaningless as they are swallowed up in a widespread collapse of civilization and the destruction of all human society. For this reason, if we encounter a great thinker who can clearly understand where history has been and see where we are headed today but who nevertheless says that although disaster is possible it is not inevitable, we ought to pay attention. We should be delighted to find someone who is fully aware of the danger of a culturewide catastrophe but still challenges us to hope that this does not have to be our fate and, indeed, that dramatic improvements are *possible* provided we clearly understand where we are now and can see the right path to follow to make our future hopeful rather than hopeless.

Among the great thinkers of the twentieth century, there is one who stands out: Pitirim A. Sorokin (1889–1968). While not minimizing the extent of our problems, he offers hope that the problems can be solved and the crisis resolved. Indeed, he believes that this hopeful prospect is *likely*, provided we have the discernment to see and follow the right road out of the impasse of our late second millennium culture. In 1941 Sorokin, an expatriate Russian scholar, published a book entitled *The Crisis of Our Culture*. It summed up several decades of some of the most comprehensive and diligent analysis of cultural systems and their development. Strikingly, Sorokin's detailed predictions of the direction our society would take in the remainder of the century have turned out to be correct, with very few exceptions. The accuracy of his short-term predictions, which far outstrips that of most other prognosticators, can encourage us to hope that Sorokin's long-range forecasts may also prove true in the end. Unlike the *Untergang* (decline) predicted by Spengler and others, Sorokin's predictions are hopeful. It is not necessary for our society and our world to plunge into a general catastrophe; in fact, the prospects for avoiding one are actually good.

Only a decade ago, many military strategists and other thinkers expected a devastating thermonuclear war between the two superpowers—the United States and the Soviet Union. However, the Soviet Union has now dissolved into its component republics and no longer threatens the West with nuclear war. Our cultural pessimists are no longer predicting a worldwide conflagration ignited by national rivalries but rather a worsening of certain systemic problems, such as population growth and the exhaustion of natural resources, seeing nothing for us in the long-run but planetwide disasters.

Against this background, Sorokin's views are encouraging. While he foresees that disaster will come if we follow certain wrong paths, he believes that it can be avoided and that the human race can take another important step in the fulfillment of what he calls "man's unique creative mission on this planet." In order to avoid catastrophe and to fulfill that mission, an understanding of the crisis is necessary; in order to understand, a measure of grace is required, and grace is not something that we can manipulate or generate on our own—it must come from God. If we do understand our situation, and receive the grace to choose the right paths and to follow them, both individually and as a society, then the twilight in which we find ourselves will turn out to be the twilight before a new dawn, not before the full darkness of night.

Mere humans, no matter how learned, cannot demand or generate the "grace of understanding." That is in God's hands. Yet perhaps we can disclose facts and illuminate relationships in such a way that understanding will be made easier and finding the right paths more possible. No man's work, nor the work of any group or even of whole societies, is sufficient in itself to solve what is a systemwide crisis of the greatest magnitude. Sorokin has helped us to see what the crisis is, not to paralyze us by the awful vision but to inspire us to search for ways to resolve it. In attempting to continue his work and to impart his vision to readers half a century after him, I am conscious of standing on the shoulders of a giant. By standing on those shoulders, I may be able to see farther than he himself could, but if it were not for him, there are many things that I would not be seeing at all.

Harold O. J. Brown
Advent, A.D. 1995

xiii

1

THE AGONY OF
WESTERN CULTURE

Whom the Gods would destroy, they first make mad.

Euripides

THE TWENTIETH CENTURY IS ALMOST OVER. This second millennium has witnessed the expansion of our Western culture—a culture that began in an obscure eastern corner of the great Roman Empire. The distinct culture of Judaism was transformed into Christianity and rapidly permeated the Hellenistic world. Today there is hardly a spot on earth where Christianity's influence is not felt. Western culture as we know it began with the rise of the religion founded by a Palestinian prophet.

Today most of the world's calendars count their years from his birth. The division of history into years B.C. ("before Christ") and A.D. (*Anno Domini*, "in the year of the Lord") prevails almost everywhere in the world, a symbol of the degree to which Western culture—shaped as it was by Christianity—sets the standards for the whole world. Although in recent years there has been a move to replace B.C. and A.D. with B.C.E., "before the common era," and C.E., "common era," omitting the word *Christ* and the concept *Lord*, this cannot conceal the fact that most of the world still follows the West in thinking that something of universal importance began with Jesus Christ.

THE NARROW WEST AND THE BROAD WEST

When discussing Western culture, it is necessary to realize that it includes much more than what until recently was called "the Western world," or "the free world." "Western culture" is essentially the product of Christianity, and in this sense it includes Greece, Eastern Europe, and much of the former Soviet Union—although for forty years the latter two were cut off from Western Europe and the United States. The common tendency to refer to Western Europe and the United States as "the West" does not point to their culture but to their political and military power and defensive alliance following World War II. The broader meaning of *West* includes Latin America as well as Eastern Europe and Russia.

In a sense, Asian countries such as Singapore (founded by the British), Korea (where Christianity has become so prominent), and the Philippines also partly belong to the West. But even as parts of Asia become "the West," in the United States Western culture seems to be breaking up. American immigration policies after World War II brought in a great influx of Asians and Middle Easterners, adherents of non-Western religions. Instead of seeking their harmonious integration into Western culture—something that most of them want—America at the end of the twentieth century is self-critical, ashamed of its history, and ready to welcome a kind of cultural pandemonium under the slogans "pluralism" and "multiculturalism."

From a religious perspective, the conversion of non-Westerners to Christianity might promise to strengthen and preserve Western culture, but the propagation of Christianity has become odious and increasingly inconceivable to the new elites who rule the West. Immigration has taken on different forms in Western Europe, but there too the culture is in some danger of disintegrating. If we understand the term rightly, it makes sense to speak of *the agony of Western culture. Agony* means a life-and-death struggle, a struggle that may well lead to death but can also lead to victory.

The agony of our culture is intense and especially dangerous in the United States, a nation that is at the same time both the most Western and the least Western part of the West. It is the most Western part because that is where fundamental characteristics of Western society—including the Christian religion, experimental science, and freedom of inquiry—are most firmly established and have triumphed most completely. It is also the least Western part because that is where every tradition and value that has made the West the world's dominant culture is readily bartered, sold, or discarded when anything more efficient or convenient is proposed in its stead.

The significance of the United States for the West in the narrow sense was and is immense, for American military power held the expansionist schemes of the Soviet Union at bay until that great superpower collapsed under its own internal tensions. For forty years the Cold War between the United States and the USSR threatened to erupt into intercontinental violence, which could have devastated the entire world.

If this had happened, it would not have been East against West, or Asia against Europe, but it would have been a civil war within the West, a kind of *internal* conflict within Western culture. The two rival branches of the same Western, "Christian" civilization—namely, the materialistic, capitalistic, nominally Christian United States and the materialistic, Marxist, officially atheistic Soviet Union—could have destroyed each other and the rest of the planet with them. In other words, the same Western culture that had been setting standards for most of the rest of the world during the last two centuries might well have destroyed itself and taken the world with it before the new millennium; there might have been no new millennium.[1]

Western culture formed the modern world; Western powers might have destroyed it but mercifully have not done so yet. Unfortunately, having not destroyed the world in a nuclear holocaust, Western culture seems on the verge of destroying itself in a self-inflicted delirium. This is precisely what the brilliant German teacher, Oswald Spengler (1880–1936), prophesied in the closing

---

[1] The difference between the power bloc and culture of the USSR on the one hand and those of Western Europe and the United States on the other is so often referred to as a conflict between East and West that people fail to see that it is a conflict *within* Western culture between two degenerate versions of its Christian heritage. Marxism originated in a Christian context and rebelled vehemently against it; the rebellion in the West has been less violent, but officialdom in America is almost as hostile to Christianity as the Communist rulers of the old USSR.

years of World War I: the dying of Western civilization.[2] Even though Spengler exalted the culture of his native Germany and dedicated his great work to the German army (not realizing that its defeat was imminent), his judgment of Western culture as it was then and was to become was pessimistic. Spengler believed that civilizations and cultures, like all living beings, are born, grow, mature, decline, and ultimately die. As far as Western civilization is concerned, our time of decline and decay is upon us and cannot be reversed. Perhaps part of the immense popularity of *The Decline of the West* resulted from the fact that his statement that decline is inevitable gave rationalization and justification for the orgy of degeneracy and self-indulgence that spread across the West after World War I.[3]

Despite all its excesses, Germany and her fate are in many ways central to the Christian West. Just as Greece, although conquered and occupied, placed its stamp upon the Roman Empire, Germany, defeated, divided, and only now reunited on a portion of its former territory, placed its stamp upon the spirit of Western culture. The Protestant Reformation, which shattered the spiritual unity of the West, began there; the Enlightenment flourished there; modern science achieved some of its most important triumphs there; and, finally, Germany launched a war that destroyed much of the culture it had helped to shape and toppled Western civilization from its unchallenged worldwide eminence.

Oswald Spengler grew up when Germany was a Christian empire and lived to see it become a pagan dictatorship. Admired by Hitler, Spengler did not return the admiration but saw in the Nazi ruler one of the new Caesars whom he thought would hasten the decline of the West. If he had lived another dozen years, Spengler would have experienced an even greater disaster than he anticipated: the destruction of most of Germany's thousand-year-old culture in

---

[2] Oswald Spengler, *The Decline of the West*, trans. Francis Atkinson (New York: Knopf, 1928). The German word translated "decline," *Untergang*, is stronger; it literally means "going under."

[3] The conservative Roman Catholic scholar E. Michael Jones, in *Degenerate Moderns* (San Francisco: Ignatius, 1993), argues that much that passed for modern science and scholarship, including the work of Margaret Mead, Ruth Benedict, and Sigmund Freud, was simply rationalized sexual degeneracy. The simplicity of this analysis should not deceive us into overlooking the very evident connection between the desire for licentious freedom and the presentation of scholarly and scientific theories that claim that such conduct is not merely justifiable but desirable and commendable.

the holocaust that Hitler unleashed. All that was to happen during those twelve years would only have strengthened Spengler's conviction that the West is doomed to fade from world history.

Spengler was not a Christian, and his prophecies of decline do not include the catastrophic demonic and divine interventions foreseen in several Christian visions, such as that of the best-selling, fundamentalist, futurologist Hal Lindsay. Lindsay's spectacularly successful 1971 book, *The Late, Great Planet Earth* was ignored by the intellectual world and the secular media, but it nevertheless sold over twenty million copies in various languages. Read by a different class of readers from those who struggled through Spengler, Lindsay also fostered the feeling that the world as we know it is at the end of its tether. He gave the present world order hardly ten more years to live before coming to a fiery end in the battle of Armageddon.[4]

Prophecies of doom have a fascination for most of us. They tend to become self-fulfilling when they cause us to lose hope and to fail to make the choices that might make the future brighter. Fortunately, doomsayers such as Spengler and Lindsay, although they are many, are not the only ones trying to discern the future of our culture.

Only nine years younger than Spengler, Pitirim A. Sorokin lived thirty years longer. Sentenced to death under the last czar, Nicholas II, Sorokin was later released and became the private secretary of Aleksandr Kerenski, the president of the short-lived liberal Russian republic that was overthrown by the Bolsheviks. Sentenced to death again, Sorokin was pardoned by Lenin but later was exiled. He came to the United States, where he spent the last four decades of his life, chiefly at Harvard University. Sorokin lived to see Marxist totalitarianism spread across Eastern Europe and much of Asia, and at the time of his death, the Soviet Union and Communist China were still pursing their expansionist policies of subversion and conquest.

Based on what was happening around him, Sorokin should have had every reason to be pessimistic about Western culture; little or nothing pointed to

---

[4] Hal Lindsay, *The Late, Great Planet Earth* (Grand Rapids, Mich.: Zondervan, 1971).

recovery or renewal. Instead he thought he saw in human potential and in Western civilization the seeds of a new dawn. How could he do this? He examined a vast sweep of human cultures, observing their phases of birth and death, growth and aging, decline and renewal. There he discerned patterns that can be transferred to our own culture, offering more hopeful prospects than those of Spengler or Lindsay. But there was another reason: Sorokin believed in God and took seriously the idea that God has a mission for the human race on earth, a mission that he himself will help us to fulfill if the task seems too great for our unaided powers. If there is such a God, and if he does have such a mission for mankind, then Western culture may well be in agony, but it does not have to die. If there were no such God and no such mission, then the future of the West and the human race as a whole would be bleak indeed. This present work is inspired not only by the thoroughness, reliability, and brilliance of Sorokin's analysis but also by the shared conviction that there is a God and that he is concerned about the future of our race.

Sorokin did not live long enough to observe the softening and collapse of the Soviet Union—the monstrous power that for so long had threatened to lash out and destroy or enslave us. The breakup of the Communist empire in the years 1989–91 should have generated a wave of euphoria and optimism throughout the West. Instead, the West plods sulkily along, with hardly a momentary flash of exultation over its deliverance from imminent destruction. The reason is stated by Aleksandr Solzhenitsyn: "Men have forgotten God."

Sorokin was neither a priest nor a prophet, at least not in the religious sense of the word, but he did not forget God. Forget God, and one may as well forget Sorokin's hope and most of his work. Leave God out, and the reader may as well lay this book aside. Remember God, and the facts Sorokin marshaled, which are revised and brought up to date in the present work, will indeed lay before us the prospect of a brilliant new dawn.

Many confident predictors of the future rather quickly lost their luster when events proved them wrong. Orwell's worldwide totalitarianism did not come in 1984, although some think that it will still come. The Great Tribulation and the battle of Armageddon that Lindsay deemed so near has yet to begin. Sorokin's less dramatic prophecies have a better record. He published

The Crisis of Our Age in 1941 and reissued it unchanged in 1956.[5] It was brought out again half a century later (1992), still unchanged. Virtually every detail of Sorokin's predictions has been fulfilled except the main one—his expectation that our culture will finally find the way out of its systemwide crisis and instead of a fiery *dies irae* (day of wrath) will experience a new dawn.

We should keep our eyes and ears open to catch the sights and sounds of renewal in the midst of the swirling visions and cacophonous sounds of our cultural agony. There is an agony that precedes death, but there is also an agony that is the crisis before recovery. Sorokin's work warns us against making the paralyzing mistake of thinking that our agony—which we cannot help but feel—inevitably means that the day of the West, and perhaps of Christianity, is done. Because Sorokin's analysis has proved so reliable in its details, the note of hope on which he ends *The Crisis of Our Age* grows stronger with the passing years. With most writers, such as Spengler and Orwell, one hopes desperately that they are wrong; with Sorokin, one dares to hope that he is right.

The first impression of Pitirim Sorokin is that he too was a historical pessimist preoccupied with the crisis of our civilization and that he anticipated its inevitable collapse. He by no means underestimated the severity and extent of the crisis; indeed, he described it in great detail. Like Spengler, Sorokin saw regularities and repetitive patterns in history, but unlike Spengler, he did not see the history of civilizations as paralleling the lifecycle of organisms. Every biological organism, including every human being, must eventually die. Human society, however, is not a biological organism. There are similarities, but there are also differences. With biological organisms, similar risk factors will produce similar diseases. Within sociocultural systems, similar causative factors in similar situations will likely bring about similar developments, but *it is not inevitable*. Changes of direction are possible, and the future of any particular society is not foreordained.

---

[5] Pitirim A. Sorokin, *The Crisis of Our Age* (1941; reprint, Garden City, N.Y.: Doubleday, 1956).

7

CULTURE AS A SUPERSYSTEM

We readily recognize that there are links and interactions between various aspects of culture. Literature is linked to music and to the visual arts; medical science is linked to biology, chemistry, economics, and even politics. Education is linked to politics, law, religion, and the economy. Even sports and recreation are linked to the economy and politics. One of Sorokin's fundamental axioms (which he simply presupposes and does not bother to prove) is the conviction that this linkage goes far beyond the relationships where it is evident, such as that between medicine and the physical sciences, but ultimately involves all aspects of a developed culture. Every vigorous culture is integrated; he calls this a *sociocultural supersystem*. The various aspects of culture—the arts, entertainment, systems of truth, law, ethics, medicine, religion, politics, and economic and family life— are all interconnected. Developments in one invariably influence the others; problems in one cannot be addressed or corrected without sooner or later affecting all of the others.

Our society is flooded with bits or "bites" of information, seemingly unrelated data that appear to demand our attention, one after another, tumbling over one another in a chaotic, disorganized way: urban terrorism, family breakdown, government deficits, epidemics, educational stagnation, pornography, sexual confusion, etc. It is absolutely essential to recognize the interconnectedness of these phenomena. When a person is suffering from severe blood loss, a transfusion may be vital to his survival and should be given without delay. However, if the cause of the hemorrhage cannot be located and removed, the transfusion will give only momentary relief. Our society is hemorrhaging in many ways, and we are trying to bring relief with tourniquets, transfusions, and other remedies. While such remedies may be necessary or even crucial, they will only serve to delay the final disaster unless the basic reason for the crisis can be recognized and dealt with, addressing causes rather than symptoms alone. It is important to recognize the unity of sociocultural supersystems in order to understand what is meant by saying that an entire culture is situated in one or another of three major phases, or, occasionally, in transition between them. Our culture is one that is in transition, a transition so painful that it is not incorrect to call it an agony.

The Phases of the Supersystem

Sorokin identified three distinct phases through which cultures pass: *ideational, idealistic,* and *sensate.* Each phase has distinctive characteristics and in general runs a specific course. Virtually every human society can be found at any particular time to be in one phase or another, or in transition between two of them. Every aspect of society reflects the phase in which that society finds itself: Philosophy and religion, government and law, literature, music and the arts, family structures, and economic life are largely determined by the underlying principles of the mentality of that particular phase.

Ideational. The ideational mentality sees spiritual truth and values as virtually the only truth and values worthy of the name. God and the divine world are the highest and truest realities; the good is what God wills. The Byzantine icon of the Risen Christ—*Christos Pantokrator* (Christ the Ruler of All)—is an example of ideational art: The figure of Christ is intended to give the worshiper an impression of his heavenly glory, not to convey a realistic portrait. A culture in its ideational phase is willing to sacrifice pleasures and immediate goals for the sake of its high principles. Self-denial, asceticism, and martyrdom are natural behaviors from the ideational point of view.

Idealistic. The idealistic mentality represents a compromise between the ideational and sensate, although it inclines more to the ideational. Like an ideational culture, an idealistic culture rates spiritual truth and values above all others, but it also appreciates the realities and values of the sensory world and does not treat them as meaningless or nonexistent. In its early phases its principles and standards of behavior will resemble the ideational more than the sensate, but because it is open to the material values and attractions of the sensory world, the idealistic mentality tends to develop into the sensate form.

Sensate. The sensate mentality is the exact opposite of the ideational mentality. It is interested only in those things, usually material in nature, that appeal to or affect the senses. It seeks the imposing, the impressive, the voluptuous; it encourages self-indulgence. A huge oil canvas such as Rubens's "The Drunken Hercules" is a representative work of sensate art. Virtually all glossy magazine advertising is sensate. No apology is made for encouraging people to squander their resources on self-indulgence. Let us "eat, drink, and be merry," forgetting that "tomorrow we die." Sensate culture and sensate art go beyond simple materialism in that materialism merely defines matter as the only reality; the sensate mentality becomes enthusiastic about it.

Western culture, as we shall show, is in the last stages of the sensate phase, or, to use Sorokin's expression, it is a late, degenerate sensate culture. By *degenerate* he means that many aspects of culture that were once well-defined, well-coordinated, and productive have begun to lose their former balance and harmony, becoming shriveled or bloated, nonfunctional or counterproductive. Later when we describe various aspects of our late sensate culture, it will become apparent that many of them are degenerate not only in the technical sense that they no longer form part of a well-functioning, integrated whole, but also in the sense that they are morally blameworthy and merit condemnation.[6]

Historical Perspective

As we look back into history, we see that many cultures have simply vanished, but some have survived major threats and have flourished again. Egyptian culture lasted in recognizable form for more than two thousand years; Mesopotamian culture also endured for centuries. China's civilization is still older, and perhaps not even the sweeping, brutally cruel measures of Communism will bring it to an end.

Compared to such millennial cultures, the culture of the United States is much younger. It is only as a branch of Western Christian culture that American culture can boast an impressive history and tradition. If the culture of the United States succeeds in cutting itself off from its sources—as so many influential forces in America seem to want it to do—it may soon cease to be a recognizable culture. Because of the strategic importance of the American culture for the West as a whole, any collapse of culture in the United States could

---

[6] One of Sorokin's traits is directness. He uses terms that say what he means without worrying about the potentially inflammatory implications of such language. The term *degenerate* has a technical meaning and does not necessarily imply condemnation, although Sorokin does not conceal his disapproval of the direction of contemporary society.

have a devastating effect on the heartlands of the West in Europe, especially because Europe is also showing signs of a deepening crisis of cultural identity. All of Western culture is in transition, a transition that we may properly call a crisis. The crisis did not begin in the United States, but because of the speed with which developments in America spread around the world, the American crisis aggravates already existing tendencies of European culture to degenerate and disintegrate.

European civilization entered its sensate phase in the late fifteenth century, coinciding with the beginning of the modern era. After almost six hundred years, it seems to many people that even modernity is behind us and that the entire West is entering a new and different world, unlike anything mankind has ever known—an exciting challenge for some, a frightening prospect for others. The mid-twentieth century was a time of the apparently unstoppable forward march of science. The end of the century is a time of resurgent spirituality and occultism to a degree that would have been unimaginable half a century ago. In the eyes of many, nothing in our culture looks familiar any longer; the boundary markers are changed every day. As the late Margaret Mead liked to say of people thirty and over, "We are all immigrants in the world of the young."

If Sorokin is right, the boundary markers are indeed being moved, but the disorientation that we feel does not signal the advent of something truly new but rather the kind of shift that has taken place more than once in the past. If we understand the parallels of the past, we may recognize dangers to which we would otherwise succumb and seize opportunities that we might otherwise let slip.

Modern sensate Western culture has not been in existence quite as long as the sensate culture of ancient Rome was before the impact of Christianity caused its great shift, but things move faster now. May we expect the kind of constructive renewal that created medieval Christian civilization out of the ruins of pagan Rome and the barbarian invasions? And if so, where will it come from? Does Western Christian Civilization have the resources to renew itself, or has it entered a late, degenerate phase from which it cannot recover?

As we view the historic panorama of cultures as they rise, develop, flourish, and ultimately fall, it is important to notice not only change but also continuity. There have been societies that were violently overthrown and blotted out—for

11

example, the wealthy merchant culture centered around Carthage in North Africa, which was crushed by Rome. A few seem to have vanished without being militarily subjugated, but no culture disappears without leaving traces. The story of Egyptian civilization spans almost three thousand years, and it might appear to follow Spengler's biological model, passing from birth and youth through old age to death. (Ancient Egyptian culture had effectively vanished even before Augustus Caesar brought the land under Roman control.) Yet our own Western civilization has retained some memory of Egypt, for example, in Verdi's opera *Aida* and in symbols such as the pyramid on the official seal of the United States and the obelisk called the Washington Monument.

The history of Egypt does not offer a good parallel to ours. Rome interests us more; its history offers both promise and threat. The Roman Empire in the West offers a wonderful illustration of the organizing and administrative genius of pre-Christian Western civilization, and at the same time a perfect example of the collapse that can come with the exhaustion of the sensate phase of a civilization. Imperial, pagan Rome collapsed, but Europe did not die with it. There was a transformation from which the invading barbarian tribes also learned and out of which a new and more humane culture arose.

This precisely parallels the danger and the challenge facing Western culture today. The decline of pagan Rome saw the dawn of Western Christian civilization—the first phase of the new sociocultural system to which we still belong. Where are we now, and where is our civilization headed? Are we doomed to fall in our own day as Rome fell before the Germanic barbarians? Or will we see a revitalized culture arise where declining sensate values currently rule?

In order to answer those questions, it is helpful to observe the features of our civilization that parallel the Roman experience as well as those that differ. Rome was not only the culminating phase of late Hellenistic, Mediterranean paganism, it was also the birthplace of a new world civilization called Christendom, of which we are the heirs. At the end of the Roman Empire, the sensate system that prevailed had become so degenerate it could no longer sustain itself. A new outlook, the new sociocultural system based on Christianity, replaced the pagan system of the Graeco-Roman world. The sensate worldview that extolled the appetites of the senses gave way to an ideational outlook that challenged the people to "seek first the kingdom of God and his righteousness."

This was the beginning of a new civilization that with all its variety and diversity nevertheless has remained a unity until the present.

In the fifteen centuries since its beginning, Western culture has passed through a series of changes until now, like the Rome of A.D. 200, it has reached what Sorokin calls a degenerate late sensate phase. In this condition, Western civilization, like that of Rome in decline, can no longer continue. Countless thinkers have recognized this. If we followed Spengler's organic model, we would have to agree that our culture has reached its late old age and soon must die. Sorokin did not accept the organic model. His position was that our culture and civilization do not have to die, but if they are not to do so, they must experience a recovery and renewal on the scale that Europe experienced as pagan Rome declined and Christianity began. The fatigued, jaded Roman world received and accepted a tremendous new vision; so far, ours has nothing comparable.[7]

THE GRACE OF UNDERSTANDING

The late sensate phase of Western culture has reached its final stages, and it cannot continue. However, civilization need not perish with it. There is a possibility of a far-reaching transformation that would avert the total disaster Sorokin calls the *dies irae* and lead instead to a true renewal. For pagan Rome, the transformation came with Christianity. Sorokin held that renewal can come only if we receive what he calls the "grace of understanding" and, assisted by that grace, make the right decisions. Can this grace of understanding come through elements already present, from the Judeo-Christian sources that once before changed the world? Or are they too exhausted? Inasmuch as a spiritual reorientation is one of the conditions that Sorokin sees as necessary for renewal, it is appropriate to use a familiar Christian term and speak of the possible *revival* of Western civilization—not in a strictly religious sense, but certainly not without a religious component.

---

[7] In addition to explicitly quoting and footnoting Sorokin's works, I have not infrequently borrowed his concepts and his language throughout this work. I acknowledge my indebtedness to Sorokin; however, it would become excessively tedious to acknowledge that indebtedness at every point.

If the grace of understanding is necessary to prevent a civilization-wide sociocultural disaster and to make renewal possible, what is it that we need to understand? On the one hand, we need to understand the full extent of the crisis in which we find ourselves, and not make the mistake of trivializing it, as though it could be resolved by making a few changes here and there in the structure of our social, economic, and political order. If we do not recognize its seriousness, we will wear ourselves out with adjustments and cosmetic changes, thereby making the disaster unavoidable. On the other hand, we must not make the mistake of seeing the present crisis as hopeless and therefore fail to make the kind of changes that could save us from a fiery ordeal.

As early as 1926, Sorokin made comments of this nature:

> Every important aspect of the life, organization, and culture of Western society is in extraordinary crisis. . . . Its body and mind are sick and there is hardly a spot on its body which is not sore, nor any nervous fibre which functions soundly. . . . We are living, thinking, and acting at the end of a brilliant, six-hundred-year long Sensate day. The oblique rays of the sun still illumine the glory of the passing epoch. But the light is fading, and in the deepening shadows it becomes more and more difficult to see clearly and to orient ourselves safely in the confusions of the twilight. The night of the transitory period begins to loom before us, with its nightmares, frightening shadows, and heart-rending horrors. Beyond it, however, the dawn of a new great Ideational culture is probably waiting to greet the men of the future.[8]

During the years following World War II, as the dream of united nations happily cooperating for world peace and development faded in the context of the Cold War, author after author produced dire visions of the future, the best known being George Orwell's *Nineteen Eighty-Four*. With his three slogans, "War is peace," "Slavery is freedom," and "Ignorance is strength," Orwell described an increasingly bleak and dismal future for the human race. Futurologists from many disciplines disagreed as to how the changes would be brought about, but they essentially agreed in seeing a bleak future for mankind.

---

[8] Cited from Sorokin, *Social and Cultural Dynamics*, vol. 3 (New York: American Book Company, 1937), 535, but the author had made the same statements in slightly different form from 1926 onward, before the stock market crash, the Depression, and the outbreak of World War II.

The year 1984 passed without incident, but the world continued to labor under the threat of the alternatives of a fiery nuclear Armageddon or a gradual crushing of freedom with the relentless advances of totalitarian Communism. Then, abruptly and (for most people) totally unexpectedly, the Soviet Empire began to break up. The European satellites of the Soviet Union began to change, some peaceably, such as the German Democratic Republic, or, as in Romania, through a bloody coup d'état. Finally, the Soviet Union itself disintegrated.

Much of the world breathed a sigh of relief. The sword of Damocles that hung over the entire earth seemed to have been sheathed. Military budgets could be reduced, troops withdrawn from areas where massive forces had confronted one another. The conflict between Israel, its Arab neighbors, and its own Palestinian minority seemed close to resolution after smoldering for almost half a century. The abundant banquet of a modern prosperity could be enjoyed in tranquility, at least by the rich countries of the earth. Unfortunately, the evils that confronted humanity in general and our own society in particular do not seem to have ended with the disappearance of the immediate military danger. When Iraq sought to enrich itself at the expense of its tiny neighbor other powers united to destroy its army and to drive it back onto its own soil— a step supposedly expressive of a New World Order.

With no immediate threat of a major war on the horizon, rulers and ruled alike thought that they could turn away from external dangers and concentrate on their own internal problems. Curiously, however, after the initial sigh of relief, the populations of the major countries do not seem to have become more content and happier. Instead they remain caught up in turmoil of many kinds, wracked by apprehensions, filled with anxiety. There is a frenzied pursuit of pleasure by both the rich and the less affluent, as though the motto of all the world had become the old Epicurean proverb: "Eat, drink, and be merry, for tomorrow we die."

Does this mean that the systemwide crisis described by Sorokin in 1941, when the European conflict was becoming generalized into total world war, has ended and that we have entered a period of tranquility and stability? No, it does not, for the 1939–45 war was only a severe paroxysm, not the crisis itself. The war illustrated the crisis, but even if war had been averted, the crisis would nevertheless be with us. It does not require formal declarations of war between great powers, the marshaling of vast armies, great naval flotillas, and immense bomber fleets to produce the kind of disasters of which Sorokin wrote. He wrote these lines in 1941, in the midst of an expanding, worldwide conflagration, but what he said then is still true today, even though the great powers themselves are formally at peace:

> The crisis is here in all its stark and unquestionable reality. We are in the midst of an enormous conflagration burning everything into ashes. In a few weeks millions of human lives are uprooted; in a few hours century-old cities are demolished; in a few days, kingdoms are erased. Red human blood flows in broad streams from one end of the earth to another. Ever-expanding misery spreads its gloomy shadow over larger and larger areas. The fortunes, happiness, and comfort of untold millions have disappeared. Peace, security, and safety have vanished. Prosperity and well-being have become in many countries but a memory; freedom, a mere myth. Western culture is covered by a blackout. A great tornado sweeps over the whole of mankind.
>
> If the explosion of the crisis is thus undeniable, its nature, its causes, and its consequences are much less certain. We read and hear daily a dozen different opinions and diagnoses.[9]

In the 1990s, half a century later, the only thing that is missing from Sorokin's description of crisis is the direct clash of great powers in technological war: "*In a few days, kingdoms are erased.*" In a matter of hours in 1989, the German Democratic Republic came to an end, and two years later the same thing happened to the much larger and vastly more powerful Soviet Union. More peacefully, in three days the once firmly established white Republic of South Africa was transformed into something new, with the ultimate outcome yet to be seen.

"*Red human blood flows in broad streams from one end of the earth to another.*" 1991 saw the outbreak of fratricidal civil war in disintegrating Yugoslavia, and 1994 brought death to hundreds of thousands in Rwanda. "*In a few weeks, millions of human lives are uprooted.*" Hundreds of thousands of Rwandans fled to miserable refugee camps in neighboring countries. Streams of refugees filled the waters off the coasts of Cuba and Haiti, some fortunate ones reaching land in Florida only to be confined in isolated, makeshift refugee camps.

---

[9] Pitirim A. Sorokin, *The Crisis of Our Age*, 2nd ed. (Oxford; Oneworld, 1992), 14–15.

"Peace, security, and safety have vanished." Even as the world's most advanced military power launched a vast array of sea, air, and land forces to overthrow bloody tyranny and install what it called democracy in a tiny island country, the death toll from planned murder and random violence in its own cities reached staggering proportions. Whole areas of formerly brilliant metropolises have come to resemble battlefields, where strangers do not dare to venture and the residents are in constant danger. Epidemics that formerly ravaged entire populations, such as smallpox, cholera, and typhoid fever, have been checked or even eliminated, yet other dangers have risen to take their place. Even the old plague reappeared, as AIDS proves to be a scourge that is even more implacable than most varieties of cancer. Millions of unborn babies are destroyed in the womb. In the Netherlands thousands of sick and elderly people are being put away by euthanasia and physician-assisted suicide, and similar things are beginning in the U.S. and elsewhere. The certainties and security that most people in the developed countries have come to take for granted are disappearing; economic security is not the only thing that is fragile. Life itself is frequently at risk.

"Prosperity and well-being have become in many countries but a memory." In countries that once were totalitarian dictatorships, the return of political and economic freedom has aggravated rather than alleviated economic distress. In countries that remain free and to all appearances enjoy prosperity, such as the United States, immense trade deficits and public debt appear to threaten a catastrophe that can at best be postponed but not averted.

An Unavoidable Explosion?

The impending economic disaster and mass starvation that an expanding population was expected to produce have not yet happened. Optimists, who are few in number, think they can be averted. Pessimists warn that the longer they are postponed, the worse they will be when they inevitably occur. Between the two, the majority of people continue to enjoy a measure of affluence and diversion, trying to forget that "tomorrow we die."

That we are in a situation of crisis is assumed on all sides. What differs is our understanding of the nature of the crisis and our expectation of what can or ought to be done about it. Many are like the early Christians about whom Peter writes,

"Ever since our fathers died, everything goes on as it has since the beginning of creation (2 Pet. 3:4 NIV)." Western culture has withstood the Black Plague, smallpox and cholera epidemics, the French Revolution, the industrial revolution, the Napoleonic Wars, the American Civil War, economic crises, two world wars, the Bolshevik Revolution, and the Cold War. Thus there is some justification for thinking that it can overcome its present difficulties. Such optimism does not ignore dangers but relativizes and trivializes them, expecting them to pass.

We seek to identify and isolate specific problems and to blame them on individuals or groups, on economic factors that we can influence, or on climatic changes to which we can adjust. Our age is particularly fond of blaming evil individuals for its difficulties. During World War II, the villains were Hitler, Tojo, and Mussolini. Once they were eliminated, it was assumed the crisis would be past. Unfortunately, these moral monsters found successors, perhaps even more murderous than themselves, in Stalin and Mao Zedong. These too have vanished from the stage, but their places have been taken by lesser tyrants. It is interesting to observe the sweeping terms in which the menace they pose is portrayed by the media: Saddam Hussein temporarily took center stage, briefly appearing as a monster whose removal would end a crisis. Even a small-scale dictator such as Lt. General Raoul Cédras in Haiti could for a few months in 1993 be portrayed as a threat to the peace of the hemisphere if not of the entire world. One may wonder why the media and the leaders of great powers can work themselves into a frenzy over such a petty tyrant. Perhaps it is because they intuitively realize that the crisis has not ended with the passing of Hitler, Stalin, Mao or other lesser bullies such as Hussein. Since they are in the habit of identifying the crisis with a particular human villain, they search frantically for someone they can make into the monster of the hour.

The mistake lies in failing to recognize that these undeniable difficulties are not individual and isolated problems that can be resolved one after another. Rather they are part of a systemwide crisis that can only be resolved by a systemwide transformation. That society is in a time of crisis cannot be denied, but as Sorokin states, "These diagnosticians . . . prescribe as the cure such medicine as a slight or substantial readjustment of economic conditions, from a rearrangement of money, or banking, or social security to the elimination of private property. . . . Through these and similar measures they hope to correct the maladjustment, to eradicate the evil, and to return to the bliss of 'bigger and better' prosperity, to the sunshine of secure peace, to . . . progress."[10] In contemporary terms, the adjustments are such things as health insurance, employer contributions to health care costs, bilingual education, gun control, dancing lessons, and midnight basketball. "Such is one—probably the most prevalent—diagnosis of the crisis, its roots, and its cure,"[11] as something that gifted leaders, possessing good will and given great authority and funding, can resolve. This diagnosis must be rejected, for it recognizes only a few symptoms, not the disease itself.

The other diagnosis seems more realistic, but it has the disadvantage that it sees no hope and can do no more than reinforce our sense of impending disaster. The current pattern of culture that we call Western civilization has had its day and must withdraw gracefully or under compulsion from the stage of history. Whereas only a few years ago, bemused by technological progress, we could still speak hopefully of the "revolution of rising expectations," we now have to recognize this as a deluded dream, one that must be replaced by the acceptance of defeat and decline. The only reasonable course for our civilization lies in doing what we can to postpone defeat and to make it as painless as possible.

This has been the attitude of many of the most eminent politicians of the West, especially during the later phases of the Cold War. Surprisingly, the apparent victory of the West in that conflict has not altered it. Instead, no longer threatened by potentially superior enemy forces, we continue our anxious retreat. The onward march of Western civilization, characterized as it often was by arrogance and disdain for other societies, has now faltered and must stop altogether. The Western world must abase itself before other cultures, both high and primitive. "Western Civ has got to go," as students at Stanford University chanted, to be replaced by multiculturalism and political correctness. Those making such statements and prescribing such attitudes are generally prominent individuals in well-protected situations, whose comfort and social standing is unlikely to be challenged in the near future. Those who oppose

---

[10] Ibid., 15.

[11] Ibid.

them—the traditional middle classes, the blue-collar workers, the farmers, and others—are derided as arrogant reactionaries and are often rendered leaderless by the defection of their most talented and intellectually trained members to the cause of multiculturalism and commitment to the inferiority of the West.

According to this view, the present crisis with all its symptoms is merely the beginning of the inevitable end. Such a pessimistic view takes on the nature of a self-fulfilling prophecy by creating defeatism among those who might still seek to be creative and constructive, leading many to abandon the effort. Anyone with ears to hear can confirm that it is being loudly proclaimed by college presidents and professors, by ministers and journalists, by statesmen and politicians. Sorokin had already made this observation in 1941. The only thing that has changed is that now it is often done with a kind of "prideful self-satisfaction," to use Father R. L. Bruckberger's term, "like eunuchs proud of being castrated."[12]

Wrong on Both Counts

The analyses of both the optimists and the pessimists are wrong. The crisis we face is not a matter than can be dealt with by simple adjustment. Neither is it a complex of problems and difficulties that can be addressed and solved individually. It simultaneously involves the whole of Western culture and all of its institutions, from national governments and international organizations to the smallest units of society, even to individuals. The arts and sciences, morals and religion, economics, attitudes toward work and saving, philosophy and law, manners, the family, marriage and sexual customs, in short, everything in the life of the Western world is unstable and changing. Sorokin quite correctly calls it the disintegration of the fundamental form of Western culture and society dominant for the last four centuries.[13]

Pessimistic though this diagnosis may sound, and bleak though the outlook for our civilization may appear to be, it is not correct to say that this sickness of the West is inevitably a sickness unto death. If it continues as it is presently

---

[12] R. L. Bruckberger, *La Révelation de Jésus Christ* (Paris: Grasset, 1983).

[13] See Sorokin, *Crisis*, chap. 1.

going, it will be, but it need not be. Western culture and civilization have reached a crucial period, but it need not be the point at which decline and defeat have become irreversible; it can and ought to be a turning point, the beginning of a great new phase. This brings us back to the two things necessary for this to happen: *understanding* and *grace*. We can work for understanding; we cannot work for grace. If our Creator still has a purpose for the human race, however, we have reason to expect that he will not withhold his grace.

A UNIFIED SYSTEM

It is essential to remember this important fact: Each culture represents an integrated system, a so-called sociocultural supersystem. Of course no human culture is one-dimensional; indeed, even the most primitive cultures are complex. Each human culture presents a multiplicity of aspects: It has laws and customs, some form of government and administration, an economic system, patterns of family structure, educational practices, popular and fine arts, a system or systems of truth, and a religion, or something that takes the place of religion.

When we look at an ancient or unfamiliar culture such as that of ancient Egypt or the pre-Columbian Aztecs, we readily see it as a cultural unity because we are so much farther from it than from our own society. We have no problem speaking of "ancient Egyptian culture" or "Aztec culture." When we think of our own society, which is so much closer to us, we more easily see the variety, the tensions, and the contradictions.

Because we live in the midst of the European-American cultural world, we are more aware of its diversity than its unity. We have no universally recognizable symbols for Western culture, such as the pyramids for ancient Egypt or the Parthenon for Greece; however, there are symbols that exemplify it—for example, the churches and cathedrals that mark the skyline of so many towns and older cities. As recently as the early 1950s, church spires stood out prominently on the skyline of Boston, Massachusetts, although now they are lost among the skyscrapers. Pyramids and churches have in common the fact that they point to immortality and thus symbolize the interest of the society in that which is permanent and lasting, although in the one case it was to the fictional immortality of a divine pharaoh, while in the other it was to God as the giver of life.

21

The pyramids were built to outlast both peoples and cultures and did not rely on worshipers for their continuing existence. Although weathered by the centuries and defaced by generations of irreverent vandals, they still stand, two millennia after the civilization that produced them has vanished. Churches, by contrast, need people. The great cathedrals and churches of Europe remained the central points of most cities until the second half of our century, despite the fact that many of them no longer functioned as centers of lively worship. Now, however, even the largest cathedrals are increasingly overshadowed by office buildings and other secular structures; some smaller ones have been expropriated or sold and put to other uses as museums, concert halls, libraries, even dance halls. Some have been transformed into places of worship for non-Christian religions, in the same way that a few ancient Roman and Greek temples were made into Christian churches.

The fact that these structures have lost their central place in America and are losing it in Europe is symbolic of the incipient disintegration of the Western cultural world.[14] This disintegration is going on everywhere although in different ways and at varying speeds. There is a contrast between North America, especially the United States, on the one hand and Europe on the other. Europe has the structures and monuments of Christian civilization and still observes most of the holidays of the church year, but religious life in Europe is at a low ebb. In the United States, there are far more people who actively participate in and profess Christianity than in Europe. As Alexis de Tocqueville observed early in the last century, there is no other country in the world where Christian faith has so vigorously taken hold of as many people as in the United States.[15] There has never been an established national church in the United States (the last state church was disestablished in 1832), which is probably one reason for the continuing vitality of religion in America.

---

[14] This is not to suggest that the central location of churches or their prominence on the town skyline is of crucial importance to the unity of our culture but merely that the older pattern reflected certain central, unifying values of our culture.

[15] Alexis de Tocqueville, *Democracy in America*, trans. Henry Reeve (New Rochelle, N.Y.: Arlington House, 1966).

While Europe has slowly but surely drifted away from its Christian base, in the United States the drift was hardly evident until the 1960s, when a series of Supreme Court decisions abruptly placed the federal government in a posture of hostility to religion. As a result, changes in American culture that had remained hidden suddenly became evident, and the pace of change accelerated. In some respects, American culture has become more disoriented than European, where a veneer of Christian tradition still remains. Despite the large number of people in the United States who are serious about their Christian commitments, such traditional marks of a Christian society as Sunday closings and religious holidays have been all but eradicated. In general, however, one can say that both Europe and North America are in the last phase of the sensate sociocultural system. The fate that awaits both continents if there is no substantial change is the same, and the transformation needed to avoid the *dies irae* and recover a vision of our divine mission and purpose in existence is the same for both.

A DISAPPEARING HERITAGE

In surveying the great city of Washington, D.C., one is immediately struck by the conscious attempt of the architects and city planners to establish ties to the great republic of Rome as well as to the democratic heritage of Greece. The upper house of the legislature is called the Senate; the building in which the legislature sits is the Capitol. The rostrum of the Speaker of the House is flanked by the *fasces*, the symbol of authority in the Roman republic.

Yet the symbols of Christianity are missing in Washington, despite the fact that Christianity and the biblical tradition played a prominent role in American life when our country was founded. Most of the early leaders of the United States took a Christian orientation for granted, and no one thought that religious expression should be excluded from public life.

This lack of Christian symbols reveals the fact that in the eighteenth and nineteenth centuries, Western society was consciously moving away from what remained of its idealistic culture and becoming more explicitly and consciously sensate throughout. During the French Revolution, there was a violent rejection of the Roman Catholic Church and of Christianity, although Robespierre thought it necessary to preserve religion in the form of his cult of the Supreme Being. The man who turned the French Republic into an Empire, Napoleon, utilized religion and the papacy in the effort to consolidate his short-lived imperial system.

The concept that a society can get along totally without religion is quite new. From France, the United States inherited a certain tendency to rationalize in the French sense—to seek to carry the theoretical principles of government to their logical conclusions. This has led in the United States to transforming the principle of non-establishment (of a state church) to a radical separation of church and state, which by the end of the twentieth century has increasingly come to mean the radical exclusion of all that is religious, and particularly of all that is Christian, from visibility in public life.

This gradual abandonment of the Christian heritage of Western nations has now become a deliberate rejection. As such, it marks the final stage in the repudiation of an idealistic view of life and the world—one that believed in spiritual reality and in the personal God of the Bible, without disdaining the material realities and values of God's Creation—and its replacement with a sensate materialism that recognizes no reality but that which can be seen, heard, smelled, and felt. There was a period of at least three centuries when the emerging sensate culture still had room for idealistic values and a measure of respect for those who held them. This period is now coming to its shuddering end. Nowhere is this plainer than in the area of the arts, both in the things the arts produce and in the way the culture and the political establishment responds to them.

2

THE CRISIS IN
THE ARTS

*The fine arts are one of the most sensitive mirrors of
the society and culture of which they are an
important part.*

Pitirim Sorokin

DOES ART IMITATE LIFE, OR DOES LIFE IMITATE ART? Does violence in movies and on television cause violence among teenagers and children, or is it only a mirror of reality? Do nudity and explicit sexuality in the entertainment media encourage imitation, or do they merely portray changing mores? Does the constant repetition of words formerly considered obscene and blasphemous change speech and destroy courtesy and civility, or is it merely an authentic and accurate rendition of real life? Will the increasingly favorable portrayal of homosexuality in the media cause young people to embrace that lifestyle, or is it merely being fair to those who are "naturally" predisposed to it? These and other questions reveal the importance of what is going on in the arts to the culture as a whole.

The arts reflect the fundamental orientation of society as well as the particular views and behavior patterns of its members; at the same time, they spread and reinforce such views and patterns. All of the arts in the West, including popular art and its extreme forms, are becoming increasingly chaotic and disoriented, and in this respect they both reflect and intensify the chaotic and disorienting tendencies in society and culture.[1] In short, when we understand what is going on in the world of art today, we shall understand a great deal about the present condition and the probable future of our late sensate sociocultural system.

THE ARTS: CAUSE OR EFFECT?

Every culture has had its characteristic forms of artistic, musical, and literary expression. In the past, these forms were usually regarded as expressions of the spirit or mentality of an age rather than as the forces that shaped or created it. Friedrich Schiller asserted that it is the spirit that shapes the body.[2] The spirit that pervades the arts and entertainment of the West today is shaping a culture of which only the degenerate can be proud.[3] Before the age of mass media, access to the arts, to music, and even to literature was limited. To enjoy a painting or a sculpture, a person went where it was located. For music, an individual played or sang for personal enjoyment or went to a hall or home where music was being performed. Before printing, access to literature was likewise limited. People went to poetry readings, listened to storytellers, learned stories by heart, purchased a precious hand-copied manuscript or found one in a library. Literature first became widely accessible with the advent of movable type and the printing of books, magazines, pamphlets, and newspapers in great numbers. Only in this century did the techniques of recording, film, television, and video make art, music, and literature in all their forms—from the highest and most

---

[1] Even when classic works are presented, they may be modernized or altered in such a way that they no longer communicate the vision of the original author. Shakespeare is not necessarily falsified by being performed in modern dress, but when Macbeth is made into a woman, something quite foreign has been made of the bard's work.

[2] This phrase from Schiller's celebrated drama *Wallenstein* is on the facade of the Busch-Reisinger Museum at Harvard University (*Wallensteins Tod*, act 3, scene 13).

[3] Sorokin wrote: "If we are forced to accept [contemporary art] as a faithful representation of human society, then man and his culture must certainly forfeit our respect and admiration." Pitirim A. Sorokin, *The Crisis of Our Age*, 2d. ed. (Oxford: Oneworld, 1992), 56.

cultivated to the lowest and crudest—accessible to virtually every member of society, even teenagers and young children.

People no longer become educated and acquire cultivation in order to appreciate music, literature, and art; what passes for such things floods in upon the young and immature, interfering with education and supplanting cultivated tastes with primitivism and decadence. Allan Bloom's surprising bestseller, *The Closing of the American Mind*, compellingly describes the devastating impact of rock music in the academies (even the elite schools) where the most favored young people of America are supposed to acquire education and cultivate good taste, but no longer can do so.

The music, drama, and spectacles that were previously enjoyed only by those who could afford tickets to concerts and the theater are now readily available to almost everyone almost everywhere. This vastly increased availability of every form of art has come about at a time when most of the restraints on artistic expression—whether legal, moral, or merely conventional—have been overthrown in the name of freedom of expression. The consequence in art is the same as in economics: Bad art, like bad money, drives out the good.

This has led to a paradoxical situation, especially acute in the United States in the last third of the twentieth century. On the one hand, since the 1960s we have experienced the liberation of pornography and the elimination of virtually all restrictions on obscenity and blasphemy in the print and electronic media, with the result that not only entertainment but public discourse and everyday speech have descended into what earlier times would have called the gutter.[4] This is not merely excused but praised and promoted by almost everyone in the media, education, and government. Those who urge caution, express concerns, or suggest restrictions or controls are immediately denounced as advocates of censorship and thought control.

The intellectual and cultural elites of the West defend the right of media and entertainment moguls to profit by hawking images of violence, unrestrained sexual license, blasphemy, and degeneracy of every kind. Yet such

---

[4] The only restrictions that remain in force are those against prayer or the expression of religious sentiments or moral convictions in any forum that is under government control, such as schools or public buildings.

things are not confined to the screen, the television set, and the printed page, but are encountered in real life in the form of sexual harassment and abuse of both women and children, spreading an atmosphere of distress and misery bordering on despair. Families and legal and public health authorities lament the wave of atrocity and barbarism that seems to be sweeping over an entire society.[5] On the one hand a large segment of the political, intellectual, and media worlds demand unrestricted freedom of expression, often including the abolition of every restriction on any act that can be considered an artistic expression—from naked dancing and sex acts consummated on stage or screen, to trampling or burning the American flag. On the other hand, there is a continual outcry from victims and their advocates for a level of restrictions and controls that in an earlier age would have been considered unnecessary. Self-restraint, modesty, and decency are ridiculed and discarded as relics of a bygone age.

Appeals by those who have been wounded or injured are ignored except when such a demand serves a momentary need of an elite or promotes a currently fashionable cause such as "diversity" or "multiculturalism." In the present climate of "anything goes" there is little chance to suppress art that is obscene, pornographic, cruel, and depraved. No matter how flagrantly offensive the material or the performance, and no matter how mild the restrictions proposed (e.g. merely withholding public funding from obscene or blasphemous art without preventing or punishing anything or anyone) there is always an immediate and anguished outcry from the opinion makers: "Censorship!"

In modern America the tendencies to suppression and control do not target things that are truly cruel and depraved. Instead suppression is aimed at things that were formerly considered edifying, touching, and uplifting, such as religious symbols, affirmations of faith, references to God or salvation. The Ten Commandments, which once were taken for granted as the foundation of public law and justice in the United States, have been removed from schoolrooms and courtrooms. The tendencies to censorship are not limited to religious matters. Portrayals of noble or self-sacrificing figures, wholesome role models,

---

[5] It is often urged that these offenses are not really increasing but merely being better and more fully reported, but this assertion seems extremely naive and is becoming less believable every day.

and romantic or sentimental figures from history and legend are prohibited or, if permitted, are shown only in distorted and dishonoring forms.

Speech and thought control extend to things that were once normal or innocuous, including even familiar, nonpejorative words indicating an individual's sex, such as *stewardess, policeman,* and *mailman.*[6] The customary use of the words *man* and *men* and the pronouns *he, his,* and *him* in a generic sense to refer to either sex is being increasingly banned as insensitive at best, sexist and patriarchal at worst.[7] Students are told that their theses will not be accepted and writers hear that their works will not be printed unless they conform to the newspeak demands of "sensitive" language. While obscene, pornographic displays on stage and screen, and lyrics that call for abuse and torture are defended in the courts and exalted by media critics, innocent flirtatious behavior can be banned and punished as sexual harassment. A mere accusation of offensive or suggestive language can cost a person his job and ruin his career—a fate more likely to befall a man than a woman.

Formerly respected and innocent symbols of certain religious or political groups, such as the cross, the Christmas tree, or the Confederate flag have to be banned from every place where they might come into public view. They are banned from public property on the pretext that they would imply official endorsement of religion and from the workplace on the grounds that they might create discomfort among those who do not share the views they symbolize. The

---

6 Indeed, even the use of the word *sex* is being banned in many circles to be replaced by *gender*. This is on the grounds that sex is a biological category suggesting something determined by nature, while *gender* reflects a social convention and can be whatever you want it to be.

7 Because some of the ordinary titles of respect carried connotations of sex and marital or social status, in the United States titles and terms of respect such as *sir* and *ma'am* are increasingly disregarded and abandoned. With the appointment of the first woman to the United States Supreme Court in 1981, the old title *Mr. Justice* was abandoned. Instead of adopting the plausible *Madam Justice* for Mrs. O'Connor, both male and female members of the court are now called by the generic term *Justice*.

Usage varies from country to country, but in general one can also observe a decline in formality throughout Europe. For example, although Sweden still has a king, since the 1960s the monarch may be addressed by using the informal *du* rather than the older, polite *ni*. A decline in formality or formalism is not evil in itself, but if it implies that neither a person's age, profession, nor accomplishment merit any form of conventional recognition, it diminishes civility and leads to increasingly chaotic social relationships.

net effect, of course, is to spread the impression that religious commitment is nothing more than a peculiar and shameful hobby.

Thus modern Western society, especially but not only in North America, is increasingly schizophrenic, using one hand to grasp out for licentiousness, obscenity, and crudeness without limits, while using the other to stifle expressions of piety and reverence and to tear down symbols of traditional values. Our sociocultural system is not merely drifting but plunging into a chaotic no man's land where all recognized standards of taste, decency, and manners have not merely vanished but are vigorously trampled on wherever they may be found.

ARTS AND FINE ARTS

In *The Crisis of Our Age*, as well as in other works, Sorokin uses the expression "the fine arts," but his observations apply equally to popular culture: "What society and culture are, such will their fine arts be."[8] Actually, his remarks apply to everything in the world of entertainment and even the news media, for news often becomes entertainment, and entertainment makes news. Sorokin still worked within the old assumption that the members of high society should and frequently would exhibit moral and social virtues and be examples for the rest of society. Nevertheless, he would not have been surprised by revelations that United States senators and others in high office have wallowed in moral degeneracy, nor by the fact that some of them have been subjected to pharisaical condemnation by the same media that praise similar or greater depravity on the part of favored entertainers.

Sorokin contended that the more refined products of culture, literature, and the fine arts should have an uplifting effect on the general culture. The lower classes of society were assumed to have lower standards in many areas of life, including both conduct and artistic tastes, and popular culture was held to be cruder and less demanding than the truly fine arts. The example of the fine arts and the behavior of the distinguished classes of society ought in principle to have an uplifting effect on the whole culture. The higher forms of

---

[8] Sorokin, *Crisis*, 26.

art, music, literature, and theater should ideally have a moral, educational, and edifying impact on the general public, particularly by comparison with the amusements of the mob, such as sports spectacles, carnivals, bawdy songs, and vulgar entertainments. Unfortunately, in our day the upper or higher echelons of the world of culture, business, and politics (identified by celebrity and media attention) set the standards for the masses in degenerate conduct and degrading behavior patterns. Supposedly great artists approve and endorse the debasement of art even if they do not themselves engage in it.[9]

If by the terms *society* and *culture* we mean only *high society* and *refined culture* (the realms to which the fine arts traditionally belong and where they are cultivated and supported), we shall be seeing only part of the true picture. Instead of furnishing examples of integrity, altruism, and decency to the broad masses, the highest-ranking and most celebrated members of society, including royalty and political leaders, are increasingly ready to become patrons of the crude, the obscene, and the pornographic in the arts. At times they even seem willing to offer their own lives as the subject matter.

The sort of vulgarity and licentiousness that used to be relegated to back rooms and low dives can now be found on the greatest stages, the "court theaters" of our degenerate democratic society. In an effort to exhibit the common touch, princes and presidents fraternize with the debasers of values and shower them with praise and honors. Instead of elevating tastes and lifting standards, presidents and prime ministers show by their own behavior that "anything goes" in art and perhaps in life as well.

The Latin proverb, *de gustibus non disputandum est* (there is to be no disputing about tastes) should not frighten us into failing to notice that an egg is rotten or that milk has gone sour. We must not shrink back from speaking frankly about the condition of the arts at the end of this second millennium. Sorokin's willingness to criticize the sacred cows of art and entertainment permitted him to show that the

---

[9] For additional insight, see the work of critic Michael Medved, *Hollywood vs. America* (New York: HarperCollins, 1992). In Chicago a leading figure in the artistic world, Mme. Ardis Kranik, director of the city's famed Lyric Opera, has come out in vehement and indignant defense of the late Robert Mapplethorpe and his degenerate pornographic art, denouncing the reluctance of the federal government to fund similar art as censorship and repression.

arts are not merely a weathervane indicating the way the cultural wind is blowing, but also a rudder, determining the direction that is being taken by whole societies and cultures.

THE THREE FORMS OF THE ARTS:
IDEATIONAL, IDEALISTIC, AND SENSATE

Because every culture is an integrated system, the arts will also exhibit the basic characteristics of the phase in which the whole culture stands: ideational, idealistic, or sensate. Frequently the arts are somewhat in advance of the general culture; when they become chaotic and lose their integrating principles, it is likely that the rest of the culture will soon follow.

Cultures pass through different phases, but at any given time each culture can be found somewhere on the spectrum that moves from the purely spiritual orientation of the ideational to the systematic materialism of the sensate. There are transitional periods, during which it may not be apparent what a culture will become. Our present Western culture is in such a transitional period and is experiencing the inconsistencies and contradictions of its late sensate phase as well as the stirrings of something new, perhaps—but not necessarily—of something very good that lies ahead. The arts on the whole offer more evidence for disintegration than for renewal, but even there we can look for hopeful signs, precisely because when the whole culture shifts the arts cannot fail to be part of the shift.

The Internal Consistency of Each of the Three Systems

As long as a system remains integrated, its effect is felt throughout every aspect of the society. For this reason, when a sociocultural system begins to disintegrate, the change affects not merely certain institutions, but everything. Sorokin observed that when a culture is predominantly sensate, sensate also will be its dominant fine arts, and when a culture is unintegrated, chaotic, and eclectic so also will be its fine arts.

For several centuries, our sensate culture was integrated, but during recent decades, evidence of chaos and disorder has been growing. For more than four centuries our fine arts have been predominantly sensate; through the past century and a half they have gradually become degenerate and chaotic. What originally was appreciated as innovative and exciting became tiresome and boring; every few years something new had to be offered. As time went on, the pace of change increased, and the innovations had to become more and more daring, with every new change hailed as artistic progress. To criticize or reject any new thing is taken as evidence of Philistinism and lack of artistic sensitivity.

Our literati and artists encourage us to think of *l'art pour l'art*—art for art's sake—as though the arts existed in a world of their own, on a spiritual plane above common life. Unfortunately for those who would see the arts as autonomous, on examination it becomes evident that the arts are intricately bound up with the rest of society and culture. They cannot assume a particular form unless the society is ready for it, and they cannot appear to challenge society or to protest against it without themselves being part of it. The protest songs of the antiwar movement that swept the United States as well as other nations in the 1960s both expressed public feelings and also exerted an influence upon them. In an ideational or idealistic culture, the message of the songs—that nothing is worth dying for—could hardly have caught on. However, in the sensate culture of the decade, the sentiment made headway and influenced large masses of people.[10]

Ideational Art

In its content as well as in its type, ideational articulates the major premise of ideational culture, that the true, indeed the only reality-value is God. Therefore the topic of ideational art is the supersensory Kingdom of God. Its "heroes" are

---

[10] Ideational and idealistic cultures can inspire people to volunteer for war and other hazardous duties much more readily than can the sensate society. Even a materialistic society such as the USSR found it useful to evoke the highly ideational heritage of Russian Orthodoxy to stir up enthusiasm for the struggle with Hitler—who for his part created a fraudulent idealistic vision to motivate his people for war.

God and other deities, angels, saints and sinners, the soul, as well as the mysteries of Creation, Incarnation, Redemption, Crucifixion and Salvation, and other transcendental events. It is religious through and through. [11]

The art of the ideational culture may appear crude and unskilled to the eye. This is sometimes taken to mean that the culture is primitive or undeveloped. Yet this is a misunderstanding. Ideational art does not fail to produce realistic representations of things in the material world because its artists lack the skills to do so but because they do not try to capture the real world of the senses, much less to elevate and exalt it. Instead they try to point the viewers to heavenly, supernatural realities. The subjects of ideational art are divine or angelic beings, scenes in heaven or hell. No effort is made to portray them realistically, in part because they cannot be seen by the eye to be copied, and in part because an overly realistic representation would cause observers to confuse them with earthly subjects and not to realize that they belong to a transcendent, supersensory world.

When ideational art does portray historical events it is typically highly stylized; it symbolizes rather than accurately represents. Consider the adoration of the Magi as recorded in the Gospel of Matthew. Had a photographer been there, presumably he could have made lifelike photographs. But a lifelike photo or a detailed painting would not have communicated what the ideational artist wanted to say. An ideational painting explains what the feast of the Epiphany celebrates, namely, that the Gentiles were also looking forward to the coming of Christ. A lifelike painting would have fastened the attention of the viewer on the particular individuals involved instead of seeing the Magi as symbolic of the Gentile nations. There is no realistic way to depict this supernatural message on canvas, so the artist must paint symbolic figures.

The paramount example of art of this type is the icon painting of the Eastern Orthodox churches. Icons are still being produced today—a reminder of an older,

---

[11] Sorokin, *Crisis*, 27. The term *supersensory* rather than *supernatural* is used to emphasize the fact that such realities cannot be perceived by the five senses. From the ideational perspective, supersensory realities are the most natural of all.

ideational culture that is being deliberately preserved, against the trend of the times. They seek to portray a reality so superior to the materials and techniques available to the artist that any attempt to portray it realistically would be doomed to failure from the start.

For this reason ideational art does not offer landscapes, real people, or still-life tableaux. "Its object is not to amuse, entertain or give pleasure, but to bring the believer into a closer union with God. . . . Its emotional tone is pious, ethereal, and ascetic. . . . Its style is and must be symbolic. . . . It suggests a marvelous soul dressed in shabby clothes."[12] Ideational art is clearly intended to convey a message, to instruct the viewers, indeed, to lead them into a religious or spiritual experience. Because religious truth is seen as permanent and unchanging, ideational artists do not seek to be original but treat the same themes in the same fashion, so that they are often seen as copyists rather than as creative artists. Ideational art seldom appeals to the human sense of physical beauty, for it does not find its value in those things that appeal to the five human senses but in that which transcends them.

Idealistic Art

There is a natural contact point between the sensory realities of earth and the supersensory reality of God. If God is indeed the Creator of the universe, than it is reasonable to assume that at certain points the universe will point to its Author: "The heavens declare the glory of God; and the firmament sheweth his handywork" (Ps. 19:1 KJV).

Idealistic art portrays the reality of the sensory world, but only its sublimest and noblest aspects. It shows nothing that is ugly and vulgar. It can use accurate representational art to convey symbolic meaning. The idealistic artist is not yet the priest of a new, sensate pseudoreligion of *l'art pour l'art*, but is merely the *primus inter pares* (first among equals) of his community. His art

---

[12] Sorokin, *Crisis*, 27.

represents "a marvelous synthesis of the ideational and the noblest forms of sensate art."[13] When it portrays the beauty of the created world, idealistic art does so to remind the viewer of the glory of God who created it.

Sensate Art

As one might expect, sensate art is virtually the opposite of ideational art; it is totally dependent on an appeal to the senses. Unlike ideational art, which is not concerned with giving an accurate representation of the real world, sensate art, particularly in its early phase, presents realistic representation: portraits, landscapes, real or imaginary events of the real world. It tends to begin with important and impressive figures and events such as monarchs, battles, coronations, treaties, or storms at sea. For a time sensate art may continue to portray actual events of idealistic significance: Jesus calming the waves, the coronation of the Holy Roman Emperor. Even the dome of the United States Capitol building portrays George Washington's ascent into heaven. For many decades, sensate art attempted to inspire and exalt its audience not by directing attention to religious doctrines but by pointing to the excellence of this world and of the most prominent representatives of humanity. Early sensate art often did touch upon higher spiritual realities, but it did so not to bring about a moral or spiritual transformation in the beholder but simply to be pleasing, stimulating, or entertaining.

Even though it began with subjects familiar to ideational and idealistic art, sensate art did not remain tied to them. Michelangelo, working early in the sensate phase, produced works that seem to be idealistic as well as sensate—for example his great paintings in the Sistine Chapel of the Vatican. His art represents the transition from the idealistic world (to which he was still formally committed and from which, through the pope, he received commissions)

---

[13] Ibid., 28–29. There is also a kind of art that does not fit into any of these three categories, which we may describe as a kind of mechanical reproduction without internal or external unity. This form, which Sorokin designates as eclectic art, an art bazaar, has become more and more common in the second half of our century as a consequence of the technological developments that permit endless reproduction, duplication, modification, and proliferation without requiring any technical skill of the artist.

to the emergent sensate culture. The fleshly nudes of Rubens are unambiguously sensate; they attract the viewer not to the contemplation of any spiritualized human ideal but to the excitement the flesh can offer

In its early phases sensate art exalted the human form, the apparent innocence and charm of childhood, the physical beauty and strength of youth and early maturity, the voluptuous attractions of the well-formed human body, and dignified and stately old age. It also portrayed idyllic landscapes, storms at sea, rustic village festivals, and noble animals. Accuracy and lifelike representation were emphasized, with the intention of delighting the eye and giving pleasure to the beholder. In these early phases it is difficult to draw a clear line between sensate and idealistic art, because early sensate art tends to concentrate on the most admirable aspects of the real world and even to idealize them. In its overripe stage, however, sensate art descends from the heights of high politics, bourgeois citizens in council, or even peasants at work or play and turns instead to common or debased subjects such as prostitutes, beggars, criminals, madmen, sick and dying persons, slum scenes, even cadavers. Most recently the degenerate sensate period has been producing such things as the larger than life soup cans of Andy Warhol and the homoerotic pornography of Robert Mapplethorpe.[14]

In contrast to ideational art, which seeks to concentrate the attention of the beholder on eternal things, sensate art seeks to entertain, divert, and fascinate. In its overripe phase, it will seek to captivate and enslave the viewer, perhaps to entice him or her to plunge into direct sensate self-gratification. Pornography offers a crass example of this, but much contemporary advertising serves a similar purpose, although in a more refined way.

The key ideas of sensate art are:

1. attachment to the real world

2. the desire to fascinate and to entertain

---

[14] Mapplethorpe (who died of AIDS in 1989), after demonstrating unique artistic ability as a photographer, turned his attention to such bizarre subjects as one man urinating into another's mouth and a self-portrait of himself naked with the handle of a bullwhip protruding from his anus.

In its late phase, sensate art is primarily a commercial product, intended to attract and to produce profit. While ideational art is static, sensate art is fluid. It may seem strange to name both Michelangelo and Picasso as representatives of sensate art, for the one painted and sculpted realistically while the other became a prime practitioner of abstraction. The term *sensate art* may seem too broad to be useful, for it embraces not only the high art of masters such as Rubens and Tintoretto, the Impressionists, the Expressionists, the less than realistic art of modern painters such as Paul Gaugin and Franz Marc, abstract art of various kinds, and surrealism, but also the pop art of figures such as Andy Warhol. Perhaps the main thing that these so different artists have in common is a disinterest in the spiritual and a preoccupation with the present world of empirical reality, whether it is perceived as beautiful or as absurd.

Sensate art has abandoned the idea that there are any supersensory values to be reflected; ultimately it rejects the idea that there is anything noble or praiseworthy at all. It has turned away from the concept that art should serve the function of lifting the heart and mind of the viewer to what is eternal; instead it seeks to bind the viewer to the present, to personal experience, to the control of the senses. One may tend to lose oneself in the beauty of this world through the beautiful landscapes or Romantic allegories of the Hudson River School, for example, or one may be given the impression that the world is meaningless or absurd in the art of Picasso or Francis Bacon, but in sensate art one is never pointed to a world of permanent and abiding values. To Paul's lines, "Whatever is true, whatever is noble, whatever is right, whatever is pure, whatever is lovely, whatever is admirable—if anything is excellent or praiseworthy, think about such things" (Phil. 4:8, NIV), sensate art retorts, "Nothing is!" Because art has become sacrosanct to much of the opinion-making elite of modern culture, hardly anyone dares to say that such things as a crude drawing of a soup can (Warhol) or even a photo plunged into a jar of urine (Serrano) are not really art.

Sensate art aims to stimulate, to excite, to attract. It seeks to draw the beholder or hearer into the real world of sensory satisfaction—or, in some cases, of sensory disgust and revulsion—but not to lift him above the world to the realm of spiritual contemplation and fulfillment. Divorced from religion, morals, and other values, and with no educational or edifying intent, it really does become *l'art pour l'art*—art for art's sake. Whereas ideational art habitually represented its human subjects in modest attire, usually in clothing that corresponded to what the subjects symbolized, sensate art quickly turned to voluptuous nudity, sometimes difficult to distinguish from pornography.[15]

The sensate form of art may continue to represent the external world in a realistic manner over a period of centuries, but in its later phases it often becomes impressionistic, expressionistic, and finally surrealistic, giving way to fantasy, absurdity, and illusion. In its early stages, its goal was to make the physical world attractive to the beholder, to entice him or her into the contemplation or enjoyment of the sensual pleasures the world offers. But each new product must offer something new and in order to do this, sensate art is inevitably drawn in the direction of *Steigerung* (intensification), using ever more striking and dramatic images, sounds, and techniques in order to catch the imagination of viewers and draw them into its spell.

Because its purpose is entertainment, and because people are more easily amused by the comical and ridiculous than by the noble and edifying, sensate art readily resorts to comedy, farce, satire, and ridicule. In order to avoid boring the viewer or hearer, it constantly changes, always looking for something new and exciting. As Sorokin says, "Since it does not symbolize any supersensory value, it stands and falls by its external appearance . . . [making] lavish use of pomp and circumstance, colossality, stunning techniques, and other means of external adornment. . . . "[16] Nowhere is this more evident than in the colossal motion pictures of our day or in the neopagan spectacles such as the half-time show that accompanies the Super Bowl football game.

---

[15] It is, of course, possible to portray the naked human form in a relatively chaste way, appealing more to an artistic appreciation of beauty than to any lascivious interest. Much sensate art, even that of great masters such as Peter Paul Rubens, even though not pornographic, is nevertheless suggestive of concupiscence and debauchery. In magazines, as in the motion pictures of recent decades, pornography began by displaying nudes in poses that were suggestive but not explicit and has proceeded to ever more explicit depictions of both normal and perverted sexual activities.

[16] Sorokin, *Crisis*, 28–29.

Although in the ideational phase painting an icon was thought of as an act of worship, in our sensate age, both old and new icons have quite naturally become objects of commerce. Sensate art is primarily produced by a class of professional artists and depends for its success on an uncritical public and a fawning media. As time goes on, all of the distorting and grotesque characteristics of sensate art are increasingly exaggerated. Instead of commissioning works destined to become timeless art, as earlier patrons did, modern tycoons bid immense sums at auctions for the famous works of the past and even for trivial possessions of famous people—an unconscious attestation of the loss of true creativity that is a characteristic of the degenerate phase of our sensate culture.

Art Through the Ages

Although they may have left no written records, so-called primitive cultures have frequently produced artifacts that show them to be fundamentally ideational. Examples of simple forms of ideational art can be found in the distant past in the geometric art of the Neolithic era as well as in the present or recent past among African tribes and the Zuni Indians. The ideational also dominates in Taoist art, Buddhist culture, Tibet and Brahmanic India, ancient Egypt, and Greece from the ninth to the beginning of the fifth century B.C.

Periods of sensate art are also widely distributed. They include the representational art of the Old Stone Age, much of Assyrian history, Egypt from the later stages of the Old Kingdom, much of the Creto-Mycenaean culture, and the Graeco-Roman world during the Hellenistic period until the end of the Empire in the West. The art of our own culture has been increasingly sensate since the Renaissance.

Artifacts from the idealistic system are less frequently found because it tends to be a transitional form, even though once established it may last for several centuries. It is well represented in Greece of the fifth century B.C. and in the late European medieval world, in periods when the ideational system had lost its dominance and before the sensate system had come into being.

It is important to recognize that these different phases—ideational, idealistic, and sensate—alternate with one another; one is not "higher" or "more primitive" than the others. The particular phase does not indicate the level of civilization of a people nor the technical skill of its artists and craftsmen but rather reflects the *mentality* of the culture. This refers not merely to the way its members think and analyze but to their whole way of perceiving, interpreting, and understanding their world and reality.

Because we live in a culture that has been sensate for several centuries, we inevitably look at the products of other cultures and other times through our own sensate eyes. Ideational art naturally strikes us as more primitive than sensate art because as sensate men and women we do not have a feeling for the supersensory and divine realities that inspire it. We can learn to appreciate an ideational culture in the way one can appreciate an exhibit in a museum, but it is hard for us to think of ourselves as ever being at home in it. This is part of the explanation for the apprehension and loathing expressed by the opinion-making elements of the sensate culture for every expression of religious conviction.

It is easy for a sensate culture to dismiss ideational art as primitive. When people in our own sensate society grow bored and jaded with the latest refinements of sensate art, they may turn back to ideational art as a faddish alternative, but very seldom will their exotic tastes lead them to any appreciation of the spiritual realities that inspire it.

To dismiss the artistic productions of ideational and idealistic cultures as crude and lacking in skill is a serious misunderstanding. It fails to take into account that even in the early Stone Age, artists could accurately represent things they were interested in, such as animals and hunting scenes. It is customary for most of us to think of primitive man as living in a world full of spiritual beings, gods and goddesses, and supernatural powers that do not exist. We think of sophisticated peoples as being more sceptical, realistic, and less naive. Yet, this would be an oversimplification. As far as we can judge from available evidence, very early humans were quite aware of sensory reality. The cave paintings of the Old Stone Age reflect a sharp awareness of the temporal world and do not suggest an interest in supersensory reality. Therefore, it appears correct to speak of that culture, simple though it was, as sensate. In other words, it is a mistake to suppose that because a culture was early and primitive, it was less aware of the sensory world and lived in the unreal world of supersensory and spiritual realities.

Earliest Human Art

Because the Western culture that we know began with an ideational phase sixteen centuries ago, we tend to asssume that the earliest phase of any culture will be ideational, in other words, that it is natural for primitive man to think in terms of the divine and of spiritual realities. Hence, we may expect primitive art to be essentially religious.

In fact, however, this is not always the case. Sorokin's evidence reveals that even early man could and in some cases did have a sensate worldview. The Old and New Stone Ages (Paleolithic and Neolithic eras) have left no written documentation or treatises explaining how they looked on the world and on reality, but we can draw some conclusions from the artifacts and artistic evidence they have left behind. This evidence, although scanty, suggests that the primitive culture of the Old Stone Age was sensate, while that of the New Stone Age had become ideational. Even though both of the early cultures are primitive in our eyes, they understood reality in ways as different as the difference between late Hellenistic paganism and early Christianity.[17]

Although we do not know much about the pre-Homeric culture of Crete and Mycenaean Greece in the second millennium B.C., we have enough evidence to see that its orientation was primarily sensate. Its art and the few literary remains that have been deciphered show a worldly, hedonistic approach to reality. The famous Vaphio cup reveals a distinctly sensate orientation. Myths from this vanished culture, such as the story of Theseus and the Minotaur, reflect a skeptical

---

[17] If it is surprising that the earlier Stone Age was sensate, preoccupied with material realities, consider that our present late modern or postmodern period appears to be turning away from material and objective realities, from the world of the hard sciences, despite all of its accomplishments in that realm. To the surprise of many, we are experiencing an upsurge of mysticism through the New Age movement. Natural science in the modern sense owed its beginning to the Christian theological conviction that the world was the work of an intelligent, all-wise Creator, and for that reason it could be investigated and to some extent understood by humans made in the image of God. Christianity is not materialistic in the sense of considering the material world the supreme reality, but it does hold that the Creator's handiwork is objectively real and can profitably be investigated by what we call the scientific method. The scientific method will not survive indefinitely, however, when a culture loses its faith in God the Creator as the author of objective reality. The culture will turn to worlds of illusion, as in the current New Age movement. Paradoxical as it may seem, the rise of modern science was initiated not by the kind of skepticism that believes only in what can be seen and felt but by confident Christian faith in an orderly creation by a wise God.

attitude that had no place for supersensory realities. In other words, it was a sensate culture. A few centuries later, on the same soil, we encounter the ideational culture of Homer. The *Iliad* portrays a world in which the gods were in touch with humans; a world in which man lived, to use John H. Finley Jr.'s expression, "in the eye of God, not *Who's Who*."[18] The sculptures of this period show us the gods and goddesses in stylized, symbolic form; icons in stone, as it were, representing power, wisdom, and other attributes, rather than as the perfect examples of human beauty that we find in the later periods of Greek culture, both idealistic and sensate.

More Recent Parallels

Even a glance at these early eastern Mediterranean cultures reminds us that the sensate phase with its worldly sophistication and skepticism about the reality of a supersensory, divine order is not necessarily the end phase of a culture but may be followed by an ideational outlook that once again sees divine realities as paramount. This happened in the transition from early Cretan-Mycenaean culture to that of Homer's Greece, and it happened again in a period about which we have much fuller evidence, at the end of Graeco-Roman paganism.

Although modern popular culture does not promote a careful and systematic study of history, most of us have some awareness of the Hellenistic background of Western civilization, having been exposed to both fact and fiction about the glory of Greece and the grandeur of Rome. Novels and films such as *Ben Hur* and *The Robe* have enough historical accuracy to give us an impression both of the magnificence of sensate Roman culture and also of its cynical worldliness. However, Roman institutions and structures were overwhelmed by barbarian invasions or simply broke down because of internal weakness and fatigue. We call the period that followed the fall of Rome the Dark Ages—a designation that misses the fact that it was really the dawn of the new culture, in the twilight of which we still live today.[19]

---

18 This expression comes from the late John H. Finley Jr.'s lectures in his popular Harvard College course, "Humanities 2."

19 Recent scholarship has begun to rehabilitate the Dark Ages and to recognize that civilization by no means ended with the fall of Rome.

The new dawn of emerging Christian civilization is seen in the transition in art that became evident in the fourth century A.D., a clear change from the increasingly degenerate sensate art of the late Graeco-Roman period to an ideational approach reflecting faith in God and divine reality—art that for centuries would characterize Western Christendom. It is a mistake to think that early Christian art is less representational and realistic than late Hellenistic art because the artists of the period no longer possessed adequate skill and technique. It looks different because the artists had turned their gaze away from man toward God and his glory, to themes that could not be represented realistically even though they were believed to be very real indeed.

THE SIGNIFICANCE OF THE SHIFTS
BETWEEN SUPERSYSTEMS

If we do not consider the great historians such as Spengler, Toynbee, and Sorokin but simply think of the common understanding of the arts and culture in general, we have a simpler picture. Each of these three great thinkers dealt with the rise and fall of cultures—in other words, with cycles of history. Most contemporary people, at least in the West, do not think in terms of cycles but are deeply imbued with the idea of progress, which we tend to see largely in terms of technology and comfort rather than in the realm of ideas or spiritual values. If our comforts have increased, we consider this progress. If our ethics and morals have deteriorated and our arts have become increasingly degenerate and pornographic at the same time, we accept it as part of progress: "You can't turn back the clock."

For this reason, it is natural for our age to regret the passing of the magnificent sensate culture that built the Coliseum and the Pantheon and to look upon the early Christian phase as a decline. Little basilicas, dark Romanesque chapels, and rude castles cannot compare with those great Roman edifices, nor do hymns and Christian tracts interest us like the heroic epics and torrid love poetry of the classical era. Hardly anything produced in the Dark and Middle Ages seems really impressive to us—with the possible exception of the great cathedrals.

From history books, museums, and motion picture epics we have an impression of the artistic excellence and architectural triumphs of classical Greek and pagan Roman civilization. We have seen pictures of the statues of Praxiteles, the busts of Julius and Augustus Caesar, Greek and Roman temples, the Roman Forum, and the Colosseum where so many gladiators and early Christian martyrs met death. Then we have seen images of Germanic barbarians and Viking pirates raiding, burning, and destroying cities and towns in Roman Europe, succeeded by far less heroic impressions of rudely clad saints in the desert and monkish scribes in monasteries. We have seen, if not the objects themselves, pictures of the statues of saints with unexpressive faces and bodily forms indistinguishable under flowing garments, the stiff paintings of the Virgin Mother and Child, of worshiping saints with halos, of martyrs in unrealistic poses of noble suffering, contrasting with the noble nudes of classical art. We have compared, at least in imagination, the huts of Frankish peasants and the rude castles of German robber barons to the magnificent palaces that once graced the Seven Hills of Rome, and we have compared the gargoyles on medieval cathedrals to the beautiful idols of the goddess Aphrodite and the gods Apollo and Hermes.

We have seen the transition from the stiff and formal religious paintings of the thirteenth century to the beautiful, lifelike representational art of the Renaissance, which produced statues such as Michelangelo's David, in no way inferior to those of classical Greece. The art of da Vinci, Raphael, Titian, Dürer, Rembrandt, and the Dutch Masters, followed by a succession of painters all over Europe, seems to represent a fresh discovery of talent and technique unknown to the painters of saints and sacred scenes in earlier centuries. If this is all that we see, it is easy to look on the world of medieval Christendom—the Age of Faith, as some histories define it—as an obscure period between the brilliance of Graeco-Roman civilization and the new clarity of the Renaissance. This superficial understanding is shared by many in our contemporary culture, who either condemn medieval Christendom as a period of backwardness and ignorance (in the case of non-Christians) or apologize for it (in the case of Christians).

NOTABLE SHIFTS IN THE NATURE OF THE ARTS

Shifts in the cultural supersystem produce shifts in the forms of the arts, which promote shifts in the entire sociocultural system. If we consider the cultural world with which we are most familiar—Western civilization from the Greeks through imperial Rome to the present—we observe the three major shifts already mentioned:

1. from ideational to sensate art with an idealistic interval, between the ages of Homer and that of Alexander the Great;

2. from sensate back to ideational after the fourth century of the Christian era;

3. from ideational to sensate, once again with an idealistic interval, beginning in the later Middle Ages.

We should examine them not only for their own sakes, as contributions to our understanding of human civilization, but also in order to help us understand the contemporary crisis in our modern Western culture.[20]

Sorokin offers a succinct description of the first transition:

Beginning with the end of the sixth century B.C., we note a decline of ideational art in all its aspects and the emergence of an idealistic art which reaches its climax in the fifth century B.C. with Phidias, Aeschylus, Sophocles, and Pindar. It is probably the example *par excellence* of idealistic art. Exemplified by the Parthenon, it is half religious and half empirical. From the sensory world it derives only its noble types and positive values. It is an idealizing, typological art. Its portraits are beautiful types—not realistic representations of a given individual. It is marred by nothing low, vulgar, or debasing. Its idealism manifests itself in the artist's excellent knowledge of human anatomy and of the means of rendering it in an ideal form; in the type of persons represented; in their posters; in the abstract treatment of the human type. There are no concrete portraits, no ugliness, no defective traits. We are introduced to immortals or idealized mortals; the aged are rejuvenated; infants are depicted as grown up; the women reveal few traits that are specifically womanish, and appear in the guise of athletes. There is no concrete landscape. The postures and expressions are free from anything violent,

---

[20] As recently as the end of the Second World War, Asian and African nations, and notably defeated Japan, equated "Westernization" with the modernization they considered necessary for their own survival, and therefore sought to learn and adopt Western ways. It is interesting and embarrassing to note that, hardly half a century later, some contemporary Asian societies, such as Singapore, now identify "Western values" with social and moral degeneracy and work hard to keep them out.

from excessive emotion and distorting passion. They are calm and imperturbable, like the gods. Even the dead reflect the same serene beauty.[21]

The art and literature of Greece during this idealistic period was committed to the promotion of moral, civic, and religious values. It was not intended to reflect the day-to-day reality of life with all the disappointment, frustration, suffering, and anxiety that ordinary people experience. Its purpose was to hold up the best examples of human virtues: courage, wisdom, dignity, prowess in war, athletic ability, and beauty and grace of the physical form. Its goal was to promote the pursuit of excellence, which was thought of not as making new sports records or amassing great wealth but in terms of character, wisdom, and virtue. The virtues of public figures were extolled for popular imitation; their blemishes were covered over.

The great tragedies of Aeschylus, Sophocles, and Euripides centered on the way in which even a small failing—the tragic flaw—in an otherwise noble character could bring inexorable disaster. The reader habituated to respond in the cynical, debunking way of modern, sensate America will naturally object, "That's unrealistic. Life is not like that." That is precisely the point: It is not realistic but idealistic. It is not intended to observe and report the failings and failures that are all too common to our species but rather to show what noble and virtuous standards can and sometimes have been achieved, and to encourage the general public, beginning with the young, to strive for them.[22] The artists and poets of this era had not yet become entrepreneurs like their parallels during the sensate period; the arts at this point were for *amateurs* (from the Latin word for "lovers") not professionals, as were the athletes of the time.[23]

---

[21] *Sorokin*, Crisis, 32.

[22] Traditionally, Christianity, with its doctrine of original sin, has been critical of the moral accomplishments and virtues of the "noble pagans," pointing out that the best of them "fall short of the glory of God" (Rom. 3:23). It is true that no human being is free from flaws and failings, but some people struggle to overcome them and others abandon the struggle, or even revel in their faults.

[23] In the idealistic culture, athletics too was primarily the province of amateurs, but it was not long before sports and games became professional. Once this happens, it becomes increasingly rare for even the best athletes to inspire virtue in the young. This is not so much because athletes become less virtuous as because the culture has changed: Virtue is no longer something to be recognized, much less admired and imitated.

THE ARTS REFLECT THE SPIRIT OF THE AGE

The arts, both the fine arts and popular arts, express the artists' understanding of the world and of our place in it; the form they take reveals what the respective artists consider true or false, meaningful or absurd, beautiful or ugly, noble or base. Art will gain a following if and only if what it represents or says corresponds to what its audience believes, senses, or feels. When contact has been established, the art plays a double role, both reflecting and helping to shape the sociocultural system around it. Often art functions like a magnifying glass or a loudspeaker, making things already present in a culture bigger and louder; in the process, it can also stimulate further growth or exaggeration of the trends it reflects. What artists do is always a function of the sociocultural supersystem in which they live and work, and as such it reflects that system's approach to reality:

- In the ideational cultures of the past, the arts portrayed divine and spiritual realities as the only reality
- Idealistic art continues to portray them as the highest realities.
- In sensate systems, divine and spiritual subjects are replaced by earthly, material ones.

The arts reflect not only the fashions and tastes of a culture—what it considers important and attractive—but also its fundamental view of reality, what it thinks about truth and what things it thinks to be true. The art of a culture is inevitably related to its systems of truth.

3

THE CRISIS IN
SYSTEMS OF TRUTH

The wisdom of this world is foolishness with God.

1 Corinthians 3:19 KJV

EVER SINCE THE RENAISSANCE, the world has been fascinated by the rapid increase of human knowledge. Our scientists have discovered one new truth after another and revealed secret after secret previously hidden from human view. By a strange paradox, however, the more we learn, the more perplexed our society seems to be growing about what is *real*, what is *true*. "Science is not concerned with reality. . . . It is not for us as scientists to worry about 'reality.'"[1] There is a kind of scientific or intellectual fatigue setting in. Instead of the search for truth that characterized modernism, we are in the era of postmodernism, where reality is fluid and truth depends entirely on the beholder.

Sorokin asserted that in the degenerate phase of a sensate culture, the pace of scientific inventions and discoveries would slacken. Late in his life

---

[1] Sorokin cites this statement by an anonymous young scientist at the beginning of his third chapter. Pitirim A. Sorokin, *The Crisis of Our Age*, 2d ed. (Oxford: Oneworld, 1992), 66–67.

he acknowledged that the contrary was happening: Inventions and discoveries have continued to proliferate at an exponential rate. There do seem to be signs that the onward march of science is stagnating, however. The exploration of space, which reached a high point with the moon landing the year after Sorokin's death, has slowed down. Medical science continues to make progress, but it is encountering frustrating obstacles. Cures are found for familiar diseases, but new maladies have appeared and previously suppressed ones are reappearing. Fewer babies die in infancy, and the average life span is increasing, but the maximum age attainable by humans does not seem to have advanced much. "As for the days of our life, they contain seventy years, or if due to strength, eighty years" (Ps. 90:10). Prestigious medical journals feature the discovery of new abortifacients and report physician-assisted suicide as though they were great accomplishments.

Every few years we are confronted with a new generation of computers and software; it is becoming possible to process more and more data in ever shorter times. Unfortunately, as time goes on, more of the data are to be found only in the machines and fewer in the human mind. The human mind is being challenged more and more aggressively with mounting floods of data that threaten to overwhelm it entirely—a kind of information overload in which it does not know data but only knows where to find data.[2] The time of the Renaissance man is past, when a person could attain a high degree of mastery in several scientific and scholarly disciplines.

Pontius Pilate asked Jesus, "What is truth?" (John 18:38). Sorokin observes that Pilate's question is perennial. It would take a superhuman, omniscient Mind to provide an answer valid for every culture and for all mankind. But Pilate was a skeptic and probably did not believe that such a Mind existed, or that if it did, it would not give an answer in a form we could understand. In other words, he implied that truth is not attainable.

---

[2] When future historians look back upon the closing decades of our millennium and the first years of the next, it may be that Sorokin will have been right after all, for it seems that more and more of the discoveries and innovations are being made by computers and not by human minds. The store of human knowledge is indeed increasing exponentially, but more and more of it is stored in computer data banks and less and less in our brains. The day may come when hardly anyone actually *knows* a single thing, although large numbers of people will know which file to access to find out virtually anything and everything.

It is important to put Pilate's words into perspective. Every human acquisition of truth is partial and incomplete. All human efforts are subject to error. Reasonable people through the centuries have always known that human knowledge is limited: We can know only in part. However, it is important to recognize that while we cannot know fully and exhaustively, we can know at least some things with certainty. The Christian in particular is committed to the conviction that this "omniscient Mind" really does exist and can and does communicate truth to us. This is the doctrine of the Word of God; a doctrine that makes good sense if one is persuaded that God is real and personal.

If God is real and truly is the "Creator of heaven and earth and of all things visible and invisible," as the Nicene Creed (A.D. 325) puts it, then there ought to be a principle of rationality and coherence in the universe that will permit us, despite our flawed intellects and proneness to error, to discover solid truths. If the universe is the work of a supremely wise Creator, then it is reasonable to expect that it has a structure and an order that we, his creatures, can comprehend at least in part. If it is true, as biblical theology teaches, that we humans are made in God's image, then it is even more reasonable to expect that we will be able to understand the Creator's handiwork at least to some extent.

Things are as they are either because God made them that way or because, after he made them, factors such as human sin intervened to alter them. This concept is fundamental to the great monotheistic faiths. There is a divinely established Order of Being, and this order is sufficiently stable so that we can examine it, learn about it, and make trustworthy predictions based upon it.

The belief in the wise Creator provided the necessary presupposition for the rise of modern science; historians and philosophers of science such as Alfred North Whitehead (1861–1947) and Stanley L. Jaki (1924–present) have shown this. Experimental science in the modern sense of the word arose because people believed in a wise Creator and an orderly Creation, a conviction that they derived primarily from the Bible and Christian teaching. Once science became well established in circles where the Christian understanding of the unity of truth prevailed, scientists of other faiths (or no faith) could and did make valuable contributions. Nevertheless, science as we know it would hardly have begun if it had not been for the Christian conviction that an all-wise Creator made the world and endowed us, his creatures, with sufficient wisdom to understand it, at least in part.

THREE APPROACHES TO TRUTH

Like other aspects of culture, a different approach to truth characterizes each of the three main supersystems, at least to the extent that the culture and its representatives believe that such a thing as truth exists and can be known.

Ideational Truth

For an ideational culture, truth depends on God. Whatever God reveals is true: His statements to us, properly understood as he intended, are infallible in principle and in reality. In the great monotheistic religions, this expresses itself in terms of the infallibility of Scripture (i.e., of the Bible or the Koran, understood as the very word of God). Even ideational cultures that lack a written revelation maintain that the truths of the gods are absolute and cannot be altered or modified by human activity.

The absoluteness and immutability of divine reality is the source of the tragic conflict in many early Greek dramas. The Greeks had no sacred book like the Bible to tell them that killing a parent is a grievous crime and will be punished inexorably, but they did not need it. In the great tragedies, the *Oresteia* of Aeschylus and Sophocles' *Oedipus Cycle*, Orestes and Oedipus learn truth through tragic experience; their fates proclaim it to the audience. The course of tragedy is inexorable: Once a fatal mistake has been committed, nothing can be done to reverse it.

Because divine truths are absolute and unchanging, people in an ideational culture are often willing to die for their faith. The promise of eternal bliss in heaven and the threat of eternal damnation in hell seem surer and longer-lasting than any pleasures or pains this world can promise or threaten.

Sensate Truth

A sensate culture, by contrast, believes only what it can prove or thinks that it can prove, and trusts only what it can test or thinks that it can test. It is common, although not inevitable, for people in a sensate culture to become cynical about values, unwilling to make sacrifices for anything as intangible as a spiritual truth or a religious ideal. When sensate cultures need soldiers, they often have to resort to mercenaries, who find the thought of pay and plunder attractive enough to risk suffering and death.

In our own sensate culture, even the professional military forces of the United States have come to resemble mercenaries. They are no longer recruited primarily on the basis of patriotism or love of country but with the explicit promise of substantial benefits and an implied commitment that if they have to fight at all, it will be against inferior enemies and with the odds on their side. Like mercenary armies of the past, American forces are frequently engaged in places where America's national interests are not at stake, to protect the interests of others. They differ from mercenaries of the past, however, in that the other entity does not pay them; they serve at their own nation's expense.

Idealistic Truth

The idealistic approach to truth is a kind of synthesis: with regard to the phenomena of the material world, it accepts the evidence of the senses and of our measuring instruments. With regard to supersensory reality, it depends on divine revelation. An idealistic culture can be very productive in the areas of mathematics, logic, and philosophy, which depend not on divine revelation but on the synthetic ability of human reason. An idealistic system of truth resembles an ideational system in that it too holds spiritual truths to be the highest truths, but because it also prizes the evidence of the senses, it may gradually become more sensate with the passage of time. Sensate truth, based on immediate sense perceptions, may ultimately thrust idealistic truth aside or place it in a separate realm, called "religious truth"— a realm that is not connected with actual reality. Under these conditions, the "truths" of science are considered facts, while what once were considered truths of faith become mere opinions or viewpoints.

A Fourth Possibility: No Truth

By a twist that seemed strange only a few years ago, modern man is becoming *postmodern*. He is no longer committed to the concepts of real truth and objective reality, as was the case only a few decades ago. Although a sensate system will initially value the truths of science and experience, as it becomes overripe it will come to doubt its own evidence even with respect to scientific truths and material facts. Fifty years ago it was customary to describe religious convictions and moral standards as only "beliefs" or "opinions" without any foundation in reality like that of the natural sciences. Today there is a growing trend to dismiss even the assured facts and scientific evidence of the natural sciences as interpretations that will naturally vary from observer to observer. This gives rise to a skepticism that denies truth exists at all or, if it does exist, that it can be known—or, even if it can be known, that it can be expressed and communicated. This is generally called postmodernism.

The hermeneutics of thinkers such as Jacques Derrida and Michel Foucault challenges the concept of *objective* meaning of a text. In order to interpret it, a reader must deconstruct it, identifying the dominant conceptual structures that underlie it and interpreting it according to his or her own perspective. This does not mean that a text has *no* meaning at all but rather that the meaning is dependent on the perspective of the reader. Such an approach makes intellectual inquiry and the communication of learning and meaning so difficult that its appeal is usually limited to a small circle; many simply give up seeking truth.

No longer sure of the truths of even the natural sciences, postmodern Western man sees everything as dependent on his own understanding and interpretation of reality. From a few decades in which Western man showed virtually unlimited confidence in the ability of science to lead him into all truth, now he has come to doubt that there is such a thing as truth or, if it exists, that it can be known. Instead of becoming totally skeptical and immersing himself entirely in material reality, postmodern man is beginning to create for himself a world filled with spiritual presences, disembodied beings, astral selves, alternative medicine, and all manner of beliefs that would have been dismissed as absurd superstitions only a few years ago.

As Sorokin points out, "Mankind cannot live and act under the conditions of such a system."[3] A variation of this radical skepticism, which denies that anything is really true, is the new fashion of multiculturalism, which in effect pretends that everything is true, depending on the time, place, and circumstances.

THE CRISIS IN THE SYSTEMS OF TRUTH

The crisis in the systems of truth expresses itself in an irreconcilable clash between the idealistic and ideational systems on the one hand and the sensate system on the other. What appears to be rock-solid truth from the ideational perspective is derided as foolishness and superstition from the perspective of sensate truth. Religious convictions for which thousands willingly suffered martyrdom are dismissed as dangerous illusions. On the other hand, what sensate truth sees as established facts of science, history, and worldly experience can be held as trivial and insignificant or even found false and illusory from the perspective of ideational truth. The sensate worldview says, "Eat, drink, and be merry, for tomorrow we die," expecting that death is the end. The ideational view says, "It is given to man once to die, and after that, the judgment." What does it profit one to accumulate riches or honors if these are destined to perish and one will suffer eternal lostness for ignoring the truth of God?

In a sensate culture truths that are fundamental to an idealistic or ideational system are not so much disputed as found to be irrelevant or meaningless— for example, the Christian doctrine of the Trinity. Those who held a rival ideational system, such as Muslims, contended fiercely (frequently resorting to armed force) that such a doctrine is false and blasphemous because it conflicted with their own understanding of ideational truth, "God is One."[4] Sorokin

---

[3] Sorokin, *Crisis*, 68.

[4] Of course orthodox Christianity also asserts that God is one and sees its doctrine of the Trinity as preserving rather than endangering this conviction.

observes, "Many a revealed truth of religion is utterly false from the point of view of an exclusive truth of the senses, and vice versa. This explains the sharp clash of these systems of truth that marks especially the periods of decline of the one and the rise of the other."[5]

Toward the end of the last sensate era before our own, in the first three centuries of imperial rule in Rome, the rising Christian worldview was considered not merely unproved and unfounded, but ignorant, superstitious, and self-deceived. The best pagan thinkers had only harsh criticisms for it:

> Tacitus called it "dangerous superstition, infamous and abominable."
>
> Pliny characterized it as "nothing but a debased superstition carried to an extreme."
>
> Marcus Aurelius said that it resulted from an unreasoning and unbalanced spirit of opposition.

As Sorokin comments, "From the point of view of sensory truth, the Christian truth of faith, revelation, and God—indeed, the whole Christian religion and movement—could not appear other than an absurdity and a superstition."[6]

The clash between the sensate system of late paganism and the ideational truth of Christianity, based on divine revelation, went on for centuries until the complete triumph of Christianity throughout the territory of the Roman Empire in about the sixth century. To some extent, the church superseded the empire, and a restored culture based on the truths of faith rather than of the senses began to create modern Europe. The rise of Islam during and after the seventh century was an almost fatal threat to Christendom but not to ideational culture, for the Muslims also held firmly to the concept of the truth of faith, even though the content of their faith differed from that of their Christian adversaries.

From India in the east to the Atlantic Ocean in the west, from the Sahara in the south to the Hebrides in the North, ideational truth held sway. When the

---

[5] Sorokin, *Crisis*, 69.

[6] Ibid.

intellectual triumph of Islam in Syria, Egypt, and North Africa speedily followed the Arab conquests, it was not a question of one fundamental type of cultural supersystem replacing another but, more simply, of the elimination of certain doctrines and their replacement by different ones of a similar type.[7]

Although our attention is primarily focused on Christianity, we can observe a similar development of culture from ideational through idealistic to sensate in the Muslim world. Arabic and Turkish culture, while formally committed to the ideational truth of Islam, became sensate even more rapidly than the culture of Christendom (although after the Renaissance, Christendom caught up with the Muslim world and overtook it, and for a time brought much of it under its own colonial or imperial control).[8] The sophisticated Muslim cultures of Egypt, the Near East, and Muslim Spain became highly sensate, but when the European powers began to dominate them, they experienced a shift in the direction of ideational truth and values. Since World War II and the end of the colonial period in Africa, the Muslim world has experienced a vigorous reaction against the sensate culture that it mistakenly takes to be the product of the infidel West and of Christianity, a reaction known by the somewhat misleading name of Muslim fundamentalism.[9]

Military triumphs, imperial expansion, and economic prosperity have frequently facilitated a shift from the ideational or idealistic view that makes the truth of God paramount and the wisdom of this world less significant to the sensate view that only facts matter—the "truths" that can be measured,

---

[7] After World War II, many individuals who had been active Nazis signed up as Communists, although the Nazis and the Communists were bitter enemies during the war. It was not a case of a fundamental change of philosophy or faith but merely as it were of coloration, from black to red.

[8] After its brilliant conquests of the Persian Empire and of much of what had been Roman, the Muslim world was both wealthier and more cosmopolitan than the Crisian, for it was in contact not only with the Christian culture of Byzantium but with the high cultures of Asia. Wealth and sophistication, by comparison with the ruder conditions of Western Europe, no doubt facilitated the rise of sensate thinking in the Muslim world. The Byzantine Empire centered in Constantinople was hardly less sophisticated during this period (eighth through eleventh centuries), but because it was constantly engaged in fighting for its life against first Arabs, then Turks, and much of the time against Slavs from the north, it did not experience the same sensate development.

[9] The term *fundamentalism* was coined early in the twentieth century to represent a particular school of Christianity, which had only doctrinal and social interests but no inclination to force its view upon society by means of violence.

weighed, and preferably turned to profit. Loss of power may initiate a shift in the other direction. The last great shift from sensate to ideational truth came about in Rome when imperial power and security were waning; it was not accompanied by violence. In the Christian West today, the dominance of the sensate worldview is stronger and enjoys the support of the institutions of government, education, and information. Nevertheless, here too there are signs of a resurgence of an ideational approach to truth; so far they have not been accompanied by anything like the violence that has been associated with Muslim fundamentalism.

It would be wrong to see the readiness to engage in violence and terrorist acts as the most significant feature of Muslim fundamentalism, for that might give the false impression that what is at stake in the minds of the activists is nothing more than worldly power and the control of government. In reality these are only incidental aspects of the movement. What is crucial to them is *truth*. Modern sensate culture, to some extent forced upon them by the West and to some extent cultivated in their own sophisticated and decadent circles, denies the truth of Allah. For that reason, it must at least be banished from Muslim lands, if not eradicated everywhere.

Fundamentalists—Christian as well as Muslim—have kept or returned to the foundational conviction that the highest truth, virtually the only truth, is that of revelation. In Western Christendom, particularly in those lands where liberalism has prevailed, people have grown unaccustomed to using force to resolve intellectual and religious disputes, although the Nazis and the Marxists certainly did not shun it. The resurgence of fundamentalism is only a minority phenomenon for the time being, even in the Muslim world, but the fact that it exists at all in the modern or postmodern world is further evidence that the sensate cultural system is nearing exhaustion.

When sensate truth fails, when men and women in increasing numbers no longer find its one-dimensional approach to reality satisfying, something will inevitably arise to take its place. Will it be a return to a new dawn with a commitment to the truths of God, to the dignity of man made in the divine image, and to a creative mission here on earth? Or will the loss of such stability as even sensate truth possesses initiate a slide into chaos and barbarism? Part of the answer lies in our own hands.

DIVINE REVELATION AND HUMAN SCIENCE

The rise of modern science coincides roughly with the transition from the idealistic culture of the later Middle Ages to the sensate sociocultural system that has prevailed since then. The conflict between faith and reason, between theology and the natural sciences, arose precisely because both systems claim to be committed to truth, and both believe (or until recently believed) in the unity of truth, properly understood. What one discipline discovers to be true will not cease to be true when viewed from the perspective of another discipline. For both ideational and idealistic systems, divine revelation is absolutely true. Truths that can be discovered through the senses necessarily will be in harmony with revelation. If they do not seem to harmonize, either there is a misunderstanding, or they are simply not truths at all. For the sensate system, the things that the human mind discovers about the material world are absolutely true. All three systems have a high idea of truth. When they reach substantially conflicting results, controversy is inevitable.

Initially, certain scientists began to challenge specific religious doctrines because they came to the conclusion that they were not true. Truth remained the criterion for the acceptance or rejection of religious beliefs. If true, they should be accepted by natural scientists and by theologians. If false, they should be rejected by theologians as well as by natural scientists. An expanding sensate culture thought that it had discovered many things contrary to the truths taught by religion, and bitter conflicts ensued, especially from the mid-nineteenth century to the present day. For several centuries, Christians committed to their own idealistic or ideational truths felt secure enough to reject the sensate challenges, but with the passage of time and the increasing pervasiveness of sensate culture, many of them either gave up the disputed doctrines or abandoned Christianity altogether.

During the Thirty Years' War (1618–48), the willingness of Christians to fight and die for the truths of Christianity was tested and to a large extent exhausted.[10] The sensate view of truth was already taking hold when the

---

[10] Religion was not the only cause of the Thirty Years' War, but it embittered the conflict and made reasonable compromises impossible.

religious controversies began. As the cost of mutual slaughter for the sake of religious truths grew ever higher, people became disillusioned and were ready to turn to the truths of the senses.

In the eighteenth-century Age of Reason, revelation was no longer trusted as reliable, absolute truth. Indeed, it came to be considered unnecessary or even dangerous, causing religious wars. Human reason was proposed as a sufficient guide for the good life.

In the nineteenth century, biblical criticism and Darwin's evolutionary theory made the concept of divinely revealed truth seem even less credible. Nevertheless, men continued to believe that truth exists; they simply no longer accepted what the Bible or other religious revelation taught as a reliable guide to it. In this phase of sensate culture, the material world was held to be the highest, indeed, the only reality, and the knowledge that we can gain of this world, especially through science, was taken to be unquestionable, reliable truth. Science took the place of the guiding light that Christians had seen in divine revelation and was viewed as a more reliable guide.

DISILLUSIONMENT WITH TRUTH

In the middle of the twentieth century, arguments against religious doctrine were often based on real or supposed evidence from the natural sciences and expressed in language such as: "That's not true. The evidence contradicts it." However, as the twentieth century passed, people became disillusioned with the natural sciences and increasingly less ready to give full credit to what the sciences presented as evidence. Einstein's concept of relativity and Heisenberg's uncertainty principle, although hardly widely understood, made it plain that there are limits to the power of science to make objective observations that are not influenced by the subjectivity of the scientists. Even scientific truths, hitherto thought to be objective by their very nature, began to be seen as subjective, to vary with the observer. The existentialist movement in philosophy found human existence absurd. It was succeeded by postmodernism, which challenged all received interpretations and understandings. All truth became relative, which is to say relatively unreliable and absolutely worthless.

This seems to be an innate problem of the sensate approach to truth: Thinking that the material world alone is the source of truth and that it can be adequately understood by using our senses and the instruments and tools that our science and technology can develop, we become increasingly frustrated as we encounter both the limits and the built-in error factors in science; we begin to lose confidence in the reality of truth itself. If truth lies in the subjectivity of the beholder, then neither material evidence nor reliable divine revelation is required to authenticate a claim. Either anything suffices or nothing suffices. As applied to religion, religious doctrines were no longer exalted as objectively and absolutely true nor denounced as objectively false; instead they were praised as "true for you," or "true for me." They could also be rejected because, "They do nothing for me," or, "I can't relate to them."

This new approach has now permeated every area of life in our late sensate culture. Where only a short time ago medicine trusted only the most scientifically verifiable claims, now alternative methods of treatment are being promoted and taken seriously with little or no demand for experimental support, let alone verification. In religion, without a universally reliable standard of truth by which to measure it, the most fundamental religious doctrine came to be seen as little more than a question of preference or of taste. Consequently, there could no longer be any absolute principles of ethics and morals; these too became questions of taste, preference, even mood. The modern world, which self-confidently assumed that it could discover the ultimate truths of all reality through science, aided by the newest and most precise instruments and the newly discovered potential of the computer, instead has had to recognize that virtually every question to which it thinks it has found an answer raises more questions that are unanswerable.

Science has never been able to answer the ultimate question of *why* things are as they are, but for a time it was so successful in explaining *how* they came to be that it gave the impression it was actually answering the ultimate question. Now, in this degenerate phase of our sensate culture, people are losing confidence in science just as they have already lost confidence in religion. If the modern era was characterized by an exaggerated confidence in science and scientific truth, the present generation is not only losing that confidence but is beginning to think that even to look for it was a mistake. We are now in the frame of reference called postmodernism. This development is character-istic of a late sensate culture, although it has never previously appeared in exactly the form that we find today.

This radical skepticism alternates between thinking that nothing is real and claiming that reality is whatever we want it to be, much like Milton's Satan in *Paradise Lost*:

> *The mind is its own place, and in itself*
> *Can make a Heaven of Hell, a Hell of Heaven.*

In Milton's thought, this boast represented a demonic delusion, but from the postmodern viewpoint, it may be a self-evident truth. Reader-response criticism denies that texts mean anything in themselves: everything depends on the reac-tion of the reader. This replacement of the idea of objective truth with the concept of reader response (truth is always relative to the observer) is a radically new approach to doctrinal dispute and differences of religious conviction. When an apparent clash of views arises, the contenders no longer accuse one another of being mistaken; instead they mutually agree, "That is true for you, and what I believe is true for me." This may seem more charitable and tolerant than the older view, which holds that mutually contradictory assertions cannot both be true at the same time, but the tremendous disadvantage is that it does not reckon with reality. If this brief life is all there is, if, as Catullus wrote, after it there is only *Nox perpetua una dormienda*—"one endless night that we must sleep"—then it surely makes sense to live this life entirely for one's own interests, saying, "Devil take the hindmost!" If, however, it really is "given to man once to die, and after that the judgment," then such an attitude is self-destructive.

Ideational cultures see truth only as the truth of God, of the divine order, know-able through revelation or inspiration. Idealistic cultures accept other truths, but continue to value the truth of God as the highest and most important kind of truth. Sensate cultures find truth only in the hard facts of the material world, which at the outset seem solid and reliable but, as time goes on and the culture becomes decadent, come to be seen as mere interpretations, and nothing solid remains.

The crisis in the systems of truth has affected all of the intellectual disci-plines except the hard experimental sciences, and even there its impact is being felt. In American law, for example, the principle of trial by jury was adopted as the best way to determine the guilt or innocence of an accused person. Now the jury system has become something like a theater audience, awarding "innocent" or "guilty" verdicts to the best defender or prosecutor. The quest for the actual truth of the charges becomes lost and irrelevant. A defendant will be punished or released not on the basis of personal guilt or innocence, but on the basis of the jury's response. What is important is how the jury *feels* about a defendant and his or her victims. In personal injury suits, the amount of damages supposedly suffered by a plaintiff becomes irrelevant; what counts is the jury's readiness to see one party as a *victim* and the other as the *oppressor*.

In the area of philosophy—traditionally the search for truth in the pursuit of wisdom—one current trend of postmodernism implies or actually denies that objective truth can ever be determined. Observers can only react to what they perceive on the basis of certain inherited categories, and their conclusions represent only the way they apply their categories to their perceptions; it does not represent anything we could properly call truth. Another approach, the "Vienna Circle" of logical positivism inaugurated by Rudolf Carnap, teaches that any statement that cannot be verified experimentally is meaningless. This contention would make most human philosophy meaningless; indeed, Carnap's own doctrine cannot be verified experimentally.

In psychology, behaviorism tells us that our most precious intellectual achievements are simply the products of conditioning, stimulus, and response. There is no question of discovering objective truth. What this approach cannot tell us is whether its debunking of the traditional quest for truth in law and philosophy means that no such thing as truth exists, or whether its own debunking is merely the behaviorists' response to the conditioning and stimuli they have received. This approach has no way of dealing with the possibility that it is itself fundamentally flawed and suffering from self-imposed blindness, unable to see reality other than through the distorting lenses of some highly unsuitable spectacles. Form has become more important than facts. Instead of making an earnest effort to ascertain the truth in a particular situation, we divert ourselves by endless inquiries into method and by trying to manipulate the procedures or the searchers.

4

THE CRISIS IN RELIGION

For each man's mind is like a labyrinth, so that it is no wonder that individual nations were drawn aside into various falsehoods; and not only this, but individual men, almost, had their own gods.

John Calvin

THE CRISIS IN THE SYSTEMS OF TRUTH has had a dramatic effect on religion in the West. Three great religions influenced Western culture. Judaism was the beginning; it shaped the point of departure for the religion of Western civilization, Christianity. Islam, which has a number of common features with both Judaism and Christianity, has affected the West primarily as a challenge to the Christian faith. Because the late sensate sociocultural system of the West doubts the very existence of truth, it undermines the credibility and the *raison d'être* of the great religion of the West, Christianity. Every major Christian confession makes the same claim: to teach objective truths, not merely subjective interpretations, about God, man, and the world.

GENERIC RELIGION?

Because all religions deal with the supersensory world and consequently cannot be tested like the propositions of the natural sciences, there is a tendency in popular thinking to create a category called "religion" and to place Christianity in it, lumping it together with other religions of all kinds. All of these are then in opposition to facts, science, and truth. Paradoxically, a culture that doubts its own ability to know truth acts as though it can be quite sure of its conviction that religion in general—especially religions with truth claims and Christianity in particular—cannot help us to find truth.

To put all the faiths and doctrines into one category—religion—and to set that category off against science and history is extremely misleading.[1] It is commonly said by people unfamiliar with religion that all religions are alike, or that all religions seek the same things. This can be meant in a positive sense, said in the hope of persuading people of different religions to unite for a common moral good. It can also be meant negatively, as a criticism and rejection of religion: All religions are alike; all are equally invalid and equally worthless. By putting all religious beliefs and practices (some of which are obviously foolish or destructive) into a single category, those who are militantly antireligious can argue that religion ought to be suppressed altogether or at least reduced to the level of a private interest or hobby. A culture that is concerned about truth will not discard all religions without examination, for it is conceivable that one or more of them does teach truth. To lump all religions and their doctrines and practices together as generic religion makes no sense, whether it is done to praise the religions or to condemn them.

To reject all religions in principle or to assert that all are equally irrelevant is something that is possible only in the kind of sensate culture that dismisses all spiritual and religious truth by definition. A person who is religious in the usual sense of the word in that he or she actually believes certain doctrines to be absolutely and universally true cannot avoid conflicts with the surrounding sensate

---

[1] In the United States, the First Amendment to the Constitution, which forbids Congress to make "an establishment of religion," is interpreted to mean that government may not draw any theological distinctions. It cannot declare certain religions or religious practices acceptable and others unacceptable. This in effect lumps all religions together, from the great traditional religions of the West to the most exotic cults. Because there are at least a few religious practices that no modern, human government can endorse (such as *sati*, burning a widow on her husband's funeral pyre), the implication is that no practice that is even remotely religious, such as singing carols at Christmas, can be tolerated. Indeed, even the words *Christmas vacation* have been replaced in many public schools by *winter holidays*.

culture, because sensate culture denies the existence of such truth. If the sensate culture claimed to be adequate and competent only for dealing with the material aspects of life and was willing to grant that there are areas in which religion, or a particular religion, is more competent than the surrounding culture, it would no longer be a fully sensate culture. It would be a compromise, in other words, a kind of idealistic culture. As long as the sensate culture of the West was only partially integrated and unified, people could live in it and to a greater or lesser degree still maintain the beliefs and practices of a religion that actually hearkened back to the ideational or idealistic system of the past. But as the sensate culture becomes more total, it places religious people in a conflict situation in which they must either abandon their religion, repudiate the culture, or somehow find a way to live in a situation of constant tension.

PUSHING RELIGION TO THE FRINGE

The proliferation of the mass media, the creation of the global village of which Marshall McLuhan wrote,[2] will ultimately require all traditional religions to be pushed to the fringe of society. Unless the sensate culture itself undergoes the kind of shift that will permit supersensory reality and values to be recognized and reaffirmed once again, it will grow increasingly hostile to religion, and not only to religion but to objective moral standards of all kinds.

When religious groups compromise their foundational beliefs in order to coexist with the late sensate culture rather than challenging it or standing against it, they in effect consent to their own liquidation. Those for whom the Christian religion or any traditional religion is vitally important must recognize that the conflict with the sensate culture will eventually result either in the suppression of all religious truth claims or in a substantial transformation of the culture. In our day, the momentum seems to be for the suppression of religious truth, but this momentum is not irreversible.

Specific aspects of our sensate culture clash with fundamental principles

---

[2] Marshall McLuhan, *The Gutenberg Galaxy* (Toronto: University of Toronto Press, 1962).

of several religions (e.g., the exaltation of sexual license in the entertainment media conflicts with the religious call for sexual self-control). However, this is not the root cause of the hostility of sensate culture to religion. It is rather that the sensate culture has a view of truth that derides as superstition any religion that claims its doctrines are true.

For those who want to affirm religion, it is not logical to say that all religions are equally valid, for while there are fundamental points of agreement between many religions, there are also some direct contradictions between religions:

- The three great monotheistic religions—Judaism, Christianity, and Islam—all believe in one God and have many moral precepts in common, but they disagree vigorously about God's nature and some of his attributes.

- The moral precepts of Christianity and Buddhism are similar in many ways, but Christianity believes in one God while Buddhism believes in no God—it is atheistic.

- In both Christianity and the religion of the Aztecs, God or the gods was said to value the human heart, but with a fundamental difference. Christianity, following Judaism, says, "You shall love the Lord your God with all your heart" (Matt. 22:37; see also Deut. 13:3) and calls upon believers to give their hearts to God. In Aztec religion the human heart had to be offered in quite a different way. It was "gods' food," and was plucked out of the living victim's body and offered to an idol so that the gods would continue to preserve the world.

Most religions do have some things in common, particularly in the realm of precepts for a moral life, but it is clearly false to assert that all religions are fundamentally alike or that they all seek the same things.

SUPERSENSORY TRUTH: THE ONLY TRUTH?

An ideational culture considers the truth of faith—divine truth—to be the only truth. Idealistic cultures also accept other kinds of truth but consider divine truth higher than any other. A sensate culture, by contrast, accepts only the truths of the senses. For this reason, one might expect a sensate culture to be profoundly irreligious and to have little or no religious faith and practice.

Although Western culture has been sensate for centuries, this is clearly not the case. There are two reasons for this:

1. Although the dominant culture rejects all religion as superstition, it has not yet taken control of the minds of every person in it. Millions are, so to speak, backward or reactionary in that they have not yet bought into the skepticism of the sensate mentality. If everyone had been, there would be no crisis in religion in our contemporary sensate culture, for there would be no religion.

2. As the Hebrew Scripture proclaims and Jesus reaffirmed, "Man shall not live on bread alone" (Matt. 4:4; see also Deut. 8:3). When the culture ridicules traditional religions and drives them to the fringes, millions of people, feeling a void in their lives, will resurrect ancient or exotic religions or fashion new ones to their own liking.

The fact is that our sensate culture is full of religions, but is losing the religions that created it. Human beings have such a strong religious impulse that it is all but impossible for most people to have no religion at all. They may not call it religion, but they have it nevertheless. As G. K. Chesterton put it, "The man who does not believe in God does not believe in nothing; he will believe in anything." Religions abound in sensate cultures, but because the sensate understanding of truth depends on measurable sensory evidence, while religion in general deals with the supersensory, it does not evaluate religious beliefs in terms of truth but in terms of how they make their adherents feel, how they meet needs. What is important is no longer the objective reality of God or of the powers and forces that religion venerates but the subjective satisfaction that it can give to its adherents.

Because sensate culture presupposes that there is no such thing as a supersensory realm of reality that is inaccessible to the senses but that can be known through divine revelation or human spirituality, it is evident that sensate culture will not be hospitable to a religion such as Christianity that emphasizes the objective truth of divine revelation. This fact has created the paradoxical situation that now prevails throughout Western Christendom: The culture of the West was created on an ideational basis. As it shifted into a more idealistic phase, it still continued to exalt the supremacy of divine truth. Now, with the culture as a whole in its sensate phase, there is a schizophrenic conflict between the religious aspects of the culture and those people who are still rooted in the objective truth of faith on the one hand and the mass of the sensate culture and those who accept only the truths of the senses on the other hand.

The crisis in religion in the West at the end of the second millennium of Christianity does not lie in the clash of doctrines that divide the Christian confessions (such as papal infallibility and biblical inerrancy) but rather in the radical sensate approach to truth. For if nothing spiritual can be known to be true, then all religions that make truth claims must be thrown out. If they are not totally discarded, they may be cultivated as a mere hobby like gardening or golf but certainly cannot serve as a foundation for one's life.

Any historically revealed religion stands or falls by the objective truth of its doctrinal claims. Christianity is the paramount example of such a religion and the one most relevant to Western civilization. Some of the dogmatic assertions of Christianity, like some of those of Judaism and Islam, are based on historical records in which persons and events are described as having been present or taken place in real history. In a number of biblical texts we find a record of events that are so clearly located in real history that one must either accept them as factual or dismiss much of the religion as invalid.

In Judaism, for example, nothing is more significant than the Law of God, which is epitomized in the Ten Commandments. The commandments are precepts rather than doctrines and so at first glance might not seem like the sort of thing that can be challenged historically. In fact, however, the Decalogue begins with a historical statement: "I am the LORD your God, who brought you out of the land of Egypt, out of the house of slavery. You shall have no other gods before Me" (Exod. 20:2). Thus the Law is tied to a report of a historical event, the memory of which is celebrated every year at Passover. Is that memory reliable? Did Moses actually lead the Hebrews out of Egypt at God's command, aided by several spectacular acts of divine intervention? If so, then the Ten Commandments come from God and are clearly binding.

70

If not, why should commandments that a small group of people mistakenly ascribed to God be binding on people of various races and languages three thousand and more years later?

THE PROBLEM OF CHRISTIANITY

Western culture is unthinkable without Christianity, with which it began and with which it is impregnated and saturated, although the influence of Christianity on the culture grows weaker year by year. Although Christian preachers, teachers, and evangelists claimed from the outset that the Gospel ought to be accepted because it is literally true, the benefits that Christian ethics can bring to a culture do not depend on everyone or even a majority in that culture actually believing the religion is true. There is a certain civilizing value in Christianity that has appealed to rulers and governors from an early date, presumably to the Emperor Constantine himself.

Christian moral teachings have value for anyone, Christian or not—a fact often recognized by teachers of other great religions. However, the serious Christian sees these teachings as normative because they come from Christ, the risen Lord. At no time in the history of the world since Christ has the majority of mankind accepted the stories about Jesus' resurrection as reliable and his claims as warranted, even though most of his moral precepts are so central to human experience that they coincide in many respects with the teachings of other religions as well as with the thinking of most moralists. The difficulty is that the civilizing and cultural value of Christianity is available only when its tenets are widely if not universally believed and accepted, at least in a general sense, and they rapidly disappear when the fundamental outlines of Christian belief are no longer taken seriously by many people. Inasmuch as the sensate culture makes it extremely difficult for people to take seriously doctrines that refer to supersensory realities—to God, heaven, the soul, and salvation—it is to be expected that a sensate culture will gradually wear Christianity down, and this is indeed what has been happening.

There are practical, traditional, and sentimental reasons for people in the West to want to hold onto the cultural influences of Christianity. When many people no longer believe in Christianity and are unwilling to observe its more difficult precepts but nevertheless value the name and its cultural benefits, they put forward the most bizarre ideas as equally valid or even preferable, alternative expressions of the Christian faith.

The Christian religion ultimately stands or falls by the truth of the proclamation of the Resurrection of Christ. It is self-evident that Christianity presents Jesus as a real figure of history, situated in the context of Roman rule in Jerusalem. The Roman governor Pontius Pilate and the two kings named Herod make the intended historical context absolutely clear. If the resurrection of Jesus did not take place as it is reported in the Gospels, then believers are in the situation described by the Apostle Paul: "If Christ has not been raised, then our preaching is vain, and your faith also is vain" (1 Cor. 15:14). Generations of Christian martyrs went willingly to their deaths, confidently expecting to be raised to new life, as Christ was raised. Their emphasis was not on the quality but on the content of their faith, on the character and powers of the One in whom they believed—things that were fully demonstrated by his resurrection from the dead. Today not many people in the Western cultural world would so readily stake their lives on the resurrection of Christ, not so much because they deny that it took place as because the sensate world in which we all live simply does not reckon with religious truths of that kind. Despite this, until quite recently the majority of people in the West still embraced the civilization that grew out of resurrection faith. Western culture grew out of belief in some definite religious truths, but now Western sensate man does not believe that religious truth exists. Can it long survive?

PLURALISM AND MULTICULTURALISM

The centuries-old tendency in the West to extol the value of Christian civilization without necessarily believing in the truth of Christian doctrines has finally proved unworkable. Two key passwords or slogans in this development are *pluralism* and *multiculturalism*. The term *pluralism* was first used descriptively for a situation in which many different religions and philosophies were present side by side, with no single religion having official or factual predominance.

Recently it has come to be prescriptive—to mean a situation in which no religion or philosophy may be allowed to claim that it is true. In practice in the West, pluralism is often invoked to prevent Christians and Christianity from claiming the right to determine or direct the course of culture, to favor certain developments and trends and to oppose or suppress others. Pluralism denies to Christianity the right to exercise its traditional normative or stabilizing function in the society that it shaped and formed.

Multiculturalism also began as a descriptive term and has become a prescriptive one. Unlike pluralism, which can result when there is a massive migration of ideas, multiculturalism describes the situation that arises when the migration of people results in individuals from a variety of cultures living side by side. In the past immigrants into a culture have generally been willing to adapt themselves to that host culture, either accepting it or at least living in harmony with it. Examples of this pattern were the settlement of scattered Jews in European countries in the Diaspora, and on a smaller scale, the immigration of persecuted Huguenots from France to Switzerland, Germany, and Britain. Normally a host country assumed that immigrants would respond according to the proverb, "When in Rome, do as the Romans do."

Since World War II, multiculturalism has become prescriptive rather than descriptive. The movement of populations, including large numbers of refugees as well as those moving for reasons of business, education, or employment from non-Western cultures, has become immense at precisely the time that Western culture has undergone a crisis of self-confidence. It was in the West that the two most destructive wars in human history began.[3] It was a Western demagogue, Adolf Hitler, who proclaimed a doctrine of Nordic racial superiority so odious it made other Nordics and Caucasians in general begin to apologize for their very existence on the planet. It was the paramount Western power, the United States, that unleashed weapons of mass destruction in Asia, wiping out whole cities by atomic and by conventional firestorms. It was the United States

---

[3] The Second World War is said to have begun with the German invasion of Poland in 1939, although actually Japan was already engaged in the invasion of China. The German invasion of Russia and the Japanese attack on the United States, both in 1941, generalized the conflict, tying the European-African and Asian wars together.

that utilized all sorts of modern technological weaponry in vain against a much smaller Asian country and ultimately withdrew from Vietnam in disgrace.

Under these circumstances, people in several Western countries, especially the United States, promoted the view that all cultures are equal, with the exception of their own Western culture, which is inferior. It is denounced as cultural imperialism for Western countries to try to preserve (most critics would say "impose") Western cultural views even within their own borders. Non-Western religions brought into the West by immigrants and accepted by some Westerners must be given a hearing and treated with respectful courtesy, including the acceptance of their customs, mores, social standards, and religious holidays, while the traditional Western customs, mores, social standards, and holidays derived from Christianity must under no circumstances be imposed on the newcomers. Indeed, out of respect for the newcomers, these traditions must be shoved into the background even among those who normally hold and practice them.

THE DEMORALIZATION OF CHRISTENDOM

Pluralism and multiculturalism lead to a phenomenon that may be called the demoralization of the majority in the nominally Christian lands of Western culture. This is demoralization in both senses of the term, in that it involves a loss both of *morals*, which in the West have derived principally from the Christian religion, and of *morale*, which is lost when one is obliged constantly to apologize for the fact of one's existence and erstwhile prominence in the world. Western nations have been in the habit of praising Western and Christian civilization (and excusing their own imperial and economic aggressions) as bringing civilization, modern medicine, sanitation, and even Christianity to needy and backward regions. These excuses were often hollow and unconvincing, although sometimes they were true; in very few cases did the beneficiary nations want to do away with the advantages of Western technology and science, even as they rejected Western imperialism and economic domination. The Christian culture of the West has not prevented Western nations from being rapacious and exploitative, but it has made them aware of their own sinfulness and readier than some to admit their own misdeeds. This has led to a self-condemnation in the West, even extending to the Western churches, which accuse themselves of having been insensitive to other cultures and of pushing aside folk religions in their eagerness to make converts.

A substantial part of the Western cultural world came under the influence of Marxism, which ruled the Soviet Union for seven decades and its satellites for three. Marxism engaged in a long campaign of criticism, abuse, and slander of the Christian heritage of the West, sometimes accurately pointing out crimes and abuses, but more often simply resorting to blanket condemnation. Even though Marxism has all but vanished as an active opponent to Christianity, the damage that it did to the morals and morale of the West has not been healed.

Pluralism, multiculturalism, and Marxism have all contributed to the weakness and fragmentation of the Christian religion as a force for integration in Western culture, but the most serious weakening has come not from these influences but from the pervasive influence of the sensate system itself. During the centuries when the sensate worldview was active primarily in the realm of ideas—motivating people to think less in terms of spiritual and divine supersensory realities and values and more in terms of this world, human reason, and material things—the churches could struggle against it in the intellectual arena on more or less equal terms and could continue to influence believers, win new converts, and maintain an idealistic element in an increasingly degenerating sensate culture.

A crucial change came in this century. Some place it before World War I or between the wars, some after World War II. In any event, its effect is immense. The sensate culture has passed beyond the realm of philosophies, ideals, art, and music and has taken firm hold of morality and personal conduct. The ambient culture lives for its pleasures, denying and ridiculing the Christian concept that after death comes judgment. It easily seduces multitudes from paying attention to supersensory realities and spiritual values. In a situation in which many leading representatives of the Christian religion have lost the conviction necessary to argue against this trend, the attraction of hedonistic indulgences will not be widely resisted.

Christianity, we know, is not the only religion that claims to be based on historical fact as well as on divine revelation; both Judaism and Islam also tie faith and doctrine to historical persons and events, and both Judaism and Islam, like Christianity, can be challenged in principle by questioning their historical basis. It is only Christianity, however, that has within its own ranks hosts of religious officials and teachers who devote themselves to undermining the religion they formally profess. Priests, ministers, bishops, archbishops, professors, and entire faculties and schools of theology seem to find nothing strange in promoting skepticism, atheism, radical feminism, goddess worship, neopaganism, occultism, and even witchcraft, or in approving and praising conduct that traditional Christianity calls immoral and abominable.

SYNCRETISM

The two traditional religions of Western culture, Christianity and Judaism, declare that there is only one God and that worship of other gods is abominable idolatry. Historically, both have strenuously resisted mixing with other religions; in fact, it was the Jewish conviction that proclaiming Jesus as the Messiah unacceptably altered Jewish faith that led to the separation of Christianity from Judaism in the first century after Christ. In addition, neither religion willingly permits its adherents to practice one or more other religions or cults as well as their own. Judaism and Christianity differ in important ways, but they also share some common foundational doctrines. These common commitments permit both religions to exist side by side in the same culture without significantly disrupting it.

In the present crisis in religion, the syncretistic mixing of religion takes place at every level; the culture as a whole is permeated with the most diverse and mutually contradictory religious views. This is also the case in many (perhaps in most) Christian confessions and churches. Roman Catholicism, which Protestants and others have denounced for the severity and cruelty with which its Holy Office of the Inquisition sought out and persecuted those it thought were introducing errors and false doctrines into Christianity, now finds it impossible to discipline professors and priests who deny such essential Christian doctrines as the resurrection and the deity of Christ or who encourage the practice of alternative or experimental spirituality, such as witchcraft and goddess worship. Countless individuals who say they are Christians become fascinated with reincarnation, occultism, parapsychology, and UFOs (Unidentified Flying Objects). They mix traditional Christianity with other religions, both old and new, like Milton's fallen angels "in wand'ring mazes lost."

The prevalence of syncretism in the culture, in churches, and in individuals is only one more indication of the crisis in religion, a particularly striking aspect of the crisis in systems of truth. Because far more ordinary people are directly involved with religion than with philosophy or the systems of law, the crisis in religion is potentially more disruptive of cultural integration than almost any other factor.

5

THE CRISIS IN
ETHICS AND LAW

*He hath shewed thee, O man, what is good; and what
doth the LORD require of thee, but to do justly, and to
love mercy, and to walk humbly with thy God?*

Micah 6:8 KJV

THE LINES FROM MICAH'S PROPHECY were quoted by former President Carter in his 1977 inaugural address. They point to the oldest and most basic approach to the idea of law: Law is what God requires. This seems simple and straightforward enough. It is reflected in one of the cries that is most familiar to parents of young children: "That's not fair!" Even very young children when confronted with an unwelcome parental demand instinctively appeal to a higher law—to "fairness." Many people believe there is a supreme law—something that is higher than the momentary wishes or demands of a ruler, whether president, empress, mother, or father.[1]

There is an alternative approach that is increasingly dominant in modern society today: Law is what man wills. Indeed, law is whatever is willed by

---

[1] Even cultures that do not believe in the personal God of the Bible, who may be polytheists and think that gods and goddesses are numerous, generally think that there is a divine Law and that human laws must embody it.

whoever possesses the power to make others submit. The first approach is called *divine command ethics*, the second *ethical* or *legal positivism*. Divine command ethics is also called *metaphysical moralism*, which indicates that moral values come from outside, from above and beyond our familiar physical world.

Any society that is reasonably stable and durable is an *integrated* society—it fits together. Its arts correspond to its ideas about truth and religion, to its laws, to its family structure, even to its economics and industrial life. Despite all of its apparent variety and diversity, our society is still integrated, and consequently its laws are not freestanding but are part of a whole that embraces its arts, its social life, its understanding of truth, its moral and ethical consciousness.

Laws are formulations of a society's ethical consciousness. They express what society thinks about right and wrong and how it believes right should be rewarded and wrong should be punished. What is our ethical consciousness in what we are calling the degenerate phase of the late sensate supersystem? Which of the two fundamental approaches is ours as we near the end of the second millennium of our era?

1. *Metaphysical moralism.* Do we look to God, to a divine order that is above us and that does not depend on our desires, fears, or prejudices?

2. *Legal positivism.* Do we believe that men and women can make laws and that the concept of an unjust law is a contradiction in terms because it is the law that defines justice?

The Jewish prophet succinctly illustrates the first approach, appropriately called the ethics of *divine command.* If God is real—as every society in the Judeo-Christian-Muslim tradition firmly believes—and if he has shown us what he defines as good, then that clearly answers the question for all those who acknowledge his authority. Do you want to know what is good? God has shown you.

Micah's thought, "He hath shewed thee, O man," points us to a Law that is eternal, made in heaven, because it expresses the judgment and will of the Eternal, of the "Maker of heaven and earth, and of all things visible and invisible."[2] Human laws express the divine Law, some more, others less adequately, and are judged by how well they do so.

Micah was a Jewish prophet, but his view is not limited to the Semitic cultures. In the Indo-Aryan world we find a similar attitude among the Persians, recorded for us by another Jewish prophet, Daniel, relating an incident that took place after the Medes and the Persians conquered Babylon. When the Persian officials said to Darius, "O king, establish the injunction and sign the document so that it may not be changed, according to the law of the Medes and the Persians, which may not be revoked" (Dan. 6:8), they were not stressing the autocratic power of the Persian king—an ability to make a law that no one could change—but rather the conviction that the king would never pronounce a law "according to the law of the Medes and the Persians" unless he was fully convinced that he was speaking for heaven. Of course in such a case the king was not entitled to have second thoughts and later alter the law.

The Persian officials played a double game here, for they tricked the king into making an arbitrary pronouncement that no reasonable person could identify with the will of heaven, but once he had made it, they required him to treat it as a divine decree, which no mere man—not even the king himself—could change. The prophet Daniel, as readers will remember, disregarded the royal law, and was thrown into the lions' den, just as the law required. The lions, however, did not attack him as expected. God sent an angel to "shut the mouths of the lions," as Daniel said, "because I was found innocent in his sight" (Dan. 6:22 NIV). Because the will of heaven was so clearly demonstrated by this miraculous event the king was persuaded that his law was in fact no law, since it did not correspond to the will of heaven. Consequently he did not so much *change* the law in releasing Daniel and putting the officials into the lions' den as simply recognize that he had erred in declaring as law something that heaven clearly had not willed.

The story of Daniel shows that not only the Semitic Jews but also the Aryan Persians shared the same conviction that to be valid, human laws must correspond to the divine will. This attitude is common to most civilizations.

---

2 This description of God, from the traditional Christian Nicene Creed (A.D. 325), by saying that everything that exists was made by God, implies that God the Creator has the full authority to make rules for the creation that he has made.

Throughout all of history we humans have usually claimed that we set up statutes, write laws, and establish morality not on the basis of individual or group whims, but on the basis of what is right—what God or heaven wills. In other words, we act on the assumption that we will write our human laws and ordinances in such a way that they will conform to a higher Law: in the case of Micah's prophecy, this is the Law found in the Bible.

In the European–American cultural world, until recently all statute law, whether codified law on the Continent or common law in the English and American traditions, was intended to a greater or lesser degree to express the ethics and legal principles of the Bible. The law reflected the common conviction that humans cannot simply make laws as we see fit, but we must enact our statutes and regulations in accord with a higher standard. This basic approach to law is characteristic of both the ideational and idealistic sociocultural systems. It did not change until the rise of the sensate supersystem, and even then, because of the conservative nature of the legal process, its change has been slow.

TRANSITION IN LAW

What has begun to happen to the basic understanding of law in the transition from an idealistic to a sensate system? The recent history of Europe, and now of the United States, gives a striking demonstration. Laws lose their theoretical reference point in a higher Law and become increasingly arbitrary, even capricious. Incidentally, laws become extremely complicated, often requiring the services of specialists to understand. As long as a society believes that there is a divine Judge standing behind its laws, and as long as it assumes that every human judge knows himself answerable to the divine Judge, it can write its statutes in rather broad and general terms, knowing that the human judges will make every effort to interpret them in the light of the character and will of the divine Judge. As this confidence in a divine Lawgiver wanes, human laws necessarily become more and more complex; the legislators seek to guarantee the outcome of any legal dispute, leaving nothing to the human judge. In the absence of a divine Judge, the legislators have no confidence that the human judge will feel an obligation to look beyond his or her own desires and whims.

82

The rise of sensate culture has dramatically changed the orientation of human law from one that sought to reflect divine Law to one that simply embodies the will of the powerful lawgiver. In this late phase of sensate culture, the conflict between those who think that human laws must correspond to a higher Law and those who think that laws depend only on the will of man has not yet been fully resolved. Nevertheless, the final stage that lies ahead in the late phases of sensate culture can be clearly foreseen. We are coming more and more under the sway of the second type of law, which we call *positive law* (the philosophy behind it is *legal positivism*—the predominant legal philosophy in the Western world today). This is not at all surprising, for if there is no Power higher than man, then man himself must make all his own laws. The legal positivist approach to law has been known for centuries but has seldom enjoyed public respect. From this perspective—law is what those in power choose to make it— law is truly man-made. It is not dependent on any higher Authority or supersensory reality.

MAKING LAWS

Modern English usage, especially in the United States, tends to shun words of Latin origin. Thus when a journalist says *lawmaker* instead of *legislator* it may be simply because the former is easier to spell. Unfortunately, there is a significant difference in meaning between *legislation* and *lawmaking*.[3] When we so easily speak of humans like ourselves "making laws," we are unconsciously attributing to ourselves a power that we do not have. Of course we know that we cannot make any laws of nature, laws of physics and chemistry. But does that mean that we cannot make the laws of nations and societies?

Through the centuries of human history, people have assumed that there are certain givens in human relationships just as there are givens in the relationships of the heavenly bodies and the chemical elements. H_2O is water,

---

[3] Although speakers of English use *lawmakers* interchangeably with *legislators*, no parallel exists in French or German. The French do not say *faiseurs de lois*, nor the Germans *Gesetzmacher*, except in a sarcastic sense. See Edgar Bodenheimer, *Jurisprudence* (Cambridge, Mass.: Harvard University Press, 1972) 137.

and no human decree can make H_2O_2 or any other combination of atoms into water. Even those who do not believe that there is a Creator who has established a certain order in the universe have to recognize order when they are dealing with realities of physics and chemistry. But what about the relationships between human beings? If there is a Creator who has made us, then it is reasonable to suppose that he had a certain order in mind that his human creatures ought to respect and by which they ought to live.

It is self-evident that we cannot make the laws of nature, the laws of physics and chemistry. We cannot make the laws of biology, although we are becoming increasingly able to manipulate biology as we see fit. But there is a specific kind of law that we *can* make—or at least think that we can make. We can pass resolutions, enact statutes, and write them in the law books. The great question remains: Can we make whatever laws we please, or are we bound to respect a higher order in human affairs as we must in physics and chemistry?

In an ideational or idealistic sociocultural system, ethics and laws will appear as givens, as principles that derive from a higher order not made by mankind. This perspective fully agrees with the Roman proverb, "Law is found, not made." This ancient maxim presupposes that the laws of human conduct, like the laws of physics, are something that we humans have to learn to identify and express, not something that we can make up just as we please. From such a perspective, whenever humans attempt to change values and standards, those who object can point to a "Law above the laws" by which human acts and statutes can be judged.

The Transition from Found to Man-Made Law

As our sociocultural system moved from an idealistic to a sensate phase, people in general lost sight of any supersensory reality—such as God—to which human lawmakers would have to give an accounting and of any overarching, transcendent principles to which our human laws ought to conform. Nevertheless, for centuries the laws and regulations of Western societies have continued to reveal their original source in "found" laws. It is probably in the legal systems of Western societies that the full implications of our sensate mentality have been slowest to develop. Laws and legal structures are generally resistant to change.

Laws and statutes often remain on the books long after the ground has shifted under them and they have long since ceased to be respected and enforced. Now, however, we are witnessing an increasingly rapid transformation in the sphere of law, as the full force of the sensate mentality comes to be felt. This late shift may be especially bad because it is coming at a time when the sensate society as a whole is already overripe and nearing exhaustion; laws and legal principles may be transformed just when they need to be the way they used to be.

Three major developments in the eighteenth and nineteenth centuries weakened the age-old human confidence in unchanging, absolute principles of justice and law:

1. the voyages of discovery, which opened Europe to Asia and the New World;

2. the rise of biblical criticism, which denied that God has spoken reliably and authoritatively;

3. the theory of evolution, which by implication deprives the human race of its claim to be special and places us among the other animals.

Prior to the sixteenth century, the European world had little contact with any other major culture, with the exceptions of Judaism (which was limited in its extent) and Islam (which was often violent). Judaism and Christianity had almost identical views on moral principles, although they differed about theological doctrines. Both Judaism and Christianity have a strong conviction that God is the great Lawgiver. Islam, although different in many important respects from both, shares many of their perspectives and was derived from both. European Christians could look at Islam and consider it a wrong interpretation of shared facts. In any event Islam has an even stronger conviction that all law has its origin in God.

In addition, the fact that European Christendom had to expend so much energy defending itself against Islam during centuries of Arab and Turkish aggressions more or less forced most Europeans to take the validity of their own beliefs and assumptions for granted rather than engaging in introspective self-analysis. When a society is fighting for survival, it has no leisure for speculation about the validity of its cultural assumptions. Only later, as European and North American civilization appeared to reign more or less unchallenged, did speculative Western minds begin to question the *raison d'être* of their own culture and its laws.[4]

1. Voyages of Discovery. At the end of the fifteenth century, the Portuguese rounded the Cape of Good Hope and the Spanish discovered America. Europeans gradually became aware of the great and ancient civilizations east of the Turkish Empire, and in Central and South America two ancient, very different cultures were encountered. For the first time Europeans met civilizations older than theirs possessing intellectual and spiritual traditions that could not be dismissed as simply pagan and inferior, even though the Europeans were able to conquer and colonize several of them. In the Americas, the Spanish found cultures they could rapidly dominate, but even the roughest conquistadors could not fail to notice that the indigenous cultures were civilized and advanced, living by different principles than the ones they themselves took for granted.

By the eighteenth century there was enough contact with the high cultures of Asia, specifically of India and China, to force Europeans to abandon their naive belief in their own cultural superiority. The absolute truths of which they had been certain were relativized by the encounter with older civilizations that lived by other truths.[5]

---

[4] A clear illustration of this is given by Germany in the war years 1939–45. In retrospect, many of the doctrines and assumptions of Nazism can hardly stand up to analysis. However, when pounded by enemies on all sides, the Germans fought on as long as they could and did not devote much time to speculating whether what they ostensibly believed was worth fighting for. Similarly, the great American periods of self-questioning, of asking ourselves whether we have any right to be as we are, came about only after the United States had defeated its strongest enemies in war and America appeared to be the economic giant and trendsetter for the world.

[5] Some of these other civilizations also had an ideational or idealistic culture and believed in eternal laws similar to those respected in the West, but they had very different beliefs about the ultimate nature of divine reality. This began to unsettle Western minds, with the result that the practical similarity of many moral and ethical convictions was overlooked. C. S. Lewis discusses the similarities and the way they have been overlooked in his little book, *The Abolition of Man* (New York: Macmillan, 1953). Not long after the Spanish conquests in Central and South America, Europeans began to idealize and romanticize the pre-Columbian cultures they had overwhelmed, writing about them as though they were untouched by the corruptions and vices with which Europeans were all too familiar in their own lands.

2. *Rise of Biblical Criticism.* The Enlightenment in the eighteenth century further weakened European confidence in the absoluteness of Christianity and, therefore, in the universal applicability of its moral teachings. In addition, the doctrinal teachings of Christianity came under direct attack, often by the very faculties and professors of theology who might have been expected to defend them. By the middle of the nineteenth century, higher criticism had undermined confidence in the divine authorship and authority of the Bible, first of the Old Testament, then of the New as well. If the Bible is only the cut-and-paste handiwork of a variety of editors through the centuries, how can it demand our obedience today?

Initially the significance of this loss of self-confidence and of reliance on the truth of Christianity did not become evident. The moralists of the Enlightenment, such as G. E. Lessing (1729–81) and Immanuel Kant (1724–1804), upheld the same moral principles as those that Christianity teaches, even though the intellectuals, followed after a time by the general public, began to lose trust in the divine authority of the Bible. As this happened, it was only a matter of time before they began to lose respect for Christian principles of conduct. The effort to defend Christian morality not as based on divinely revealed commands but as the natural inclination of rational minds proved ineffectual. When there is no divine Judge to whom one must answer, one does not feel the urgency of listening to moralizing philosophers.

If the Bible is not the authoritative Word of God, can we humans still think of ourselves as created in God's image? If we are God's offspring, as both the Bible and much Western philosophy teach, reason tells us that we should seek to conform ourselves to the will of our Maker. But what happens if we are not made in God's image but are somehow the chance product of impersonal forces? Are there then any divinely ordained laws that we must try to find and by which we should live?

3. *Theory of Evolution.* The third blow to found law was struck by the publication of Charles Darwin's *The Origin of the Species* in 1856. Darwin did not deny the reality of God, but his views made God at best incidental to the origins of our race and thus implicitly denied the reasonableness of patterning our lives after what we took to be God's principles. Darwin's views quickly obtained wide popularity and became a new, obligatory orthodoxy in most secular and academic circles. If we human beings are not God's special creation, made in his image, but are only the current level of development from the most primitive life forms, how can we believe that there are absolute standards of morality and justice? Can our laws remain untouched by the evolution that everything else undergoes, ourselves included?

At the beginning of the twentieth century a further blow to enduring standards of ethics and justice was struck by the widespread acceptance of the view of Sigmund Freud, according to which moral reasoning and motivation are merely the expression of hidden drives and reflexes, largely of a sexual nature. Other reductionist doctrines and theories tended to reduce human moral reasoning to the level of mere biological processes. One example, the behaviorism preached by B. F. Skinner, proposed that there is no such thing as absolute or foundational truth underlying our intellectual convictions, but these supposed convictions are merely reactions to certain outside stimuli and have no particular truth content .[6]

If there are no laws made in heaven, by what standards should human society organize itself? We do need laws by which to organize and structure our lives, but if God has not given them, where shall they come from? There is only one answer: We must make them ourselves. Of course, if we make our own laws, they will have no more authority or force than what we ourselves posses and can assert by means of the power at our disposal. In other words, law comes to represent not the will of the Creator but the will of the strongest creatures. This became the widespread view, sometimes unexpressed but frequently explicit, of most Western societies in the first part of the twentieth century. America's great legal statesman, Oliver Wendell Holmes Jr., thought no differently in this respect from the great dictator, Adolf Hitler. Both of them believed that laws simply represent the will of the dominant majority. Holmes was a courteous, urbane, sophisticated gentleman, but his idea of law would have offered no opposition to the enactments of Hitler, who for a time reflected the will of Germany's dominant majority.

---

[6] See B. F. Skinner, *Beyond Freedom and Dignity* (New York: Knopf, 1971).

After World War II, Gustav Radbruch, once a leading German legal positivist, urged a return to concepts of natural law as well as to the moral and legal insights of Christianity. He asserted that the most dangerous revolution in history was when men discovered that they can *make* laws.[7] The older term, *legislation*—derived from the Latin *lex, legis* (law), and *latus* (moved, as in "translate")—corresponds to the view that laws are "found," as it were in heaven, and "moved" into our human law codes and statute books. This is the reason why we speak of "moving" and "motions" when proposing something in a deliberative body.

ESTABLISHING JUSTICE

Do our laws define justice? Or does justice exist apart from human law to be expressed as best we can in our laws? The case is clear for an ideational society: Human laws must conform to higher standards of justice. But what happens when laws are enacted ("made") that do not conform to justice but pervert it? Even highly spiritual people have to live in the real world and recognize the reality that exists outside of their faith and doctrinal convictions. They will, from time to time, observe that actual human laws do not conform to the higher standard. In an ideational culture, unjust laws will be criticized on the basis of the higher standard of justice and will be annulled or changed in order to make them just.

In the sensate society, which does not recognize the reality of any supersensory values, the only laws that exist in the human realm (not including the laws of nature) must be laws made by humans according to whatever principles and standards they think right and best. It is the law that creates justice. This attitude is reflected by the slogan that one often hears in the United States when the Supreme Court has handed down a decision many people find unjust: "It's the law of the land." This tendency to equate the High Court with justice as such is illustrated by the title of its members—not *Judge*, which suggests reflection upon and weighing of disputed matters, but *Justice*, which

---

[7] Bodenheimer, *Jurisprudence*, 139–42.

suggests that the justice itself is embodied in human persons. "The Justices have spoken" comes to mean, in effect, "justice itself has spoken." The High Court has spoken, and nothing more can be said.

In an ideational society, this understanding of the authority of Justices can make sense if one assumes that the high Justices, like the king of the Medes and the Persians in the Book of Daniel, speak with the authority of heaven. In a sensate society, no authority higher than these human voices is necessary, nor can such an authority exist. This is precisely the position taken by one of the leading European legal theorists of the period following World War I, the Austrian jurist Hans Kelsen. Kelsen took the position that an unjust law is a contradiction in terms, for it is the law that defines justice. If a law is lawfully and properly enacted according to correct legislative procedure, it is just, and no more can be said.[8] Although Kelsen was Jewish, Hitler gladly took advantage of his theory to assert the justice of all his enactments.

War Crimes Trials

One of the greatest legal dramas of our century was performed at Nuremberg, in war-shattered, defeated Germany: the Nuremberg war crimes trials. The mentality of the victorious powers, stirred by the anguish and thirst for vengeance of the countries and population groups that had suffered most under the tyranny of the Nazis, called for punishment of the defeated leaders. But on what grounds could the representatives of what had been a sovereign power, properly installed in office (at least as properly as those of the victorious Soviet Union) be tried for acts performed in the service of their sovereign nation? Some voices merely called for summary punishment: Round up the surviving leaders, and shoot or hang them outright. This has been done often enough in human history, and no doubt many rulers and leaders of defeated nations would have been happy to be killed speedily rather than endure the degradation and tortures that victors have often imposed.

---

[8] When Hitler annexed Austria to his German Reich, Kelsen was fortunate enough to be able to immigrate to the United States, where he revised his position somewhat: *Ordinarily*, an unjust law is a contradiction in terms, but in the extreme case, man-made laws can be unjust if they violate fundamental principles of justice. Some laws are such gross violations of natural justice and human dignity that they do not deserve to be called laws at all.

Many of the atrocities of the Nazis were committed under the cloak of national sovereignty and self-interest; some were merely arbitrary and capricious acts of cruelty. The summary execution of surviving leaders might have looked to later generations like nothing more than the victors copying the arbitrary violence of the Nazis. Therefore, there had to be formal trials to determine the guilt of the defeated leaders and to decree the appropriate punishment. Because what the Nazi government and its minions had done was not covered by any existing formal laws or conventions, a new category of offenses had to be devised: "crimes against humanity." In other words, the Nuremberg trials appealed to the common human sense that there is a law written in the heavens, which is law even if it has not been formally put into the statute books and, therefore, must be respected and can be enforced. There were flaws of many kinds in the Nuremberg trials, including the fact that the victors themselves were not altogether innocent of "crimes against humanity." Despite such flaws, the trials did at least reaffirm the principle that certain things are evil and wrong in themselves, even if human authorities have not written legislation to prohibit them. [9]

There would have been another way to justify the behavior of the Nuremberg tribunal. If it had chosen to follow Kelsen's principle of legal positivism, it could have permitted the conquering powers to make retroactive laws condemning the past conduct of the Nazi leaders, and, using these retroactive laws, punish them accordingly. Indeed some apologists for the Nuremberg trials had no difficulty with this interpretation of what they were doing.

Of course the doctrine of legal positivism cuts both ways. If the Nuremberg International Tribunal had followed Kelsen's view, then—at least from one

---

[9] The atrocities of Nazi Germany were so many and so serious that most people were ready to overlook the legal principle that it takes a law to define a crime. "Crimes against humanity" need no specific statutes to be wrong and to be punishable. Many critics, without in any sense exonerating the Nazis, were disturbed by the precedent of trying and executing people for doing things not specifically forbidden at the time they did them. Since World War II there has been a succession of attempts to use the rubric of "war crimes" to try defeated enemies with less justification than that of the original Nuremberg trials.

perspective—the so-called Nazi war criminals should have been acquitted because they were only acting as Nazi laws permitted, or even required.[10] Very few people at the time would have been satisfied with Kelsen's theory, however. Most of those who accepted the concept of war crimes trials denied that they simply reflected nothing higher than "victors' justice,"—the imposition by those who had won of whatever seemed good to them—and claimed instead that although no statutes existing at the time were violated by the accused, they were guilty before a higher law and, therefore, could justly be condemned and punished.

From the example of the Nuremberg trials, it is evident that sometimes a particular action can be justified equally well by either conflicting theory: divine law and man-made law. From the purely practical standpoint of those sentenced to be hanged, it may have made no difference. From the standpoint of those who have to live in the present, it makes a great difference whether laws are thought of as corresponding to higher principles of justice or as merely reflecting the will of those in power.

After World War II, the Nuremberg war crimes trials rejected the theory that a law is just if lawfully enacted and its corollary that what is legal by such a standard is also just. Therefore, the tribunal condemned a number of the surviving Nazi leaders to death. This concept of absolute, we might say God-given, standards of justice still lives on in human hearts and can be expressed in those rare cases that stir up the imagination to think in terms of ultimate justice rather than in what the law can be manipulated to do for someone.

In 1994 a French tribunal imitated Nuremberg on a much smaller scale, condemning seventy-eight-year-old Paul Touvier, a former Vichy militiaman, of a "crime against humanity" for the 1943 killing of seven Jewish hostages in reprisal for the killing of a French militiaman. The French court determined that the statute of limitations did not apply to "crimes against humanity," thanks to a retroactive law passed by a postwar French government, and that the presidential pardon given Touvier by President Georges Pompidou also did not apply, as Pompidou pardoned him for murder, not

---

[10] In at least some cases, however, the accused individuals had even violated existing Nazi laws in committing the deeds charged against them.

for crimes against humanity. Despite the widely shared conviction that retroactive laws are unjust (according to which Paul Touvier should not have been tried in 1994), most Frenchmen agreed that he deserved to be punished, even fifty years after the event. As with the Nuremberg precedents, there are two ways to argue that Touvier's condemnation was just:

1. On the basis of legal positivism, one can argue that the retroactive law was properly enacted and is therefore just.

2. On the basis of eternal law, one can argue that although no human statute valid at the time condemned Touvier's actions, they are wrong in the light of the higher laws of eternal and divine justice.

The case of Paul Touvier may appear insignificant by comparison with the Nuremberg trials, but it does illustrate that the concept of a standard higher than man-made laws is still with us. Although the case of one French militiaman condemned for executing seven Jewish prisoners seems trivial in the context of a war that produced tens of millions of deaths, Touvier's case also illustrates a great contemporary problem. If Touvier's action was a crime, why was it? Was it because it violated a fundamental, eternal principle of justice? If so, then it was proper to condemn him, even though his action was in accordance with the human laws in effect at the time. But if his action only became a crime because a law enacted a score of years afterwards redefined it as such, what prevents it from becoming a virtuous act at some future date if a future French or European government should rewrite the relevant laws and make the execution of hostages an appropriate way of sanctioning an assassination? Indeed, if the Vichy government, whose militiaman was assassinated, had remained in power, Touvier would hardly have had to spend the last half-century in hiding.

A Striking Example

Throughout most of the developed world, until recently most abortions were considered crimes and were forbidden by law. After World War II, one country after another relaxed abortion laws, making abortion simply a "medical procedure." For some, abortion has even become a praiseworthy act.[11] Suppose a future Court were to decide—as have earlier laws and courts—that abortion really is a crime, perhaps even a crime against humanity. Would this make all the physicians and abortion providers who enrich themselves by this procedure criminals like Touvier?

Both ideational and idealistic thought holds that if the accused Nazis, Touvier, abortionists, or anyone for that matter, are truly guilty, it is not because of human statutes in force at any particular time or enacted *ex post facto* but because certain deeds are right and others are wrong in themselves, in the sight of God. No one who is currently arguing for the prohibition of abortion envisages punishing abortionists for abortions already performed but only for those that might be done *after* a prohibition should be passed. Nevertheless, those who believe abortion (or any other deed) is a heinous act deserving of punishment undoubtedly hold this opinion because they believe it to be wrong in itself, not because it happens to be against a specific human legislative act.

THE IMPORTANCE OF THE CRISIS IN LAW

Among all the factors that contribute to the sociocultural crisis of our age, the crisis in ethics and law may well be the one that has the greatest implications for the future of our society. Theologians, philosophers, and psychologists argue about whether we humans possess true freedom of the will, but it is evident that we are called upon to make choices. In every area, choices have consequences, but in ethics and law the choices we make have consequences that can persist for centuries or perhaps even for millennia. Laws that we think we have "found" in the heavens may indeed impress us as unjust, but if so, we can argue against them on the basis of absolute standards and generally shared moral insights. Laws that are simply "made" by those in power cannot be argued against and cannot in principle be unjust. If people resent them, their only recourse is combat, whether the verbal combat of the law courts or the violent combat of rebellion.

---

[11] See Beverly Wildung Harrison, *Our Right to Choose* (Boston: Becaon Press, 1983).

CONTRASTING VIEWS OF ETHICS

Standards of ethics, whether enacted into statute laws or not, naturally correspond to the fundamental sociocultural system in which they are found.[12]

Ideational Ethics

In an ideational society, standards of right and wrong, principles of crime and punishment, will be based on supersensory values such as supernatural principles of divine justice—the decrees of God. Many familiar texts illustrate this attitude. For example, Jesus said, "Lay up for yourselves treasures in heaven, where neither moth nor rust destroys, and where thieves do not break in or steal. . . . What will a man be profited, if he gains the whole world, and forfeits his soul?" (Matt. 6:20; 16:26).

The concept that what truly counts is what happens to us in eternity has been fundamental for much of the human race throughout history. Probably at no time did all members of any society act according to this principle, but for many societies it was taken for granted that to do so would be both wise and prudent. At different times and in different places, the degree to which the political, social, and intellectual leaders have followed the standards of the sociocultural milieu or instead have set themselves above them and violated them has varied greatly.

In general, when society is in its ideational phase, the behavior of the greatest leaders has conformed, or pretended to conform, to the system. The power of ideational ethics to influence conduct depends on people believing that its theoretical foundations are true, that there is a divine Judge to whom even the greatest and most powerful of men and women will ultimately have to give account. A statement that is typical of the ideational viewpoint is that of Jesus: "For unto whomsoever much is given, of him shall much be required" (Luke 12:48 KJV). Through the centuries, countless human beings have willingly given

---

[12] The reader should bear in mind that the three supersystems are descriptions of the way cultures function, not prescriptions for how they must function. At times the distinctions between the systems are blurred, and the various aspects of a particular culture do not necessarily make the transition from one supersystem to another at the same time or with the same rapidity.

up all of the material goods of this world, even life itself, in the hope of having treasure in heaven and in order not to risk losing their eternal souls.

Although these references are from Christian texts, other major religions also have an ideational mentality. As Sorokin observes, "They all see the supreme ethical value not in this sensory world but in the supersensory world of God or the Absolute. They all regard the empirical world of the senses with all its values as a pseudo-value, or, at best, as an unimportant and subordinate value."[13]

A purely ideational system is hard to maintain because it places extremely heavy demands of self-denial on ordinary people. For a society to live according to such a value system requires a considerable level of discipline from its members, especially a willingness to defer the satisfaction of immediate needs and desires until the hereafter if necessary. In the area of ethics very few individuals and still fewer societies have been consistently ideational. Even the compromise of idealistic ethics is difficult to maintain, as indicated by the rapid collapse of a somewhat idealistic system in the United States after World War I and with increasing velocity after World War II.

Life in the real world makes demands on us that are difficult if not absolutely impossible to deny—the need for nourishment and shelter, for example—and it offers us rewards and pleasures that are not easy to spurn. Some human needs simply cannot be deferred indefinitely, and many are so strong that only the most self-disciplined and determined individuals can defer their satisfaction. A consistent ideational ethic might attempt to scorn all this-worldly interest and advancement in order to reap a great reward in the world to come, but hardly anyone is able to exist exclusively on this basis, even if one believes firmly that there will be rewards and punishments in the world to come. After all, Jesus also said of food and drink, "Your heavenly Father knows that you need them" (Matt. 6:32 NIV).

Sensate Ethics

An ethical system that regards sensory values as primary is a sensate system.

---

[13] Pitirim A. Sorokin, *The Crisis of our Age*, 2d ed. (Oxford, Oneworld, 1992), 264.

There are several varieties of sensate ethics, including utilitarianism and hedonism as well as varieties and modifications of these systems. Utilitarianism seeks the maximum happiness for the maximum number of human beings and measures happiness in terms of attaining pleasure and avoiding pain, generally defined in the realm of the senses:

> Let us eat, drink, and be merry, for tomorrow we die.

> Wine, women, and song.

> Follow thy desire, so long as thou livest. . . . Do what thou wishest on earth, and vex not thy heart.

> *Carpe diem*: Seize the day, for time is short.

> A feast is made for laughter, and wine makes life merry, but money is the answer for everything.

As Sorokin rightly observed more than half a century ago,

> Such are the eternal Chinese and Hindu, Greek and Roman, Italian and French, English and America, past and present formulae of [both] the ruder and more refined sensate systems of ethics. Their supreme aim is to increase the sum of sensate happiness, pleasure, utility, and comfort, because they do not believe in any supersensory value. Their rules are therefore not absolute but relative, expedient, and changeable, according to the persons, groups, and situations involved."[14]

Idealistic Ethics

The intermediate or mixed system, which we call idealistic, resembles the ideational in perceiving God, the Absolute, or spiritual realities as the highest value. However, it does have a place for sensory values, especially of a higher type: beauty, harmony, courage, and the like. The idealistic sociocultural system represents a compromise, but one that is closer to the ideational view than to the sensate. Ideational and idealistic ethics are similar in that both place

---

[14] Ibid., 112.

more value on supersensory realities than on those things that can be perceived and enjoyed by the senses.

Food, drink, and other so-called creature comforts appeal to our human senses, and we cannot do without them—nor ought we. However, in the realm of sensual satisfaction and creature comfort, it is but a short step from what we really need to what we simply want. As we get what we want, we may quickly become used to it and want increasingly more and different comforts. Christianity, like other higher religions, teaches that we must wait for the next life for true satisfaction of our desires as well as our needs. It is incompatible with a fully developed sensate system: it demands an ideational or idealistic approach.

THE TRANSITION FROM
IDEATIONAL TO SENSATE ETHICS

How was it possible for an ethical system that grew out of a religion with definite and apparently absolute principles to lose them and turn into a sensate system, which seeks only relative pleasures and comforts? The ideational and idealistic ethic systems both consider spiritual or sensate values the highest good—the *summum bonum*. However, they define the *summum bonum* differently:

- For the ideational system, it is God himself.

- For the idealistic system, it is the human enjoyment of God.

There is a transition between them, which may appear subtle but which involves a change in orientation that makes the transition from idealistic to sensate ethics easier and quicker than one might at first expect.

St. Thomas Aquinas, the foremost theologian of the medieval scholastic period, wrote, "The perfect happiness of man cannot be other than the vision of the divine essence." Aristotle, the pre-Christian Greek philosopher from whom Acquinas learned so much, thought in much the same way. He said that the *summum bonum* or perfectly happy life "will be higher than mere human nature, because a man will live thus, not in so far as he is a man, but in so far as there is

98

in him a divine principle. . . . We must . . . make ourselves like immortals and do all with a view to living in accordance with the highest principle in us."

For Aquinas, God himself is the *summum bonum*; the highest good for us humans is the beatific vision in God's presence, which is where we shall experience the highest possible bliss. If one determines to serve God simply for his own sake, without any thought of a reward for oneself, that is truly ideational. Virtually all of the great religions that believe in a personal God teach that he rewards those who diligently seek him and find him. In practicing self-discipline and self-denial in this earthly life, followers of those religions anticipate much greater happiness in the world to come.

One who is attracted by the diversions and pleasures of this life can sometimes be persuaded to forego them for the sake of the good (happiness, pleasure) that awaits the faithful servant of God in the hereafter. This attitude—foregoing pleasure for the moment for the sake of greater pleasure to come—is more idealistic than ideational, for it admits the reality and value of this-worldly satisfactions, but believes that the future blessedness is better and, therefore, worth waiting for.

Practically, idealistic ethics expresses itself much as ideational ethics does. Followers of both systems will usually resolve ethical issues in the same way, because they are looking to heaven for their judgment and their reward or punishment. The crucial point of contact with sensate thought lies in making the highest goal the human happiness that God can grant—the reward or punishment that he will give—rather than God himself. Once human happiness becomes our *summum bonum*, it is a short step to forsake the system that promises happiness in a future life in favor of one that seems to provide it here and now.

In the concluding scene of Engelbert Humperdink's opera *Hansel and Gretel*, the children's father, Peter, sings, "Evil cannot be ignored; virtue is its own reward." Like Humperdink's Peter, many noted ethical thinkers teach that even here and now true happiness consists in following ideational or idealistic principles. Aristotle taught that happiness, or what he would have considered worthy of being called happiness, is possible only in the context of a virtuous life. It is evident that he believed there is such a thing as a "highest principle" within us.[15] Some would say that the great ancient philosopher was naive in

---

[15] Ibid., 113.

distinguishing good from evil, virtue from vice, because he did not think himself obliged to prove that the good is good, nor that evil is evil. He could give a rational argument for making such distinctions, but he could not really provide hard evidence from the sensory world.

The psalmist wrote, "Surely, O LORD, you bless the righteous" (Ps. 5:12 NIV), but this blessing does not always come in the present life, where it can be perceived by the senses. Aristotle believed that an evil man cannot truly know love, cannot truly have friends, and, for these and other reasons, cannot have true happiness but only a counterfeit thereof. Thus the psalmist, the philosopher, and the theologian claim that virtuous living is necessary to obtain true happiness even here on earth. Unlike the ideational view that such felicity is to be found only in heaven, this idealistic approach can be tested on earth, where it does not always appear to work. This inherent weakness in the ideational approach facilitates the rise of more pragmatic sensate ethics.

Unfortunately for those who value the ideational or idealistic point of view and want to see people respect it, the reality of the next life and its anticipated rewards is guaranteed only by supersensory witness and evidence. It cannot be maintained unless the corresponding religious beliefs are widely held to be true and reliable. When the conviction that supersensory reality exists wanes, then the reasonableness of waiting for the next life for satisfaction of our needs and desires naturally disappears. Once this doubt of supersensory reality becomes widespread and effective, ideational and idealistic ethics are both doomed, and the stage is set for a move into a purely sensate frame of reference.

THE ALTERNATION OF THE SYSTEMS

These three systems of ethics have alternated throughout the history of Western civilization, from the times of Greece and Rome to the present. They have prevailed at about the same time that the corresponding systems of art and truth have been in the ascendancy[16] or, more frequently, have followed the changes in

---

[16] Ibid., 138.

art and history after an interval of a few years or decades. This is an important point, for laws change more slowly than other features of culture, and the actual state of a society may contrast with the laws that are still on the books. Ultimately, of course, the laws will come into conformity with the culture, and when this happens, the full enormity of the cultural shift will become evident.

Francis A. Schaeffer, in *Escape from Reason* and in his brief history of culture, *How Should We Then Live?*, argues that the changes appear first in the world of art and music and only later develop their full impact in the realms of ethics and law.[17] A change in ethical thinking, following recent changes in the arts, was already apparent in the fourth century B.C., when Socrates, Plato, and finally Aristotle introduced the modified idealistic view that sees in right living the road to a happy life. Belief in the reality of divine rewards and punishments is a fundamental support of both ideational and idealistic ethics.

A purely ideational system of ethics is rare. One sometimes encounters it among unusually rigorous Calvinists, who may say, "I would be willing to be damned for all eternity for the sake of the glory of God": the happiness of the individual is totally insignificant by comparison with the glory of God. Some people may assert this, and perhaps some sincerely think that they believe it, but it is a hard theory to live with.

Classic Greek tragedy reflects a similar ideational viewpoint. In the *Oedipus Cycle* of Sophocles, Oedipus must suffer although he has done all he can to avoid becoming involved in the crimes for which he is to be punished—they were imposed on him by fate. This means nothing to Sophocles; the fact that moral principles have been violated, even though unwittingly and involuntarily, means that vengeance must and will be taken. Human happiness is fleeting, and it is not the main value.

This period of transition from ideational to idealistic ethics did not last long, for by the third century B.C. sensate ethics began to prevail and continued to do so until displaced by Christianity in about the fourth century A.D. Although it sees nothing higher than the sensory world, sensate ethics has nobler as well as crasser forms. Its nobler forms do not differ that much from

---

[17] Francis A. Schaeffer, *The Collected Works of Francis Schaeffer*, 5 vols. (Wheaton, Ill.: Crossway, 1982).

idealistic ethics in their practical maxims, and this often causes observers to overlook the fundamental differences between them. Stoicism, an ethical system of the sensate period, taught a high degree of self-control, since giving in to sensual desires simply brings on dissatisfaction and degradation. More clearly pleasure-oriented but still prudent, Epicureanism taught that the senses should be gratified but that this must be done in a temperate and restrained manner because unrestrained self-indulgence brings misery rather than pleasure in the long-run. A sensate worldview does not necessarily produce gross self-indulgence, although as time goes on it will tend more and more in this direction.

Gross hedonism—the unbridled pursuit of pleasure—is the extreme form of sensate ethics. It appealed to the masses but could only be enjoyed by the wealthy and privileged. Rome's poor were not more idealistic and less self-centered by virtue of being poor; they were simply unable to afford luxurious living. In the midst of sensate self-indulgence, this made them more receptive than the rich to Christianity, the new religion that taught self-denial as a praiseworthy exercise. Perhaps it is for this reason that the Apostle Paul could write concerning those he had won to Christianity, "Not many of you were wise by human standards; not many were influential; not many were of noble birth" (1 Cor. 1:26 NIV). However, even the richest and most powerful Romans were not immune to the shifting sociocultural pattern that was replacing the sensate view of reality with a God-centered ideational one. From earliest times Christianity found converts among the rich and the ruling classes, as did some of the other more ascetic and less sensually oriented religions. It was hard even for those who possessed all of the wealth necessary to indulge their sensual appetites to be satisfied with sensory values when the society as a whole was turning to more spiritual ones.

The converse holds true as well, of course, and this is what we are experiencing in contemporary American life. It is hard even for those who are committed to otherworldly values to hold to them consistently when the entire surrounding sociocultural system is turning away from supersensory realities and grasping for those things that appeal to the senses. Western civilization still contains substantial numbers of people who believe in supersensory values, but it is hard for them to hold onto such convictions when the society around them constantly promotes materialism.

Although it began at a time when the older idealistic view was already being replaced by a sensate mentality, the Protestant Reformation of the sixteenth century reasserted an ideational worldview, placing great emphasis upon God, his will, and his Word. There is no more clearly ideational religious doctrine than the war cry of the Lutheran Reformation: "Justification by faith *alone*, without the works of the Law."[18]

The Protestant Christianity of the Reformation represented a far-reaching effort to reverse the sensate trend of European culture and to recover the original Christian conviction that supersensory values are essential. When Christianity began, its conflict with the pagan government of imperial Rome was a conflict between an ideational and a sensate system. Jesus himself told the Roman procurator Pontius Pilate, "My kingdom is not of this world" (John 18:36). Early Christianity as a movement did not have political control of territories or tribes that could revolt or wage war against imperial Rome; its battle was primarily spiritual. The Reformation launched a clash between two different understandings of ideational truth. Reformation Christianity quickly gained political control in several parts of Europe, and the conflict began to be fought with weapons. The fact that commitment to ideational and idealistic truth as expressed in religious doctrines led to bloody wars lasting for more than a century caused great disillusionment with the concept of doctrinal truth itself. Thus the ideational and idealistic revival of the Protestant Reformation only briefly impeded the shift to a fully sensate sociocultural system.

During the eighteenth century, skepticism concerning the truth and credibility of Christian doctrine grew, especially among the more educated classes in France, Britain, and Germany. From there it spread rapidly to North America. Nevertheless, many of those who were skeptical about the truth of Christian doctrines, or even denied them outright, sought to maintain Christian ethics. The Calvinist Puritanism of New England gave way to the nondogmatic religion of Unitarianism, but the Unitarians were if anything more energetic than more traditional Christians in seeking to live the kind of

---

[18] Luther added the word *alone* (German *allein*) in his translation of Romans 3:28 from the Greek, arguing that it must be inserted to give the proper sense of the original in the German of his day.

moral life that Christianity prescribed. Then with shocking abruptness, most of those who still held and practiced a variety of the Christian ethic, even though they had abandoned the doctrines of the Christian faith, suddenly turned and abandoned the ethic as well.

In 1941, and later in his 1956 work *The American Sex Revolution,* Sorokin clearly saw and predicted what was coming.[19] What has happened has more than fulfilled his predictions as in the closing years of the twentieth century the debased variety of sensate ethics has gained almost total control throughout the West. The older ideational system of ethics ruled in Europe from the fourth century to the thirteenth. After that, even though it was no longer totally dominant, it remained strong and continued to enjoy at least formal favor until recent decades. This older system is or was well known to all of us in the Western cultural world. As Sorokin writes, "Its sublimest forms are summed up in the Sermon on the Mount."

> Being derived from God, the moral values of the Christian ethics are absolute. Their cardinal principle is the all-embracing, all-bestowing, all-forgiving love of God for man, of man for God, and of man for man. Their pathos and ethos are derived from this boundless love, and from it the charismatic grace, duty, and sacrifice implied in it. Blessed by charisma, man is a child of God, and is sanctified by this relationship; regardless of his race or sex, age, or social status, he is of supreme value. Making its moral principles absolute, Christianity raises man to the highest level of sanctification, and protects him unconditionally against any use as a mere means to an end. No greater glorification or sanctification of man is possible than that vouchsafed by the ideational ethics of Christianity.
>
> From this attribute of Christian ethics followed all the medieval—either negative or indifferent—estimation of all the values of the sensory world as such, from wealth, pleasure, and utility to sensory happiness, when divorced from the supersensory value.
>
> Remember, man, that thou art dust, and returnest to dust.[20]

The self-evident presupposition behind this ethical system is that expressed in the Epistle to the Hebrews: "They admitted that they were aliens

---

[19] Pitirim A. Sorokin, *The American Sex Revolution* (Boston: Peter Sargent, 1956).

[20] Sorokin, *Crisis*, 114.

and strangers on earth. People who say such things show that they are looking for a country of their own" (Heb. 11:13–14 NIV). The most significant factor is the conviction that there is an otherworldly, supersensory reality that will be more significant, *sub specie aeternitis* (from the perspective of eternity) than the things that happen to us in the present world of time and space.

THE THREE FUNDAMENTAL SYSTEMS OF LAW

Like the ethical systems, legal systems express the value structures and relationships of the prevailing sociocultural system, although they frequently lag behind the changes in the arts and systems of truth. Jesus's Sermon on the Mount, like the Twenty-Third Psalm and the Ten Commandments, has enjoyed unchallenged prestige until almost the present day. The Ten Commandments set a standard that a reasonably determined individual ought to find possible to meet; the Sermon on the Mount, by contrast, is far more demanding. Where the commandment states, "You shall not commit adultery" (Exod. 20:14), the Sermon on the Mount says, "Anyone who looks at a woman lustfully has already committed adultery with her in his heart" (Matt. 5:27, NIV).

The moral demands of the Sermon on the Mount are high, and it is difficult, perhaps impossible, to fulfill them. The Ten Commandments, by contrast, are not altogether out of reach. The high ideational ethic of the Sermon on the Mount has been held up to people for generations as an ideal to strive for, but one that few would have scant hope of attaining. Repeatedly reaffirmed in principle, this high ideational ethic began to yield to a somewhat more flexible idealistic position from the thirteenth to the fifteenth centuries. During the course of these centuries, behavior patterns and attitudes that earlier would have been denounced and condemned became common, especially in the circles of the wealthy, the literary, and the artistic.

The Protestant Reformation was an ideational reaction, which affirmed even more rigorous ethical standards in many realms of life than the traditionalist Catholics they challenged. Several important branches of the Reformation were strongly ascetic, but because the movement undermined the doctrinal consensus of Catholicism, the Reformation did not impede the rise of sensate and utilitarian values.

An ideational culture is largely motivated by the shared convictions of the people who make it up. For this reason, as said earlier, it is not necessary for such a culture to have highly detailed laws or to spell out all that it considers desirable and undesirable. Many requirements, although taken very seriously, may remain unwritten. When an ideational society begins to write out its laws in great detail, it is evidence that the people have grown lax and need to have their religious and social duties vigorously impressed on them. Whether written or merely customary, the laws of an ideational culture conform to the Law of God or the divine order to the fullest degree possible. The concept, "to promote the general welfare," a typical goal of governments, will be understood in terms of *spiritual* welfare. The chief purpose of law will not be to increase material goods and sensory pleasure but rather to help people find their way to God, achieve union with him, and conduct themselves in accordance with his will. Its goal is to promote the glory of God or the divine order and to direct people in ways that uplift them spiritually. Their material welfare is at best secondary.

In an ideational system, crime and sin mean the same thing. The civil law is supposed to have a spiritual purpose, instructing people how they should live and sometimes even telling them what they should believe and how they should worship. Offenses against God will be crimes. As the laws of the society are presumed to reflect the will of God, any crime is thus also an offense against God. Purely religious duties such as church attendance or synagogue worship may be legal obligations, and failure to fulfill them can bring legal punishment. Other acts (such as heresy, blasphemy, marriage outside of the religious community, marriage within certain degrees of relationship, or eating and drinking certain forbidden foods and beverages), which are contrary only to religious tenets but not to natural law or the common understanding of mankind, occupy a substantial portion of the statute books and law codes. Sexual acts that are considered offenses against morality will figure prominently in the law codes of both ideational and idealistic societies (although sexual behavior and its consequences are important for social harmony and the individual well-being in any society and thus frequently are regulated by law even in sensate cultures). Laws and regulations that appear burdensome to us, used as we are to the type of liberty that prevails in a late sensate society, may be not merely endured but actually approved and appreciated by the ideational population precisely because they want to attain the promised blessedness and are not averse to being helped and guided by the government. Of course, when a sociocultural shift is in progress, then such laws and regulations appear burdensome and will be ignored and eventually abolished.

The standards of an ideational society may seem strict and harsh, but their physical harshness is often mitigated by the fact that the penalties and punishments, like the offenses, may be of a religious nature. Those who break the laws may face public confession, acts of penance, or eternal damnation in the world to come. Needless to say, if religious sanctions both in this life and in the world to come can function as effective deterrents against misdeeds and serious crimes, the need for severe punishments on earth is lessened. On the other hand, as Sorokin points out, because a misdeed offends the divine order, it must be punished even if punishing the offender does not appear to have a direct social benefit.

Ideational, Idealistic, and Sensate Systems of Law

Systems of law, like systems of ethics, are integrated under ordinary circumstances into a sociocultural supersystem and will manifest the typical features of that system according to whether it is ideational, idealistic, or sensate. An ideational culture will produce its own typical law codes, usually integrating religious principles into civil and criminal law. Law is the expression of the will of God or of the divine order, and it is primarily *jus divinum* or *jus sacrum*. Because law comes from God, it is absolute and cannot be set aside for any purpose. Statements such as this are typical:

> But if there is a man who hates his neighbor and lies in wait for him and rises up against him and strikes him so that he dies, and he flees to one of these cities [of refuge], then the elders of his city shall send and take him from there and deliver him into the hand of the avenger of blood, that he may die. You shall not pity him, but you shall purge the blood of the innocent from Israel, so that it may go well with you. (Deut. 19:11–13)

> Do not pollute the land where you are. Bloodshed pollutes the land, and atonement cannot be made for the land on which blood has been shed, except by the

blood of the one who shed it. Do not defile the land where you live and where I dwell, for I, the LORD, dwell among the Israelites. (Num. 35:33–34 NIV)

The rules of an ideational legal system cannot be challenged, because they have been handed down by the most absolute Authority of all. To question this Authority is to risk catastrophe. The usefulness of the rules is not always evident, but they must nevertheless be obeyed and not questioned. The Aztecs of pre-Columbian Mexico sacrificed thousands of captives and even volunteers to their gods every year, cutting the hearts from living bodies, because of their belief that the gods demanded this "divine food" and without it would let the world fall into chaos. The Aztecs waged war on a regular basis simply to obtain captives for this purpose.[21]

Biblical ethics can demand unquestioning, ideational obedience. God said to Abraham, "Take now your son, your only son, whom you love, Isaac, and go to the land of Moriah; and offer him there as a burnt offering on one of the mountains of which I will tell you" (Gen. 22:2). The context shows that while Abraham's God could and did demand unconditional obedience, he was satisfied with Abraham's readiness to obey even so harsh a command and did not demand that it actually be carried out: "Do not stretch out your hand against the lad and do nothing to him; for now I know that you fear God, since you have not withheld your son, your only son from Me" (Gen. 22:12).

Through the centuries, countless humans have paid a heavy price because they were convinced that the divine order demanded it. In India, until the British successfully prohibited the practice in the nineteenth century, high-ranking widows were regularly burned on the funeral pyre along with the body of their dead husband. Such laws are not intended to promote human happiness or well-being but to express human submission to the will of the gods, to a divine order. No consideration of prudence, no utilitarian call for "the greatest happiness of the greatest number" can take precedence over what God or the gods have ordained.

---

[21] One of the factors that contributed to their defeat by the Spanish was their policy of trying not to kill their opponents but to capture them alive for sacrificial purposes. The Spanish, having no such purpose in mind, regularly defeated much larger Aztec forces.

Ideational laws often protect values that do not clearly have practical importance for individuals or society.[22] It often turns out that ideationally motivated regulations promote individual health or social peace, such as the Jewish definition of certain foods as kosher and prohibition of others as unclean, or the formerly widespread American laws that kept stores closed on Sunday. Kosher regulations for food preparation and eating have definite health benefits, especially in the hot climates where they were first instituted, and obligatory Sunday closing does bring certain social benefits.[23]

In their effort to keep man in harmony with God, ideational laws provide rituals for many of the most important events of human experience, such as birth, marriage, and death, as well as for some of the less significant ones, such as birthdays and graduations. Typically, ideational law seeks to avoid any appearance of being an arbitrary human regulation that can easily be changed, such as driving on the right (or left) side of the road.

Ideational attitudes sometimes appear to persist even in a secular society that has become primarily sensate, particularly where the honor of the supreme power is concerned. In a monarchy an insult to the king's majesty may be dealt with as severely as blasphemy. Even in a republic such as the United States, certain symbolic acts will be treated with the same seriousness as sacrilege in an ideational society. Until recently, the American flag was held to be an object that had to be treated with great reverence, and even today merely voicing a threat against the President can bring incarceration and compulsory pyschiatric evaluation.

---

[22] Ideational law may have a directly or indirectly protective function. The commandment, "Thou shalt not take the name of the LORD they God in vain," is followed by the warning, "for the LORD will not hold him guiltless who taketh his name in vain" (Exod. 20:7 KJV). When false swearing or perjury becomes common, society loses a protective feature, and law in general becomes harder to enforce. When individuals blaspheme, they may inflame the deeply held religious convictions of others and cause civil strife.

[23] In the United States, Sunday closing laws have generally been overturned by secularists claiming that they establish or promote the Christian religion and hence violate the secularists' interpretation of the First Amendment to the Constitution. Most European countries have kept Sunday closing laws, not in order to support religion, but because they feel that a common day of rest is good for families and for workers.

An ideational legal system gives those living under it the impression of reliability and dependability, while at the same time it makes strict demands of them and sometimes lays heavy burdens on them. An extreme example is the sacrificial system of the pre-Columbian Aztec civilization in Mexico. In addition to the tens of thousands of captives taken in war for sacrifice, prominent families could be required to give up a beautiful child or handsome adolescent to be slain on one of the high altars. A less gruesome example of a strict demand is the obligatory fast for all Muslims in the period of Ramadan.

Christianity too, at least its more liturgical branches, has its season of fasting known as Lent. However, it has been centuries since the Lenten fasts were seriously enforced by civil law, and in recent decades the Roman Catholic church has greatly eased even its ecclesiastical regulations. In most places in the sensate culture of the West, Lent is "observed," if we may call it that, by riotous carousing and self-indulgence in the period leading up to Lent—*Carnival*, Mardi Gras, or *Fasnacht*—which is seldom followed by any penitential practices once Lent has officially begun. Sensate ethics have taken over.

In an ideational system of law, even everyday transactions such as buying and selling property are frequently accompanied by actions of a religious or ritual nature, intended to place the human transaction in the context and under the protection of the divine order. "Now in earlier times in Israel, for the redemption and transfer of property to become final, one party took off his sandal and gave it to the other. This was the method of legalizing transactions in Israel" (Ruth 4:7 NIV). Sorokin cites a similar practice from Roman law in its early ideational stage. A claimant to property under dispute opened the proceedings by holding in his hand a particular kind of stick, called a *vindicta* or *festuca* and by pronouncing a set formula: *Hanc ego rem ex jure Quiritium meam esse ago: sicut dixi, ecce tibi vinditam imposui* (I claim that this is mine under civil law, thus have I spoken, I have laid this stick on you). The defendant answered in a similar fashion; all the proceedings took on the nature of a religious ritual.[24]

---

[24] Sorokin, *Crisis*, 123.

In Israel, when a woman was accused of adultery,

> The priest shall bring her near and have her stand before the LORD, and the priest shall take holy water in an earthenware vessel; and he shall take some of the dust that is on the floor of the tabernacle and put it into the water. . . . He shall make the woman drink the water of the bitterness that brings a curse. . . . If she has defiled herself and has been unfaithful to her husband, the water which brings a curse shall go into her and cause bitterness and her abdomen will swell and her thigh will waste away, and the woman will become a curse among her people. (Num. 5:16–17, 24, 27)

The office of judge in such a system is a religious office, and disrespect for priests and judges alike was dealt with severely: "The man who shows contempt for the judge or for the priest who stands ministering there [at the place where lawsuits are tried] to the LORD your God must be put to death" (Deut. 17:12 NIV). In addition to its specific commands, ideational law embodies moral exhortation. People are called upon to treat one another as God's children, to practice sacrificial love and altruism, to show good will, and to be faithful in discharging their duties toward one another. All of this takes precedence over immediate considerations of pleasure, utility, profit, and personal contentment, although ultimately moral living will be rewarded with divine blessings in this life or hereafter, or perhaps in both.

In an ideational society, government derives its legitimacy from God or the divine. Government not sanctioned by God is illegitimate. Consequently, ideational governments are always either explicitly or implicitly theocratic.

So strong is the human conviction that a proper government must derive its authority from God that a government may continue to refer back to God long after its laws have ceased to be essentially ideational. Thus it was in the administration of President Eisenhower after World War II that the words "In God we trust" were added to United States banknotes. The British monarch still calls herself Elizabeth D. G. Regina (Elizabeth, by the grace of God Queen) on her coins.

The ideational worldview requires obedience to divine laws precisely because they are divine, not for the sake of any future benefit that will accrue to those who obey them. Idealistic legal systems strike one as a modified variety of ideational law, for they still explicitly derive their authority from God, but they place more emphasis on the practical advantages of listening to the laws of God. The kosher dietary restrictions of the Hebrew Old Testament were urged upon the people in order to make or keep them a holy people, dedicated to God. Only later did observant Jews and others take note of the fact that the purity laws frequently brought health benefits. Indian Brahmans have a strict code of ritual purity, which they follow for religious reasons, and as a result they enjoy some definite health benefits. Some practices that Hindus traditionally observe because of religious teachings, such as vegetarianism, have been adopted in other countries both by people who are attracted to Hindu ideas and by those who merely think that such personal disciplines will bring tangible benefits.

To live according to the rules of the gods in an ideational culture is certainly not easy, and for this reason truly ideational law codes generally survive only briefly. Moving to the opposite extreme, to a sensate system in which, as Cole Porter wrote, "Anything goes," appears at first to be joyfully liberating. Sadly, as the experience of ancient Rome showed and as modern sensate cultures are again coming to see, a culture cannot long endure when there are no higher standards for human behavior than the appetites and tastes of the moment.

6

SOCIAL DEGENERATION
IN THE CRISIS PERIOD

The shell of Christendom is broken. The unconquerable mind of the East, the pagan past, the industrial socialistic future confront it with their equal authority. Our whole life and mind is saturated with the slow upward filtration of a new spirit—that of an emancipated, atheistic, international democracy.

George Santayana (1913)

SANTAYANA'S OPTIMISM in 1913 was hardly justified. Instead, the incredible slaughter of World War I began the very next year, launching what became the bloodiest century in all human history. It was continuing in even greater violence, after a pause of thirty-one years, when Sorokin published *The Crisis of Our Age* in 1941. America had not yet been drawn into the conflict and life appeared to be relatively stable, at least by present-day standards. Yet for Sorokin, the wars, no matter how horrible, were not the crisis but only severe symptoms of the crisis. By the time of Sorokin's death in 1968, the problems he described had worsened in the United States, increasingly so from 1965 onward. Even then, very few foresaw the degree to which what he wrote in 1941 accurately described what would be happening to Western culture at the end of the century.[1] Anyone reading his text today has to be amazed at the accuracy of most of his predictions:

---

[1] These changes are well described by William J. Bennett, *The Index of Leading Cultural Indicators*, vol. 1 (Washington, D.C.: Heritage Foundation and Empower America, 1993).

If a person has no strong convictions as to what is right and what is wrong, if he does not believe in any God or absolute moral values, if he no longer respects contractual obligations, and, finally, if his hunger for pleasures and sensory values is paramount, what can guide and control his conduct towards other men? Nothing but his desires and lusts.[2]

From the 1950s to the 1980s, the Western world was obsessed by the specter of nuclear destruction. Books, films, and television series presented horrible scenarios (e.g., *War Games* and *The Day After*). Those who did not predict nuclear war envisaged a world dominated by spiritless totalitarianism; *Nineteen Eighty-Four*, *A Clockwork Orange*, and *Brazil* are three examples among many. The fact that this has not happened has given much of the world a false sense of security. We fail to see that these things are not what Sorokin meant by the crisis. The economies of the major industrial nations, if not flourishing, have at least survived. The sense of relief that many feel must not blind us to the fact that the crisis Sorokin foresaw has not passed but has merely left us for a moment in the deceptive calm before a coming storm.

How was it possible for him to foresee our present situation with such accuracy more than half a century ago? Although history never repeats itself exactly, human societies, like human beings, are creatures with predictable habits. When similar fundamental conditions are present, they lead to similar consequences. Such consequences are not inevitable: some alcoholics reform and change their lives; some apparently moral individuals fall into the muck and never get out of it. Humans can change. Societies can also change. This is in fact what happens in cultural shifts of the type we have been describing. The error lies in failing to recognize that cultural shifts have causes. They are created by the choices, actions, and attitudes of millions of human beings. The motivation or lack of motivation of one individual does not create a major societal change, but if huge numbers of individuals throughout a society are motivated in the same way, the society reacts accordingly.

The most dangerous thing about the mass communication technology of propaganda is not that it tells people what they must think but that it inhibits

---

[2] Pitirim A. Sorokin, *The Crisis of Our Age,* 2d. ed. (Oxford: Oneworld, 1992), 168.

independent thought. It prevents them from thinking for themselves. In the fourth decade of this century, the Nazi party made brilliant use of the new technology of mass communication—lights, films, and special effects—together with the traditional attractions of marching soldiers and massed military bands to motivate and inspire the dejected and dispirited German people. All moral inhibitions vanished. This made it possible for one midsize nation of fewer than 100 million people to challenge most of the rest of the world and look as though it might actually win.

The governments of Western countries do not have propaganda machines like Dr. Goebbels', but all of Western culture is permeated by mass communications and round-the-clock entertainment. Whole populations are effectively anesthetized; independent thinking becomes rare; slogans replace thought; and logical analysis virtually ceases to exist. Moral inhibitions vanish. Under such circumstances, the normal recuperative factors that exist in individuals and in whole cultures may be put out of action so that the constructive changes that are due, even overdue, will not occur.

When a person has neither faith in God nor any absolute moral standards, what is to deter that person from doing and taking whatever he or she pleases, regardless how it may violate the rights of others? If others oppose such "self-fulfillment," there is nothing to prevent resorting to violence. On the individual level, this can lead to crimes such as murder, robbery, theft, fraud of various kinds, and sometimes to suicide. On the societal level it leads to war, revolution, and social disintegration, which themselves are not the problem but rather symptoms of the problem. Avoiding intercontinental nuclear war, which we seem to have done for the time being, does not solve prevent social degeneration. Our culture no longer seems threatened with a devastating fiery inferno, but every passing year brings it closer to falling apart from within.

Loss of faith in God and in all moral absolutes on the societal level is a fundamental cause of the distress and evils that mark our period of sociocultural transition. Intensely religious individuals may still abound in a culture, but when the culture as a whole loses its sense of orientation, such individuals will not significantly retard the disintegration in an age of mass communication and media gigantism.

The influence of the mass media, especially mass entertainment, is a new and important factor in the incipient disintegration. It is neither society nor culture that believes in God or can lose its belief in God but rather individuals. The primary concern of most religious leaders is the persuasion and conversion of people, not the transformation of culture. However, when the religious leaders in a culture pay too little attention to what the whole culture is doing, they may be thrust into a backwater where they are not merely isolated but become increasingly impotent to spread their own convictions.

When belief in God or moral absolutes (or in both) is widespread, it influences even those who do not have a religious faith or do not hold to any absolute moral standards. Consequently, they may act with civility, decency, decorum, and even charity toward others even though they do not consciously subscribe to values that would make such conduct obligatory. When belief in God and moral absolutes fade in a society, the changing social climate will eventually intimidate even those in whom belief remains strong, as they see themselves and their convictions increasingly ridiculed.

If a society remains relatively stable, not shaken by wars, economic upheaval, or other large-scale disturbances, it is possible for substantial numbers of individuals and even groups to lose or forget their basic convictions and yet to continue to behave as society expects them to behave. For this reason, a society can preserve the appearance of stability for a considerable number of years or even decades after its fundamental convictions have eroded. This is why Western culture preserved a veneer of Christian morality long after the idealistic phase had given way to the sensate phase that is now coming to an end. When the stability and coherence of society depends on memories and habits that no longer have a solid foundation, collapse and disintegration can come with bewildering speed. There is a point to which the memory of earlier convictions—"fossilized faith"—will still motivate the people in a culture to remain within the bounds of earlier decencies, but when this point is passed things can change with incredible rapidity.

When the basic form of a culture is changing, forms of speech, styles of dress, attitudes, entertainment, and relations between parents and children, between the sexes, and between generations all change, gradually at first, then more rapidly. This has happened repeatedly throughout history. In earlier ages, even without means of mass communication and transportation, when a dominant form of culture was passing away, the conditions and basic living patterns of an entire society could be transformed with unexpected abruptness. The result is that problems that once were exceptions occurring in isolation become widespread and continual: crime, especially violent crime, mental illness, war, and revolution.

INCREASING RAPIDITY OF CHANGE

The beginning of the modern period of history coincided with the rise of printing, which facilitated the rapid spread of ideas. Both the revival of classical learning in the Renaissance and the propagation of the Bible in the Protestant Reformation challenged the millennial domination of faith and morals by the Catholic church, weakening the restraining walls of idealistic culture. The shift from a late idealistic to an early sensate culture nevertheless proceeded slowly, particularly as it affected individual conduct.

Protestantism challenged Catholic doctrines and institutional power, but it actually reinforced most Catholic moral teachings (with the exception of the requirement of clerical celibacy). Protestants, like Catholics, were taught to put the will of God first, to postpone gratification, and to endure hardships in this life in the expectation of rewards in the life to come. This position was compatible with ideational and idealistic forms of culture but not with the emerging sensate form. Sensate culture questioned and subverted traditional morals and doctrine, both Catholic and Protestant, and ultimately overthrew them. It took centuries rather than decades for the implications of this cultural shift to become effective throughout society. People and cultures move slowly, and centuries-old habits die hard; the transformation may go unnoticed for some time, but when it suddenly accelerates, nothing looks familiar any longer.

This has happened in Western culture. As the underlying sociocultural form shifted, conditions slowly became ripe for far-reaching transformations in the everyday life of ordinary people. When conditions had changed sufficiently, there was suddenly a drastic transformation. As the shift gained speed, the constantly accelerating revolution in communication and transportation caused what began as a slow slide to become an avalanche. Values and standards

117

appeared to crumble and collapse; the old certainties failed. As the Latin proverb puts it: *homo hominibus lupus*—man [becomes] a wolf to his fellowmen. People no longer recognize their common interests, for their interests have become highly individualistic and selfish. The archaic expression *lust*, which signifies inordinate desire, is an apt one to describe the self-centered drives that overrule common interests and the general welfare. Whereas in an ideational or idealistic culture lust was something to be ashamed of, in the sensate world it becomes a reason for boasting.

Large segments of society behave totally without shame in a selfish and licentious manner. Yet even now substantial numbers of people still respect the older standards and continue to act in accord with them. Religious and moral commitments keep many people out of the currents of change, unwilling to "go with the flow" despite mockery and ridicule. This is not true of the agents of public information and communication, however, for they have shifted almost totally into a late, degenerate sensate phase. They *insist* on going with the flow. This includes not only avant-garde publications and performances but also the staid metropolitan newspapers, serious magazines, and the most bourgeois-appearing television and radio newscasters and talk show hosts, and even the institutions of education at every level, from graduate school to preschool. No longer can one expect that praise and approval will be given to "whatever is true, whatever is noble, whatever is right, whatever is pure, whatever is lovely, whatever is admirable" (Phil. 4:8 NIV) nor to the persons who speak such words, perform such deeds, and exhibit such qualities. They are more apt to be ridiculed, charged with hypocrisy, and perhaps pitied as hopelessly out of date. It is not necessary to look to the cheap periodicals and tabloid newspapers to find critics who gush and rave over performances that portray and exalt violence, deceit, perversion, and even blasphemy. One finds lavish praise for such things even in leading newspapers and serious magazines. Seldom is that which is evil, distorted, or perverted described as such, much less found to be at fault.[3]

---

[3] An example can be found in the most prestigious newspaper published in the United States, the *New York Times*. As recently as 1965, the *Times* refused to accept paid advertising for a book that its editors regarded as obscene and exploitative. Now it is hardly necessary for such books to buy advertising space in the *Times*; its critics shower attention and praise on them.

AGGRESSION, VIOLENCE, AND CRIME

When a society is in an upheaval affecting all of its systems and values, individuals, groups, and ultimately whole populations lose their sense of purpose and direction. This creates conflicts characterized by growing intensity, vehemence, and violence. Individuals clash with one another, resulting in increased levels of ridicule and contempt for one another. Public discourse, even in the halls of Congress, is marked by insults that would once have been considered slander and in an earlier day would have led to duels. The vilest insults, which in simpler days might have led to mortal combat, are hurled back and forth with abandon, even at public officials, and the courts protect the offenders on the grounds of freedom of expression. Such vehemence of speech does not usually lead to violence in the hallowed halls of legislature, but the fact that it is occurring with increasing frequency there is a sign that even at high levels of society and government there is a loss of self-control. Violence of speech signifies a basic change in the attitudes of the heart.

Crimes are not only becoming more numerous, they are becoming more vicious. Robbers and burglars who formerly would not have harmed their victims after taking their money and possessions are now more likely to kill them, sometimes cruelly torturing them first. Defenseless children are not spared, and the weakness and infirmity of the elderly, instead of attracting sympathy and respect, make them preferred targets of random violence. All this is taken for granted: "Naturally that old woman was robbed and beaten. She should never have gone down that street alone." It is no longer merely the elderly and women who are afraid to walk the city streets after dark; strong young men have to be cautious. Whereas a few years ago an assault might lead to bruises, today it often ends with death. Violence and rage, when not directed toward others, are turned inward, resulting in an increase in mental illness and self-destructive activities such as drunkenness, drug abuse, sexual promiscuity, and suicide.

The institutions that traditionally provided justice, the courts, become the battleground for clashes of interest decided on almost any basis other than justice, whether it be wealth, popularity, racial or ethnic loyalty, sex, age, or the ability to hire famous lawyers. In the United States, both the criminal and civil

119

courts are in turmoil. In criminal proceedings, juries deliberate about the most atrocious murders and give verdicts of acquittal or force a mistrial because of personal sympathies or racial feelings. In civil court, juries award astronomical damages for minor problems based not on injuries actually suffered but on sympathy for the plaintiff and the wealth of the defendants. In the United States, federal and state governments making attempts to correct such abuses find themselves embroiled in bitter charges from all sides. Confidence that the courts are places where justice can be found is disappearing; it has become apparent that in many cases it is not even justice that is sought there but plunder.

The persons and agencies who previously upheld standards of decency and charity in interpersonal behavior have joined hands with those who deliberately and systematically debase them. Agencies of law enforcement and the courts are being overrun by so many serious crimes they are totally unable to check the lesser abuses that have become the order of the day. Prisoners, even violent offenders, are released from confinement because of prison overcrowding. Beyond this, courts have been aggressive in striking down many of the traditional forces that used to restrain the worst expressions of human selfishness. Religion and religious language are regularly banished from the halls where justice is supposed to reign. In 1994 the Supreme Court ruled that the Ten Commandments had to be removed from the wall of a local courthouse, where for decades they had reminded all present of the fact that there is a higher standard to respect and a higher Authority to whom all must eventually give account.

In the United States, many members of the legal profession have been diverted from the tasks of protecting the innocent, punishing the guilty, and enabling the weak to secure their rights, to what can only be called plunder. Attorneys and clients abuse tort law to enrich themselves, choosing as targets for exploitation not those who are responsible or negligent but simply wealthy individuals and corporations with little or no responsibility for an injury or loss. Physicians who are less than successful in healing a disease or repairing an injury may be plundered by attorneys and their clients for their inability to do what only God can do.[4]

---

[4] In one case, a surgeon—or rather his insurance company—was forced to pay several million dollars in damages for failure to restore to an injured man the full use of his hand. What would the

WAR

The most overwhelming and total form of violence that humans perpetrate against one another is war. Our century has been the bloodiest in human history, with wars raging across entire continents, attacking civilian populations and noncombatants with the ferocity that used to be vented only upon fighting forces. When wars become a general condition, it indicates that a culture, and perhaps even the entire world, has become unstable. Instead of outgrowing war, the world at the end of the twentieth century has performed cosmetic surgery:

- Wars are no longer fought between formations of soldiers, mighty naval armadas, or squadrons of warplanes, but in cities and in the countryside between masses of undisciplined and embittered antagonists.

- Wars are no longer called *wars*.

- Wars between nations are no longer declared but are merely waged.

World history has always been the history of war. In the Fertile Crescent of the ancient Near East, the armies of Assyria, Babylon, and Persia surged back and forth for centuries, submerging ancient cities and taking whole populations into exile, before the dynamic energy of Alexander the Great overthrew the older kingdoms and ushered in the sensate phase of culture in the Mediterranean world. The history of Rome is a history of warfare: Rome became a world empire through war and lost its empire through war. No nation in history, at no time in history, has ever been safe from aggressive war, and most nations have been tempted to launch their own wars of conquest.

Nevertheless, there is nothing inevitable about war. There have been periods when large areas of the earth have been at peace—notably, the era of the *Pax Romana*, which lasted for two centuries or more at the beginning of the Christian era. Despite repeated disillusionment, humanity continues to dream of world

---

surgeon's compensation have been had he been successful in giving the man back his hand in excellent condition? Perhaps his fee would have been large, but it would hardly have run into millions. In another case, a physician has been sentenced to prison for a medical mistake that somewhat hastened the death of a debilitated, elderly person, while other physicians are called merciful when they give their patients "assistance in suicide."

peace, while thoughtlessly cultivating attitudes of greed and selfishness that make peace merely a breathing space between wars. Although part of human nature longs for peace and harmony, these can be obtained only when people learn self-restraint and discover how to control the lusts that are in their members (see James 4:1). Self-control is never easy for humans, but it is extremely rare in an age that has totally lost sight of absolute moral principles and has forgotten all respect for a divine Judge.

World War II led to the discovery of atomic and nuclear weapons, and the atomic bomb was actually used against Japan. These horrible new weapons made it possible, for the first time, for warring nations not merely to defeat opposing armed forces, destroy cities, and massacre civilian populations, but to destroy the entire world and themselves with it. Confronted with the specter of universal destruction and the ability to destroy the entire human race, the great powers have refrained from resorting to war against each other to achieve their goals. It became evident that to do so would likely entail self-destruction.

No nuclear war has not meant a state of world peace. Weapons of mass destruction such as nuclear bombs are not needed to massacre whole populations. Even small arms and primitive weapons can wipe out thousands of human beings, as happened in Rwanda in 1994. Our century has continued to grow bloodier, far surpassing all previous centuries even without resorting again to nuclear or biological weapons, simply by using weapons we call "conventional."

Once before our sensate culture entertained the illusion that war was becoming a thing of the past, at least for the developed nations of Europe and North America. Just a century ago Napoleon's visions of conquest seemed obsolete. The end of the nineteenth century was La Belle Époque, a time of optimism and confidence. The highly developed nations of Europe and North America gullibly thought that the human race was going to enjoy progress and increasing prosperity under the inspired guidance of the West.

The awesome carnage of World War I wiped out that hope. The vision of growing peace, progress, and foreign and domestic tranquillity—the emancipated international democracy evoked by Santayana in 1913—was shattered, never to be restored. World War I was "the war to end all wars," but only twenty-one years later, the second world convulsion began. The Bolshevik October Revolution in Russia ushered in the age of totalitarian dictatorship, which only came to an end in Europe in 1991 and is still continuing in Asia. By 1941 it was already evident that the twentieth century would be the bloodiest and most brutal century in recorded history.

The second half of the century has proved no less bloody than the first half. A summary of the most significant conflicts reveals the truth:

- There have been at least three wars between Israel and her Arab neighbors in 1956, 1967, and 1973, four if one counts the fighting after the establishment of the country in 1948.

- Israel intervened violently in Lebanon in 1982 and again in 1996.

- China was involved in a bloody civil war ending in 1948.

- The Korean War broke out in 1950 and involved the United States as well as China until 1953.

- The French lost a bloody war in Indochina, ending in 1954.

- America's Vietnam debacle took place from 1965–1973. Two years later North Vietnam conquered the South.

- Cambodian Marxists inflicted an incredible genocide on their own people.

- France fought and won a second kind of civil war or "war of liberation" in her effort to retain Algeria but gave up the province in the end.

- India fought small wars with Pakistan and China.

- Iraq and Iran spent eight years in bloody conflict.

- Iraq, not chastened by huge losses in its long, struggle with Iran, invaded the neighboring state of Kuwait, calling down upon itself the destructive wrath of the United States and several allied nations.

- Civil war in Nigeria in the mid 1960s cost hundreds of thousands of lives.

- There has been a sanguinary revolution in Ethiopia and bloody civil wars in the Sudan and Somalia.

- Angola, having shaken off Portuguese control, immediately plunged into a civil war, which is still going on at the time of this writing.

- The breakup of the Soviet Union has led to relatively limited if extremely bloody outbreaks of civil war.

- The breakup of Yugoslavia has resulted in warfare that by 1996 had been going on for five years.

The world organization, the United Nations, formed in 1945 in the hope of preserving world peace, now numbers over 150 member nations, but so far it has succeeded in preserving or restoring peace only when the opposing sides are not only in agreement but are militarily weak. It has little or no success in preventing clashes between powers determined to fight.

The history of war is not flattering to the human race. War has always been destructive, extinguishing human lives, destroying property, and blighting culture. When cities are destroyed and countrysides devastated, the only profit, if we may call it that, is glory for the victors.

Why do nations go to war? It was simpler in antiquity, when at least the rulers themselves could profit by the wars they won. Tribes, cities, and nations often thought they could enrich themselves and increase their power and prestige by war. When rulers or nations go to war for glory and treasure, the effort pays off only if they have calculated correctly and win, but even winners do not always gain from their victories. The costs in blood, treasure, and culture is often far higher than expected.[5] The cost to the losers is devastating.

Modern war is always destructive, never productive. Not since 1800 has a nation or a group profited from initiating a major war.

- When Napoleon began his wars of conquest, he did not intend to leave France mourning a million dead soldiers, stripped of overseas territories, and himself an exile on St. Helena.

---

[5] Consider the Spanish conquests in Latin America. The terrible cost to the native populations is well known. But how much did Spain profit in the long-run? Its coffers filled with the plundered treasures of the Aztecs and the Incas, Spain suffered one of the earliest devastating inflations on record, unusual because it happened when Spanish money was hard (gold and silver).

- When the Southern states decided to fight for independence from the North, they did not expect to end with one-quarter of their young men dead, their cities burned and destroyed, their economy in ruins, and their governments under the heel of Reconstruction.

- When the European Powers stumbled into World War I, the Austro-Hungarian, German, and Russian emperors did not expect to be stripped of their thrones or killed, nor to see their territories broken up, their economies ruined, and the stage set for totalitarian dictatorships.

- When Britain and France intervened, they did not expect to lose a generation of young men, to saddle themselves with ever more powerful central governments, and, by the unjust peace they enacted, to be setting the stage for the even more dreadful Second World War.

- When President Woodrow Wilson plunged the United States into World War I, he did not expect to destroy the civilization of Europe and prepare the way for Hitler.

- When Hitler embarked on World War II in search of *Lebensraum* (room to live), he did not plan to die in the rubble of Berlin or to leave a divided Germany of ruined cities and blasted industries with a generation of her young men dead and ancient German territories irretrievably lost to Poles and Russians.

- When the United States became involved in Vietnam, it was not with the intention of wasting the lives of fifty thousand soldiers, leaving the Communists in control of all of Vietnam, turning Cambodia into killing fields, and calling down moral and social catastrophe in the American heartland.

- When the Soviet Union went to war to enforce its will in Afghanistan, it was not the intention of the government to lose control of the homeland and to break up the Union into more than a dozen squabbling states.

The illusion of social Darwinism that war can bring out the most heroic and the best in nations has proved a terrible deception.[6] Even the most glorious conquests have left the victors poorer than before their victories.

War Becomes Work

The first World War was an entirely new kind of war—industrialized war. Earlier wars were fought in a series of campaigns, in a few important battles. Some soldiers acquired more wealth by plunder after a victorious campaign than they could have earned in a lifetime of hard work. Being a soldier brought danger but also the chance of great rewards. But after 1914 war became a year-round, twenty-four-hours-per-day enterprise. For the first time in history (except for the sieges of fortified towns) whole armies were constantly in battle. Previously, battles had been the exceptions, breaking up long intervals of relatively peaceful military pursuits. In World War I, the fighting became constant, with only brief intervals of leave or liberty. Soldiers no longer lived in barracks or camps during long intervals between battles. Instead, they lived in trenches, constantly under bombardment, never able to draw a breath in safety.

Prior to World War II, war's devastation was largely confined to the fighting forces; civilian populations, while not secure, were spared the worst of it. Even during the United States Civil War, it was homes, farms, factories, and schools of the South that the Northern armies torched; the population was not systematically put to the sword. World War II changed that. It brought twenty-four-hour danger to the civilian populations too, at least to those of the countries at a military disadvantage, ending with the round-the-clock bombing of German cities and towns by the Western Allies and the incendiary and

---

[6] Before World War I, prominent figures in Europe and the United States argued that war is beneficial for human evolution, claiming that it facilitates "the survival of the fittest." Exactly the opposite happened. In the U.S.A. Admiral Alfred T. Mahan and General Horner Lea praised war for this reason, as did General Friedrich A. J. von Bernhardi of the German General Staff, and others in Britain and France. Claus Wagner called war "the law of nature that sums up all the laws of nature: its work of creation lies in [natural] selection." This approach was challenged by one of the leading biologists of the day, Oskar Hertwig, but without success, in *Zur Abwehr des ethischen, des sozialen, des politischen Darwinismus* (Jena, Germany: Gustav Fischer, 1918), 98–115.

atomic bomb raids on Japan. In modern war, no one can be secure—with the possible exception of the great warlords themselves, who seem to be spared by a strange kind of courtesy.

Both aggressive and defensive wars have become incredibly costly for industrialized, developed nations. The major powers have not dared to bring war to their own territories, but several (especially France, the United States, the Soviet Union, and China) have squandered blood, treasure, and respect by waging inconclusive or disastrous wars, often far from home. Sometimes the victors in war appear to have gained, as the United States appeared to do at the end of World War II. The nation emerged powerful and wealthy with its industries undamaged and its population relatively intact. Among the other winners, Britain lost her empire and while the Soviet Union appeared to gain, its gains were fleeting. The defeated nations, Germany and Japan, now have stronger economies and more wealth than their conquerors. Today, even though the major industrial powers are neither at war nor threatened by war, the spirit of anxiety and fear has never entirely vanished.

Early in World War II Sorokin wrote, "We may safely hazard the guess that as long as the transition period lasts, and until the advent of a new ideational or idealistic society and culture, war will continue to maintain its decisive role in human relationships. Even if an armistice were signed tomorrow, it would represent merely an interlude, to be followed by an even more terrible catastrophe."[7]

If by *war* we mean world war between the Great Powers, this prediction has proved wrong. But if we include the smaller powers and civil war, war still does maintain its decisive role. So far, the "even more terrible catastrophe" has not occurred. We prefer to think that it will not. At least for the time being, it appears as though war on a global scale between great nations or blocs of nations is unlikely. We should not forget, however, that there were almost one hundred years of relative peace after Napoleon's defeat at Waterloo (the Crimean War and Prussia's conflicts with Denmark, Austria, and France were only brief interludes). Many people thought that peace had definitively replaced war. It seemed that the major nations of Europe had learned to get along without war, but that hope was suddenly dashed in a horrible worldwide conflagration. In our century, it has become

---

[7] Sorokin, *Crisis*, 178.

apparent that it does not take a world war to cause misery on an immense scale. Where wars between nations have become too risky, threatening the destruction of the entire planet, revolutions and civil wars break out to fill the quota of human suffering.

Revolution

Internally, the same emotions that cause wars produce revolutions. Revolutions are generally launched with the intention or pretext of overthrowing evil and thereby improving the human condition. There is usually the hope, expressed or implied, that people will begin to behave differently after the revolution and that no additional violence will occur. In fact, in recent decades a new argument has been introduced to justify revolutionary violence: The revolutionaries define the existing governmental system, which they intend to assault, as "institutionalized" or "structural" violence and argue that their own resort to violence is only a necessary corrective, counter-violence as it were.

No doubt America's President Wilson was sincere when after having campaigned on the slogan, "He kept us out of war," he justified America's involvement in World War I by calling it the "war to end all wars." But that war only prepared the way for the next, bloodier conflict. Revolutions to end "institutionalized violence" are seldom if ever any more successful in doing so than World War I was in ending war, but the human capacity for self-deception is immense. People keep hoping. One particularly gruesome example was the 1979 "Islamic Revolution" in Iran. It overthrew an autocratic and repressive monarchy only to saddle the nation with a much crueler and more tyrannical religious totalitarianism, ruining the economy and providing the pretext for a long and bloody war with Iraq. War to end war, revolution to end oppression— one might as well speak of killing to conquer disease.

Sorokin speaks of "bloody revolutions and still bloodier wars." Perhaps the proportion has changed between wars and revolutions, and revolutions are now bloodier; in any case, the earth is still drenched in human blood.[8] The

---

[8] In addition to the bloodshed of war and revolution, since the 1970s the "silent holocaust" of abortion has cost tens of millions of unborn human lives.

128

world recoiled in horror when it learned of the Nazi genocide against Jews and other population groups before and during World War II, although the Allied powers made no attempt to stop them. Today the nations have become accustomed to hearing about revolutions and civil wars that cost hundreds of thousands or even millions of lives in a short time, such as the massacres by the Khmer Rouge in Cambodia, of Armenians by Azerbaijanis and vice versa in the former Soviet republic of Azerbaijan, by Hutus and Tutsis in Rwanda, and by the various warring factions in what used to be Yugoslavia.

In order to understand what *revolution* means and what revolutions have done in history, it is necessary to define the term, for it is used almost as ambiguously as *peace*. Revolution—as distinguished from the coup d'état, the palace revolution, civil wars, and wars of independence—is a violent upheaval that overthrows an existing order. If we consider every violent internal disturbance that has beset Greece, Rome, and Europe from the sixth century B.C. to the present, Sorokin counts over sixteen hundred. Most of these disturbances remained relatively local, were of limited duration, and did not fundamentally transform the social order.

The period of the brothers Gracchi, killed in 132 and 121 B.C., was the beginning of a civil war in Rome that really does qualify as a revolution, ending with the establishment of the empire under Augustus in 27 B.C. Entire families, clans, and classes were wiped out, the Italian countryside was depopulated, and a generalized crisis made people grateful for the restoration of order under an emperor. It is not far-fetched to see a parallel to the civil wars raging in former Yugoslavia and part of Russia, and to suppose that if they continue long enough, they may end in the kind of peace that only a tyrant can bring.

The American War of Independence was not a revolution in this sense, as the former colonies continued to develop along the lines they were already following. The French Revolution, which began in 1789, was like the Roman civil wars. It led to mass executions, to the slaughter of whole segments of the population resulting in one million deaths nationwide, to wars all over Europe, and finally to the rise of Napoleon and the establishment of an empire. It became the model for other destructive revolutions such as those in Mexico (1910), China (ending in 1949), Russia (1917), Cuba (1959), Ethiopia (1974), Cambodia (1975), Iran (1979), and many other places. There has been an orgy of murder, plunder, and human

129

disasters of every kind. States forcibly created or reestablished on the basis of national and ethnic identities, such as Czechoslovakia, Yugoslavia, and Poland after World War I, provided pretexts for World War II. Broken up into several smaller nations, Yugoslavia suffered a protracted civil war that cost tens of thousands of lives and created hundreds of thousands of refugees.

World War I brought the industrialization of warfare, which became permanent for the soldiers; the aftermath of World War II may be the industrialization of revolution, making it permanent for the population of many countries. In the United States, urban crime may come to fill the role of a revolution, making danger and misery permanent for much if not all of the population. Sorokin observes that the "war curve," measuring the incidence of wars, lags somewhat behind that of internal disturbances.[9] The generalized internal disturbances of the 1990s may foreshadow ominous developments in the future.

SUICIDE

The incidence of suicide reflects a loss of hope and despair of many kinds: People take their lives because of incurable illness or great suffering; to avoid capture, torture, and disgrace; because of loss of honor; as an act of protest. By the middle of the twentieth century, as medical science succeeded in curing or preventing some previously fatal disorders, suicide began to outpace many dreaded diseases as a cause of death, particularly among the young. For young males in America, suicide has passed accidents as a leading cause of death.

Should society accord individuals the right to decide their own deaths, to take their own lives? In ancient Greece and Rome, most authorities considered suicide acceptable or even praiseworthy under some circumstances. The Hebrew Scriptures of the Old Testament do not explicitly condemn suicide, although traditionally Judaism forbids it as the shedding of human blood. Christianity firmly condemns suicide, especially after St. Augustine (A.D. 354–430) denounced

---

[9] Sorokin, *Crisis*, 179.

it as a grievous sin. In his *Divine Comedy*, Dante placed suicides in hell. Traditionally, they were denied Christian burial, although that has changed.

In western Christendom, suicide suddenly increased in the late eighteenth and early nineteenth centuries. The great German poet Goethe devoted an entire novella, *The Sorrows of Young Werther* (1774), to suicide; his romantic treatment inspired many young persons to kill themselves. Suicide became a fad, and young men who did not intend to kill themselves at least dressed like young Werther and wore a perfume called *Eau de Werther*. Napoleon carried the book with him to Egypt. In the Romantic period of the mid-nineteenth century, suicide became more common, and Victorian England endured a wave of suicides.[10] Closer to our own day, some philosophers have praised suicide as a noble act: "Only suicide gives a free life a free end," wrote Richard N. von Coudenhove-Kalergi.[11]

While in the past suicide has frequently been dramatic, as in the Japanese ritual of seppuku or harakiri and the self-immolation of protesters in Vietnam and elsewhere, the modern tendency is to make suicide a medical procedure by euthanasia. However it is done, and whether or not it is "physician assisted," when suicide becomes common, it is another indication that the late sensate society has exhausted spiritual resources and its joy in living. "If the rate of suicide rapidly increases, it is one of the surest barometers of the failure of sensate man to attain happiness."[12] There is even the phenomenon of group suicide, as in the cyanide suicides of hundreds of followers of Jim Jones in Jonestown, Guayana, in November, 1978. The fiery deaths of more than eighty followers of David Koresh in Waco, Texas, in March, 1993 may also have been deliberate suicide.[13]

---

[10] See Olive Anderson, *Suicide in Victorian and Edwardian England* (Oxford: Clarendon, 1987), and Barbara T. Gates, *Victorian Suicide: Mad Crimes and Sad Histories* (Princeton, N.J.: Princeton University Press, 1988).

[11] Richard N. von Coudenhove-Kalergi, *Ethik und Hyperethik* (Leipzig, Germany: Der Neue Geist/Peter Reinhold, 1922), 117.

[12] Sorokin, *Crisis*, 184.

[13] It is also possible that the inferno was caused by the tactics of the attacking government forces.

MENTAL ILLNESS

Even when the destabilization of a culture does not immediately result in international or interpersonal violence, it can lead to emotional problems and mental illness on a large scale. When people in a society are not being physically destroyed by crime, war, and revolution, they may be spiritually and emotionally devastated by circumstances beyond their comprehension and control. The increase in mental illness is indicated but not fully revealed by increases in the number of psychologists, psychiatrists, and patients in mental hospitals. The extent of serious emotional and mental illnesses is only partly shown by these figures, however, for many people who are seriously disturbed either do not seek help or cannot obtain it, so that true statistics are not available.

In the United States the problem of caring for the mentally ill has become so great that laws were passed to liberate—or banish—hundreds of thousands of mentally disturbed individuals from in-patient care in hospital facilities, putting them onto the streets and greatly increasing the phenomenon known as homelessness. The great hotels and concert halls of major cities are beleaguered by flocks of homeless beggars on a scale formerly seen only in poverty-stricken cities of the Third World. Homelessness in America has reached heights unknown in earlier periods of much greater economic hardship, such as the Depression of the 1930s, chiefly for the reason that families have become smaller, have been broken up, and no longer provide a refuge even for close family members overcome by misfortune.[14] It is evident that homelessness is not caused chiefly or exclusively by overwhelming economic problems but has other, less tangible causes as well. The rise in mental illness did not occur in places where people were subjected to terrible physical dangers and stresses, such as London or Hamburg during World War II bombings, but it is taking place in the midst of affluence and luxury. The external conditions of life may appear more bearable than they were fifty or one hundred years ago, but more and more individuals

---

[14] At the same time, there is an informal support network that permits young people who are fully capable of working and supporting themselves to abandon their homes and responsibilities to float around the country living off the generosity of others, often of strangers, as well as from public welfare benefits intended for the truly unfortunate and incapacitated.

are losing their mental stability and acting in socially destructive ways. The fact that this takes place when there is no direct, excessive outward pressure on the conditions of life reveals that the malaise is not being caused by physical adversity and danger, but by less tangible factors. The shift in the foundational beliefs of the culture is important. People have lost their orientation; their ethical "fixed stars" have disappeared from the horizon, and they have no firmer standards to define right and wrong than sentiments and feelings.

The increase and pervasiveness of these devastating problems directly contradicts the foundational principles on which the sensate culture operates. Sensate culture holds that the only values are material, which means that all problems have a material cause and can be solved by material assistance.[15] The absurdity of this situation is reflected in the failure of the "War on Poverty" and related welfare programs in the United States, which have expended hundreds of billions of dollars in poverty relief since the 1960s, only to find that there are more people living in poverty and degradation today than ever before.

The rapid rise in the number of mental illnesses is accompanied by the fact that major crimes of violence frequently go unpunished, defendants being found "not guilty by reason of insanity." A defendant may be found to have been "temporarily insane" at the time of the crime, although neither before it nor afterward, having been possessed by an "irresistible impulse." Supposedly he was no more in control of himself than someone thought to be demon-possessed. In past times, the demon-possessed individual would be cured by exorcism, if possible. Today he is sent to a psychiatric hospital. "This means that Western society is rapidly becoming mentally deranged and morally unbalanced."[16]

Criminality does not inevitably or even usually indicate mental illness in the clinical sense. Crimes, particularly robbery, theft, and fraud, are often committed out of a calculated plan to profit. In the late twentieth century we are

---

[15] Because the causes of both the mental illness and the related homelessness described here are largely nonmaterial and intangible, these problems can at best be somewhat alleviated but never solved by material measures, such as increased welfare support and better public health services.

[16] Sorokin, *Crisis*, 184.

133

observing more and more crimes of pointless, despicable cruelty. Wanton, irrational acts of cruelty are celebrated in song and in films such as *Straw Dogs, Natural-Born Killers,* and *Pulp Fiction.* These films, like *The Sorrows of Young Werther* two centuries earlier, provoke imitations. The constant exhibition and glorification of violence in the entertainment media is only rarely tempered by scenes showing the capture of the criminals, the suffering of the victims, or the redress of injuries. The police are usually shown in a negative light, equally culpable and sometimes less admirable than the criminals. The phenomenon of highly organized crime making use of sophisticated technology and often engaging in legitimate business along with criminal activities has come to be a familiar subject for favorable treatment in novels and on the screen.

INCREASING BRUTALITY OF PUNISHMENT

A final element in this long series of horrors is the tendency to resort to severer and more brutal punishments as social disorder and chaos increase. Governments make increasing efforts to stifle crime by increasing the numbers of police and the severity of punishments. It may seem to many, particularly in the United States, as though this is merely being demanded but is not taking place. Corporal punishments such as flogging and torture are banned in virtually all Western societies, although they have not altogether disappeared. The death penalty has been abandoned in most Western countries, although it has been reinstituted in the United States and is increasingly applied, even though only a minority of convicted murderers is actually executed.

What is increasing at an amazing rate in the United States is the prison population. The United States actually confines more people to prison than any other Western nation, in percentages exceeded only by the former USSR and South Africa under apartheid. Yet the outcry for more prisons and longer prison sentences continues unabated in America. When in certain elements of the population one young man in four spends time in prison before the age of twenty-five, one must assume that society as a whole is suffering from severe disorientation that cannot be cured by building bigger prisons and warehousing more inmates.

It is difficult to foresee any improvement of this social degeneration on the basis of any of the programs, policies, or systems now in place. One might envisage a situation in which a disciplined, highly motivated minority could determine to "clean things up" by seizing power and establishing the dictatorship of an elite, as Rome sought to do under Augustus Caesar and his successor. Real renewal did not come to Rome through the efforts of the Caesars, however; it only came when the culture changed, renewed by the growing Christian movement.

7

THE FINAL STAGE OF
SOCIOCULTURAL
DISINTEGRATION

Bad money drives out good.

Gresham's Law

WHEN A SOCIOCULTURAL SYSTEM enters its final stage of disintegration, four symptoms usually appear:

1. an irreconcilable dualism between human pride and self-glorification on the one hand and self-contempt and self-degradation on the other hand;

2. a loss of traditional formalities in society, combined with a chaotic syncretism, in which irreconcilable elements from various cultures past and present are jumbled together without any integration;

3. emphasis on size and numbers without reference to quality;

4. a progressive exhaustion and the loss of creativity.[1]

To what extent do these features characterize Western culture today?

---

[1] Here, as at many points, we follow the analysis of Pitirim A. Sorokin, *The Crisis of Our Age,* 2d ed. (Oxford, Oneworld, 1992), 196.

THE CULTURE OF MAN'S
GLORIFICATION AND DEGRADATION

The late nineteenth and early twentieth centuries was a period of tremendous confidence in human ability and in the irrepressible march of "progress," as it was somewhat naively understood. Western culture was in the ascendant all around the world; Western science seemed to be solving the riddles of the universe one after another. It is true that certain signs of stress had already appeared, particularl y in the fine arts. In the industrialized nations, the urban proletariat lived in squalor of a different and perhaps more degrading kind than the rural poverty so widespread in earlier decades. Nevertheless, it appeared to many that the world was continually improving and that these problems were but passing interruptions to the upward course of human development. We were fully in the modern age; the primitiveness and squalor of the Middles Ages had been left behind. The poet Swinburne proclaimed, "Glory to man in the highest, for man is the maker of things." Whitman sang of himself, and Nietzsche, a sickly recluse, wrote ecstatically of the Superman.

World War I brought a sudden, overwhelming shock. Warfare became industrialized and began to consume men (and to a lesser extent women and children) on a scale previously unknown. The European Great Powers ground one another down; thrones toppled, and proud empires were dismantled (Austria-Hungary) or plunged into years of revolutionary chaos. Within twenty-five years, the twentieth century had surpassed all previous centuries in bloodiness, destruction, and wanton cruelty, but the atrocities had only begun. A temporary recovery of confidence in the 1920s was followed by the crisis of the industrial economy and worldwide depression that resulted in the Second World War. Man developed weapons that for the first time threatened the total destruction of the planet.

Against the background of these catastrophic social developments, the creative energies of musicians, artists, architects, and writers burgeoned. The growth of the mass media and means of instant communication across oceans and around the world made instant celebrity possible for a few and enabled them to become rich. Artistic productivity increased, but the results, instead of encouraging human progress, attested to an increasing disillusionment and despair, as though people were growing tired of their own existence. Instead of celebrating man and his works as the nineteenth-century poet Swinburne had done, twentieth-century art celebrated his debasement, increasingly presenting man as *Dreck* (dirt, trash), whose characteristic mentality was one of *Angst* (anxiety, dread).

In the early decades of the flowering of sensate art, princes, bishops, and even republican city-states commissioned great artists, architects, and musicians to produce works of lasting beauty, elevating and glorifying man as the crowning work of Nature or the Creator. The modern governments of the West, ostensibly or truly democratic rather than elitist, began to subsidize art that portrayed man as an orphan or monster in an impersonal, meaningless universe.[2] By some sort of perverse logic, government largess now makes it possible for art to be even more degraded and degenerate than it can be on its own in the private sectors of the economy. If the analogy with Gresham's Law holds good, it is not by depriving our culture of art, literature, and music, that its beauty will be destroyed but by flooding it with profitable or subsidized expressions of disgusting, and debased art, literature, and music. The public passes from fascination and amusement with what it previously would have considered disgusting to satiation, boredom, and finally indifference, while the artists of the age make wilder and more frenzied efforts to regain attention by more degrading spectacles and exhibitions.

During the early sensate period, the Renaissance brought a fresh appreciation of the beauty created by the artists of antiquity. The Christian understanding of people and their exalted place in God's creation remained strong, and early sensate art celebrated that which is beautiful, courageous, and noble in its subjects. Knowing that fame is fleeting but that art can endure, generous donors commissioned works of great and lasting beauty. Even large and imposing edifices, such as the palaces of Versailles in France and Schönbrunn in Austria, were constructed with rooms where people could actually live and with artistic touches that could only be appreciated close up.

As the sensate era progressed, art and architecture of this noble type lost favor. In this century, not only the totalitarian states—Italy, Germany, and the

---

[2] See the excellent discussion by the Dutch art historian H. R. Rookmaaker, *Modern Art and the Death of a Culture* (Downers Grove, Ill.: Intervarsity Press, 1970), and the more recent work by E. Michael Jones, *Degenerate Moderns* (San Francisco: Ignatius, 1993).

Soviet Union—but also the democracies, and especially the United States, began to produce colossal works often in a style imitating classical Greek and Roman architecture but characterized by increasing mediocrity and ugliness. The early, individualistic skyscrapers built in the United States found few true imitators after World War II, and America's large cities all began to look alike: jumbles of matchbox-shaped towers hundreds of feet in height, climate-controlled with windows that cannot be opened, and featureless facades.

A common characteristic of trends in art and in literature in our era is a progressive degradation of man and his culture. During the last third of this century, it has become American government policy to support the most bizarre, depraved, and disgusting forms of art, mocking traditional moral standards as well as artistic good taste, providing generous subsidies for works of art that quite literally belong in what Sorokin called the "social sewer" (such as Andres Serrano's photographs of Christ on the Cross and of the Pope immersed in glass jars filled with urine). The great museums of North America and Europe seem to vie with one another in extolling works that illustrate human degradation and perversity.

As these trends continue, it becomes more and more questionable whether, if this represents the best that it can produce, the human race deserves to survive on this planet. Our human propensity to self-degradation seems almost to justify the contentions of animal rights enthusiasts and environmentalists that the protection of animals and the environment should be a higher priority than the growth and development of the human race. "Art" of this type suggests that the human race no longer deserves even a low priority but has become a blot on the face of the earth and ought to be eliminated.

Modern Western culture has plunged into a series of destructive, self-contradictory attitudes. Starting from the assumption that human beings are not merely free but autonomous, a law unto themselves, they increasingly discover that they are not free. In the West, there are no autocratic, tyrannical dictators to demand obedience, but people are increasingly controlled by what Eric Fromm called "anonymous authorities."[3] Far from proving the conceit that man is the master of his own universe, Western culture increasingly exhibits contradictions as absurd as those which George Orwell predicted for

---

[3] Eric Fromm, *Escape from Freedom* (New York: Rinehart, 1941), 167.

the slave society of *Nineteen Eighty-Four* with its official slogans: "Freedom is Slavery," "War is Peace," and "Ignorance is Strength."

In the mid-1940s, when Orwell was writing *Nineteen Eighty-Four*, these slogans were shocking because they sounded so absurd. How could any government expect to fool anyone with such oxymorons? Today, a dozen years after Orwell's target date of 1984, we know that such slogans are no longer unbelievable. In the United States, abortion has become "choice" and "retrospective fertility control." Mercy killing first became "death with dignity" and now is "physician-assisted suicide." The absurd is becoming reality. This contradiction is becoming evident everywhere. The human race, seeking to glorify itself, pretending that it is a law unto itself and that whatever it wills or chooses to do is by definition right and good, is now declaring itself unfit to share the earth with the other living creatures and is acting in a way to prove this declaration correct.

Jesus predicted, "Everyone who exalts himself shall be humbled" (Luke 14:11). In his parable (see Luke 14:8–11), the humiliation only involved taking a lesser seat at a banquet. Today the degradation consists of having first set ourselves up as the highest and most exalted of beings, claiming virtual divine honors, and then suddenly seeing ourselves, in the words of a modern existentialist poet, as "nothing but a useless passion" (Jean-Paul Sartre).

At the beginning of the modern sensate period, the artists of the Renaissance discovered anew the beauty and nobility of the human form. During the Age of Reason and the Enlightenment, which saw a renewal of the exalted classical style in art, architecture, and letters, the dramatist and critic G. E. Lessing announced that man had "come of age." The philosopher Immanuel Kant, claiming to have refuted the traditional proofs of the existence of God, offered us "religion within the limits of reason alone." In the following century, Friedrich Nietzsche proclaimed that man should throw off the "slave morality" of weakness preached by the Christian churches and make way for the heroic ideal of the Superman.[4] There seemed to be no limits to man's arrogance and self-exaltation, but soon disillusionment set in, beginning with World

---

[4] The quotation from Gotthold Ephraim Lessing is from *The Education of the Human Race*; the Kant quotation is the title of a tractate by that great philosopher; and Nietzsche's thoughts are a basic theme in his *Thus Spake Zarathustra*.

War I, and brought to a high pitch a quarter-century later in the frenzy created by the self-chosen Master Race, which submerged much of the world in destruction and degradation never known before.

Half a century ago, Sorokin wrote,

> Our culture condemns egotisms of all kinds and boasts of the socialization and humanization of everything and everybody; in reality it displays the unbridled greed, cruelty, and egotism of individuals as well as of groups, beginning with innumerable lobbying and pressure groups and continuing through economic, political, occupational, religious, state, family, and other groups."[5]

Our present situation contains even more contradictions than those of which Sorokin wrote, for contemporary society, particularly the so-called free market, actually exalts egotism and greed under the guise of self-fulfillment, while at the same time demanding of government and social institutions the greatest concern and preferential treatment not merely for the handicapped but for those who refuse to work or learn—the lazy, immoral, and degraded members of society. Individuals as well as organizations are encouraged to make profit, success, self-gratification, and fame their highest goals.

The mass media celebrate and extol the most degraded of celebrities, murderers, pornographers, and criminal gangs; there is a mystique of "the Mob," idealizing both real and imaginary criminal organizations. When sexual libertines contract a fatal sexually transmitted disease (which they have almost certainly transmitted to others in their quest for self-fulfillment), they are extolled as noble victims, almost as martyrs, and given appointments in government, business, and education to spread their deceptive message of disease prevention. When they can be found, truly noble individuals—military heroes, selfless physicians, clergy, and even a uniquely self-sacrificing individual such as Mother Teresa—are intensely scrutinized in the hope of finding some flaw that can be blown out of all proportion in order to discourage imitation and to excuse the larger group, whose highest ideal is the pursuit of personal pleasure and convenience.

The political, educational, sports, and artistic systems elevate people who exhibit little virtue in the traditional sense of the word but who, because of

---

[5] Sorokin, *Crisis*, 197.

specialized abilities, good fortune, or the favor of the media, are exalted into prominence and become celebrities, political leaders, and even chiefs of government. Then, having exalted such morally mediocre people and placed them in the spotlight of public attention, the same media uncover and broadcast every flaw, real and imagined, that they have shown or appeared to show in their rise from obscurity. Thus the general public is progressively disillusioned and led to the conclusion that high moral conduct and the sacrifice of self for the good of others are qualities that are unknown and unattainable among human beings, or, if they exist, are found only among naive people worthy at best of condescending approval. The rare prominent individuals who profess high moral standards and dedication to one of the great religious traditions of the West can expect to be scrutinized and ridiculed if they succeed in adhering to those standards. If some inconsistency and fault, however small, can be discovered in their lives, they will be held up for public condemnation and contempt.

CHAOTIC SYNCRETISM

The architectural, musical, and literary products of an integrated culture always exhibit a high degree of consistency. A fine example of such integration is the Hellenistic culture of the Graeco-Roman world between the third century B.C. and the third century A.D. From Antioch and Alexandria in the east to the many cities of Gaul and Britain in the northwest, temples, amphitheaters, public buildings, statuary, and even medicine and science exhibited a striking uniformity of style. The same great philosophers and poets were studied and read all over the Mediterranean world. Indeed, the rapidity with which early Christianity spread around the Mediterranean basin was due less to Roman imperial rule than to the prevalence of Greek, the language of culture and trade, and to a lesser extent of Latin, the language of administration.[6]

---

[6] Many Christian writers see the cultural and administrative unity that prevailed in this period as part of what is meant by Paul's words, "When the time had fully come, God sent his Son" (Gal. 4:4 NIV).

When an integrated culture begins to disintegrate, one of the most easily recognizable symptoms is the emergence of a chaotic syncretism in the arts: style, themes, and patterns become mixed, drawing upon traditions from every conceivable culture and epoch. Sorokin cites the over-ripe sensate cultures of Greece and Rome as classical examples of such disintegration. In a familiar lament, the Roman historian Tacitus refers to the capital of the empire as "the common sink into which everything infamous and abominable flows from all corners of the world." Tacitus's lament can be echoed not merely for the great political power centers of the West (such as London, Washington, and Paris) but for every major city in the West. Every single one, without exception, functions as a "common sink," collecting what Sorokin and Tacitus would call the refuse as well as the finer products of every culture and subculture throughout the world. Indeed, thanks to the prevalence of the mass media in the West, one can say that the entire Western world has been transformed into one common sink.

Returning to the example of ancient Rome, the government, personified in its autocratic emperors, adopted an ambivalent attitude toward the growing chaotic syncretism, sometimes embracing it, sometimes trying to suppress it. The soldier-emperor Alexander Severus (A.D. 232–35) had a private temple erected in which he set up images of Zeus, Moses, Jesus, and Zoroaster. His predecessor, the morally degenerate Heliogabalus (A.D. 218–22), was murdered in the course of his abortive attempt to impose an imitation of archaic Egyptian religion at Rome. The severe persecutions of Christians and to a lesser extent of other new religions initiated by the emperors at various times were partly motivated by their wish to restore a measure of spiritual unity to their disintegrating culture. Many historians assume that although only a small minority of the population was Christian at the time, the Emperor Constantine (A.D. 306–37) accepted and fostered Christianity because he believed that it could be an integrating force.

Elements from diverse cultures can be introduced into an integrated culture without necessarily causing disruption. During the eighteenth century, as European trade with China and the East began to flourish, Chinese *objets d'art* were proudly displayed in palaces and private homes; the Austrian Empress Maria Theresa had a Chinese salon built into her palace at Schönbrunn. In the case of the Roman Empire, integration was increasingly abandoned. The empire was at the height of its power under the four "good emperors"—Trajan, Hadrian, Antoninus Pius, and Marcus Aurelius (A.D. 98–180)—but even during their reign the overripe sensate Graeco-Roman culture, to use Sorokin's words, "turned indeed into a 'common sink' or a dumping place for the most divergent elements of the most different cultures."[7]

All these currents, Sorokin observes, were not integrated into any kind of unity. At first, and for decades if not centuries, their bewildering variety provided amusement for the languid leisure classes of the capital and some of the other great cities, while the common people were treated to "bread and circuses"— free bread and gladiatorial combats. These "games" represented another and more brutal kind of syncretism: Exotic beasts from all over the world and human slaves from diverse backgrounds were pitted against each other, armed with the weapons of different armies or left unarmed, as supply and demand and the whims of the organizers dictated.

Sorokin's explanation of this phenomenon is incisive:

The reason for such a syncretism as a sign of the disintegration is evident. Any great cultural supersystem is, as we have seen, a unity integrated into one consistent whole by meaningful and causal ties. Such an integrated unity were ideational and idealistic medieval cultures, permeated by Christianity; such a unity has also been our sensate supersystem in the centuries of its emergence and growth. It had its sensate values strong and not ground into dust. It enriched itself by the elements of many cultures, whether Graeco-Roman or Arabic, Byzantine or Egyptian, Oriental or Native American. But it ingested from all these cultures *only such elements as did not contradict its soul,* and these ingested elements it modified and digested. The irreconcilable and indigestible elements of other cultures it rejected. In this sense *it was, like any great culture, highly selective and discriminatory.* At the present moment [1941] it is in a very different situation. Its values have been, as we have seen, atomized and ground into dust. Further on, created by its own genius, the new means of communication and contact into the closest interaction with practically all the cultures of all mankind. Their elements in all their astounding variety began to flow into it increasingly. Indian tobacco-smoking, Turkish baths, coffee- and tea-drinking, polo-playing, pajama-wearing, drug addiction and Oriental religious philosophy, all took root in our culture. Elements of the cultures of the Australian

---

[7] Sorokin, *Crisis,* 201.

bushmen, of Melanesian and Eskimo tribes, as well as of all historical peoples of the present and the past—Egyptian and Hindu, Chinese and Mayan, Greek and Roman, Turkish and Persian, infiltrated the sensate culture of the West and did so in ever-increasing currents.[8]

Shortly after World War II, Erich Fromm published *Escape from Freedom*, in which he explained that the end of several of the great tyrants would not mean the recovery of freedom, for society was coming under the domination of the "anonymous authorities" whose autocratic and tyrannical rule would be harder to resist than that of the tyrants because it would be largely invisible and un-recognized.[9] In today's North America, such anonymous authorities rule in the name of what is called political correctness. Some of the most cherished dictates of modern political correctness are described by the terms *pluralism, multiculturalism,* and *diversity.*

These terms may be used in a neutral sense to describe conditions in a society. Western society has become *diverse* both because of an influx of immigrants from other cultures and because of an increasing presence of "subculture," "alternative cultures," and "dropouts" in its midst. To the extent that these elements come from established cultures and preserve their inherited cultural traditions in the West, it is proper to describe them as *multicultural.* Descriptively, *pluralism* refers to a situation in which a society contains a variety of cultures, with no one culture setting the standards for the society as a whole.

These three terms can also be used in a prescriptive sense—not merely as a description of the conditions in a given society but as a pattern to be imposed on a society by persuasion, pressure, and for some, even by force. Such is the dictate of the movement known as political correctness: that pluralism, multiculturalism, and diversity be praised, encouraged, and if necessary imposed on Western culture. It should be evident to all but the most naive observer that this prescription, when made mandatory, will ultimately be a prescription for disaster.

When a biological organism is healthy, it can endure shocks of many kinds, safely digest different kinds of foods, and otherwise effectively master the diverse elements it encounters. A culture is like an organism in this respect: When

---

[8] Ibid., 201–2; emphasis added.

[9] Fromm, *Escape from Freedom*, 167.

it is in the period of its virility[10] and strength, it can assimilate, learn from, and digest many foreign elements. However, even the strongest organism will eventually succumb to too great an onslaught of intrusive influences, and as it grows older and frailer, it becomes more vulnerable. Likewise, there is a limit to what any sociocultural supersystem can accommodate even when it is in a flourishing condition, and as the culture enters what Sorokin likes to call its overripe phase, its ability to assimilate and profit from diverse influences declines. "An increasingly richer stream of heterogeneous elements brought into such a culture will remain less and less digested. More and more they will distort the style, the soul and the body of the host culture and finally will help its disintegration. That result is exactly what we now observe in contemporary Western culture."[11]

Even before World War II, the richness and variety available in Western culture was astounding. Multiple facets of various cultures could be found in it somewhere, and the variety was compounded within the great world cities such as New York and London. Yet prior to World War II the individual nations of the West still exhibited a considerable amount of cultural integrity in the smaller cities and the countryside. Crossing national frontiers in Europe—which prior to World War I was done without a passport—one could readily note the changes from one local culture to another. Half a century later, even the country towns and villages offer the spectacle of chaotic syncretism.

From music to art to dress, every style from the most sedate to the most exotic, from the most primitive to the most sophisticated is available everywhere, or at least is on film and television. The words that Sorokin wrote in 1941 were not entirely true when he published them, but they apply to contemporary Western society with an almost uncanny accuracy:

> All the mores, manners, moral rules, taboos, customs, codes, ethical systems, codes of law, of all the peoples and tribes are here, living side by side. All the religious systems, indeed, all manner of magical beliefs, are present in it. Our

---

[10] The term *virility*, from Latin vir, meaning man (male), has become a politically incorrect term to use in a positive sense, as has the related word *virtue* from the same Latin root.

[11] Sorokin, *Crisis*, 202. Sorokin's analysis at this point is so incisive and contemporary it is tempting to reprint it word for word. The interested reader should consult *Crisis*, chapter 7, pp. 196–220.

network of communication puts us in contact with them all; and all of them find somehow their devotee and apostles among us. . . . And so also with our social institutions; from the family to political regimes of all kinds, modeled along the most different patterns, they are functioning among us.[12]

The chaotic syncretism that was already evident in the first half of the twentieth century was novel enough to be recognizable, and indeed it was recognized by many others besides Sorokin. Because the culture was still somewhat integrated and apparently stable, the constant additions from other cultures were regarded by most people with more fascination than apprehension. Half a century later the syncretism and associated chaos have become so generalized that people now do not notice it, thinking it a natural condition of human culture.

For more than two centuries Germany was one of the most creative and productive cultures of the world. In Adolf Hitler's societal madness, a determined attempt was made to purge German culture of all extraneous, "foreign," "non-Nordic," "Jewish" and otherwise "decadent" elements, resulting in the tremendous intellectual, artistic, and spiritual impoverishment of the Third Reich. The Christian churches were affected to some degree, for there were efforts made to purge even them of anything Jewish, international, or weak. The churches resisted rather listlessly, but Hitler's reign proved short. After the Nazi debacle ended, there was a longing in Germany for permanent values, and the churches enjoyed renewed popularity; there was a mild religious resurgence, if not an actual revival.

It was a surprisingly short time, however, before the churches, especially the Protestant groups united as the Evangelical Church in Germany (EKD, *Evangelische Kirche in Deutschland*), themselves succumbed to chaotic syncretism. For a number of years the *Deutscher Kirchentag* (the biennial mass rally of German Protestants) has virtually excluded the traditional representatives of German faith and life. Instead it offers a gigantic "Market of Possibilities" (*Markt der Möglichkeiten*) in which all possible mores and manners are presented— except, of course, the traditional Christian mores and manners of Western culture in which Germany once played so creative a role.

---

[12] Ibid., 202–3.

During Hitler's regime one might say the rule prevailed, "Only what the Führer likes goes!" Since then a new cultural regime has been established in which, "Anything goes!" Other European countries (even the occupied ones) and of course the United States have never undergone anything like the systematic attempt to create a unified culture that characterized Hitler's rule in Germany, but like the postwar Germans, all are now experiencing the "Market of Possibilities" where "Anything goes!"

Nowhere in the world is there more syncretism and greater chaos than in the United States. Because the United States sets the trends, whatever happens there is almost immediately purchased, copied, plagiarized, or otherwise taken over throughout the world. American music, motion pictures, language, dress styles, magazines, and television programs spread each new expression of America's chaotic syncretism everywhere, virtually within hours of the time it appears in the United States. Countries with a proud cultural tradition of their own seem impotent to stem the flood of American cultural expansionism. For decades the Communist countries made a great effort to keep out all bourgeois influences and failed. Consequently, the chaotic syncretism that one sees in the United States may be somewhat more advanced than that in other countries, but most of the world will not be far behind.

Not long ago it was only in the great cities of the Western world—such as London, New York, or Paris—that one could find restaurants offering the different cuisines of the world. Now an amazing variety can be found even in small cities, and cooks everywhere are no longer bound to cooking the way grandmother did but produce everything from Polish kielbasa to South African ostrich meat in culinary styles from boiled English to Chinese stir-fry. In major cities, large and small theaters offer everything from classical Greek tragedies and the great European and American dramatists to Japanese kabuki, Chinese opera, and experimental theater performances. All across the country, network and cable television offers virtually every kind of entertainment that human ingenuity can imagine.

The religious scene is even more bewildering: Traditional forms of mainline Christianity, traditional Roman Catholicism (with Mass in Latin as well as in English), strait-laced Presbyterian worship dating from the time of the Puritans, evangelistic camp meetings, and charismatic meetings both restrained and wild vie with innumerable variations of the social Gospel, feminist spirituality, native American religion, and earth and goddess worship. Christian denominations constitute only a small fraction of the diverse religious and mystical offerings available. The other great religions—Judaism, Islam, Buddhism, and Hinduism—are all available, both in traditional versions and in exotic variations, with new ones originating in the United States on a daily basis. In addition to the competing Christian and Jewish sects and cults,[13] long-dead religions and cults are resurrected and given new life, elements of major religions are mixed and blended with one another, and totally new religions are created out of impulses old and new.

The visual arts, great museums, glossy magazines, university courses, and adult enrichment programs present everything from the primitive cave paintings of the Neolithic era through the classic art of antiquity and the Renaissance. Medieval and Byzantine religious art and iconography, the Dutch masters, French impressionists, expressionists, cubism, surrealism, and the pop art of soup cans and enlarged Sunday comic panels are presented for admiration. Every variety of music is offered, from the oldest music that can be found to African, Asian, American folk, jazz, rock, and alternative.

The bestseller lists include everything from self-help books to novels, from rewritten and frequently distorted classics through every variety of escape literature—science fiction, detective and spy thrillers, romance, satire, and pornography of every description. The great universities and colleges that once extolled the classic writings of Greece, Rome, England, France, Russia, Germany, and Spain now sometimes parallel, sometimes replace them with the works of unknown and often unintelligible writers and alternative literature. The religious book market is far from being a bulwark of stability for it offers both traditional and esoteric books of every kind, from Bibles in accurate, fanciful, and biased translations to the sacred texts of religions new and

---

[13] The terms *sect* and *cult* are often used in a pejorative sense, but here they are meant in the more technical sense: A *sect* is a branch of a particular religion that distinguishes itself by distinctive beliefs or practices but still can be reckoned to that religion; a *cult*, by contrast, may have its origin in a well-known religion but has developed such different doctrines and practices that it no longer can be identified with the group from which it originated.

old. Religious books provide techniques for finding God, discovering one's own divinity, knowing the future, healing diseases, and reaping vast material blessings.

With equal enthusiasm our culture accepts Gregorian chants and MTV; the Bible and Satanism; Thomistic philosophy and postmodernism; Freud and Augustine; classic ballet and break dancing. All of this occurs at the same time, often side by side, with no coherence or unity. Symbolic of this is the disappearance of the grand old motion picture theaters from major cities and their replacement by theater clusters, groups of six or eight projection halls in the same building offering everything from a children's movie to violent action films and coarse pornography.

What this means is that our sensate culture has broken down and lost its self-confidence. The great universities that once were the custodians and transmitters of Western culture are now more often ashamed than proud. "Western Civ," once a required course in the great accomplishments of Western civilization, has been replaced, in the name of diversity, by a hybrid collection of trivial or trumped-up accomplishments by primitive peoples and backward societies. The accomplishments of the past are dismissed as the work of DWM's—dead white males.

In this stage, the culture loses its shape and its distinctiveness and becomes formless. Creative imagination, which needs a framework of recognized standards and values at least at the outset, becomes sterile and true creativity ceases. Television scriptwriters are awarded huge salaries for producing pathetic children's programs, but among thousands of hours of television programming, one will seldom find one hour worthy of the Brothers Grimm or Hans Christian Andersen. Quantity suppresses quality, but it cannot replace it. Sorokin wrote that when a culture reaches this stage, "from the creative actor of history, it passes into a museum of historical survivals."[14]

---

[14] Sorokin, *Crisis*, 204–5.

QUANTITATIVE COLOSSALISM

If one symptom of the disintegration of a culture is the replacement of quality by quantity, another symptom is the burgeoning of colossalism in every area of life. In Greece during the sixth through the fourth centuries B.C., beauty and excellence were expressed on a modest scale. Aristotle coined the maxim, "Moderation is the best." The great intellectual and artistic accomplishments of Athens were on a small scale.

As the idealistic phase passed into the sensate phase, both Hellenistic and Roman civilization plunged into the love of quantity, of the *colossal*. It is from the 105-foot statue erected at Rhodes, the "Colossus," that we derive this term. The two-thousand-year-old ruins of the Colosseum in Rome, built without modern materials or machines, still impress visitors. The Pergamene Frieze—which once again can be seen in what was formerly East Berlin—is immense. The Mausoleum at Halicarnassus was 140 feet tall (about fifteen modern stories), and Hadrian's Tomb was large enough to be converted into a medieval castle.

Late Hellenistic and Roman cities built broad avenues and laid out lavish gardens. Huge fortunes were amassed, dwarfing those of the wealthiest individuals of the republican era. Only the Roman army was small, for the relative peace in the Mediterranean world made the immense forces of earlier years superfluous; the money it would have cost to maintain them was spent on other things. All the normal activities of society proliferated in number, size, and expense. Dramas and musical productions became huge, with vast arrays of new musical instruments. Descriptions by the great social historians Michael Rostovtzeff, Jérôme Carcopino, and others sound amazingly like accounts of modern society, all of it achieved without technology.[15] Mass education was instituted in the arts, sciences, and philosophy. Everything became available en masse: the arts, philosophies, theater, music, and "games" both bloody and athletic.

---

[15] Michael Rostovtzeff was a friend of Sorokin's and godfather to one of his sons. His *Social and Economic History of the Roman Empire*, 2d ed. rev. (Oxford: Clarendon Press, 1957) remains a classic. Jérôme Carcopino is the author of *Daily Life in Ancient Rome: The People and the City at the Height of the Empire*, trans. E. O. Lorimer (New Haven, Conn.: Yale University Press, 1940).

Developments in the modern world during the twentieth century, and particularly since World War II, have made possible the mass production of incredible quantities of consumer goods—books, magazines, records, audio cassettes, clothing, sports equipment, etc. Mass means of communication have the possibility of putting almost everyone in touch with almost everything almost at once.

These changes have been so rapid and so sweeping that many people take it for granted that our new world is totally different from everything that existed before. It is not even modern; it is postmodern.

This makes the comparison with Rome in the early Christian era all the more striking. Despite the fact that books had to be copied by hand, information spread by handwritten letters, plans for colossal works of architecture drafted with simple instruments and carried out without power tools, the tendency of sensate society in its overripe phase to turn to syncretism and colossalism was so strong that late Roman society really prefigures ours.

One might suppose that the more works of a particular genre that are produced, the greater the chance of producing something excellent. The contrary is true. Quantity does not substitute for quality, nor does it create quality. "The quantitative colossalism was but a substitute for the inability to create the great qualitative values. . . . The larger the empires grew, the more disorganized they turned out to be and the harder the lot of the citizens became. . . . The larger the crowd of philosophers, the fewer great philosophers emerged."[16]

Every American city now has a skyline of skyscrapers that rivals the Manhattan of sixty years ago. But compare the elegant lines of some of the prewar buildings like the Chrysler Building and the Empire State Building with the scores of new skyscrapers like the Sears Tower in Chicago and the World Trade Center in New York. A century ago, a few wealthy citizens could hire architects to build distinctive residences for their families and servants. Now the suburbs of every city are surrounded by "tract mansions"—huge dwellings that look more like fraternity houses than single family residences.

---

[16] Sorokin, *Crisis*, 205.

Quantity and colossalism do even less for the quality of intellectual and artistic productions. The fame of the three great Greek philosophers from the idealistic phase of Greek culture—Socrates, Plato, and Aristotle—has endured for centuries. Who can name their many imitators in the Hellenistic cities of the Roman Empire? Closer to our own time, in the late eighteenth and early nineteenth centuries before colossalism had taken hold, again the names of a few philosophers stand out, all from small German university towns: Kant, Hegel, and Fichte. Taken together, the German universities of today number their students not in thousands but in hundreds of thousands, and their faculty members not in dozens but in thousands. Will any of their philosophers' names still resound a century from now? There are dozens of playwrights producing dramas of all kinds in English. Does any one of them come close to Shakespeare?

The early centuries of Christianity produced great theologians—Origen, Augustine, Chrysostom, to name but three. The Middle Ages produced Anselm, Aquinas, and Abelard; the Reformation produced its Luther, Calvin, and Knox. Today fresh systematic theologies appear every year. But will anything from the twentieth century be remembered like the *Summa Theologica* of Aquinas or the *Institutes* of Calvin? True, there were many preachers and theologians in earlier centuries whose names have been forgotten but in nothing like today's numbers. Yet from their smaller population came those who produced works that outlast the centuries.

Colossalism has affected virtually every aspect of life in the West, and nowhere more so than in American Education. In the 1940s the college and university population of the United States had not reached two million; now it is six times that. Today more than half of American high school graduates go on to college for "higher education," although—alas—it seems that most of what the high schools teach hardly ought to be called education.

> Shall we wonder that the results of all this quantity without quality [in our culture today] are similar to those of the Hellenic and Roman cultures at the period of their quantitative colossalism, namely, a progressive decline of the constructive creativeness of our sensate culture and a rise of its destructive forces together with the cultural domination of mass mediocrity?[17]

---

[17] Sorokin, *Crisis*, 208.

MEDIOCRITY MASS PRODUCED:
THE DECLINE OF CREATIVITY

The popular fashion of praising pluralism, multiculturalism, and diversity reveals that the culture is disintegrating. When the soul of a culture is split and divided, it ceases to be loyal to itself. American culture may be the first culture in the history of the world to be committed to its own destruction. That is the significance of the event that took place—or rather failed to take place—in 1992, the 500th anniversary of Christopher Columbus' discovery of the "New World." The 400th anniversary in 1892 was celebrated with great enthusiasm all over the United States. By 1992, the forces of pluralism and multiculturalism had so embarrassed and humiliated the majority culture of America that the half-millennium anniversary was allowed to pass virtually unnoticed.[18]

In 1941 Sorokin spoke of the "feverish tempo of . . . accelerated change that excludes a creation of lasting values: yesterday's values are obsolete today; and today values will be obsolete tomorrow."[19] How can anything lasting be created in this maelstrom of constant change? The whole culture is in constant turmoil. After the reunification of Berlin, the population observes, "Berlin is one gigantic construction site." This is true because in the years 1943–45 the great city was all but leveled in hundreds of air raids, followed by direct artillery shelling during the Soviet conquest. In the United States, no such mass area bombing is needed, for we tear down our cities day by day, and rebuild them almost as rapidly. We erect great buildings of steel and reinforced concrete then tear them down to build others.

Religions and philosophies come and go almost as rapidly as office buildings and factories. Today a new cathedral is built, and tomorrow it will be demolished to create a parking garage for a sports center. Like the mythical Chronos, our culture constantly devours its own children. Even those creations

---

[18] Proportionally far less significant anniversaries, such as the fiftieth anniversary of D-Day, the Allied invasion of Normandy, and even the twenty-fifth anniversary of the Woodstock music festival received much more attention.

[19] Sorokin, *Crisis*, 208. The material in these pages is heavily indebted to Sorokin, even when no direct references are given.

and accomplishments that merit admiration (for example in religion or ethics) are devalued by the fact that they arise in the midst of a whirlwind in which everything is flying about and nothing is firmly fixed.

Our sensate culture has been productive in many fields, particularly in the sciences, technology, and medicine. In its early phases it was also highly creative in literature, music, and the arts. After the great outpouring of spiritual creativity in the Reformation of the sixteenth century, however, the sensate era became progressively less productive in the area of religion and ethics. There are ever more theologians producing ever more theologies, but with few or no exceptions, they are like dwarves standing on the shoulders of giants.[20] The Christian figures who attract attention today are the mass evangelists and television preachers. Even if a few writers were producing works worthy of the pen of an Aquinas or a Luther, their work could hardly be noticed amid the clamor of the mass popularizers of prosperity and success through mass media religion. Every success quickly breeds a host of imitators, and if in fact there is a truly creative individual in the crowd, his or her achievements will often be overlooked in the mass of mediocrity. Religion's claim to tell the meaning of human life and of human destiny is made ludicrous by pathetic mediocrities enabled by mass media.

At the same time all sorts of pseudoreligious and pseudoscientific alternatives are offered, one of the more common being the repeated attempts of a certain school of anthropologists and psychologists to reduce the "Human Animal" to the status of a "Naked Ape."[21] The highly touted sociology of the twentieth century studies primitive cultures and presents them—usually dishonestly—as happy societies of noble savages, whose mores and habits are supposedly superior to our own customs and ethics.[22] The promise and warning so common to the great

---

[20] Our century has produced one Protestant theologian whose format is large enough to permit comparison to Acquinas and Calvin, namely, Karl Barth (1886–1968).

[21] *The Human Animal* was the name of a popular series on cable television, while *The Naked Ape* (New York: Dell, 1967) was the first and most successful book of Desmond Morris, who together with many others has opposed the idea that human beings are uniquely valuable.

[22] Significant books here are Ruth Benedict, *Patterns of Culture* (Boston and New York: Houghton Mifflin, 1934); and Margaret Mead, *Coming of Age in Samoa* (New York: Blue Ribbon Books, 1928). Curiously, or perhaps not so curiously, these two, who did so much to drive all appreciation for traditional Christian values out of education, were for a time lesbian lovers. Cf. E. Michael Jones, *Degenerate Moderns*, 19–49.

monotheistic religions, that "It is appointed for men to die once and after this comes the judgment" (Heb. 9:27), places a premium on decisions and acts made during life on earth. This focus is being replaced by an increasing interest in the doctrine of reincarnation, a concept that contributed greatly to the stagnation of Indian culture over the centuries. Contrary to the gibe of Karl Marx that religion is the opiate of the people, the Christian religion has been an incredible stimulus of human endeavor. It is not at all unlikely, however, that the new religions and cults called "New Age" will in fact be opiates.

Medicine and the Sciences

The late sensate culture does still seem to be highly productive and creative in the fields of medicine and science. Yet even in these there are surprising checks and reversals. During the late 1950s and early 1960s rocket technology advanced with rapidity, and in 1969 the first human landed on the moon. It seemed as though the long-awaited "conquest of space" had begun. Since that time, however, problems of all sorts have developed, but perhaps the most significant factor is that the deteriorating sensate culture has become too self-centered to make the gigantic effort necessary to push such exploration. If there is no immediate profit to be gained—and apart from potential military exploitation, there seems to be none—what is the use of it?

Medical science continues to make great strides, but it has also encountered unexpected checks. The cost of each new medical procedure is much greater than the procedure it replaces: The CAT scan costs more than an ordinary X-ray examination, and MRI (magnetic resonance imaging) even more. Each represents an improvement, but each has become progressively more difficult for society to afford. Although the maximum length of human life has hardly increased, a greater number of people are living to an advanced age and, in the process, incurring ever greater medical costs. As a result, part of the medical, legal, and political establishments are calling for euthanasia, "a method in which killing represents a solution."[23]

---

[23] This comment was made by noted Austrian sociologist Hans Millendorfer in a lecture he delivered in Vienna, Austria, on Easter Monday 1987.

Although every year researchers in the field of medicine discover new drugs, machines, and techniques, public attention is diverted from these genuine achievements to pathetic artifices. The achievements of which medicine is coming to boast are becoming either banal or destructive: the promotion of the use of condoms to decrease the spread of sexually transmitted diseases among the promiscuous, the widespread resort to abortion as a means of dealing with "unwanted pregnancy," and an increasing fascination with the use of medical means to end human life, whether through execution by lethal injection or physician-assisted suicide. Of course, if we see in the "human animal" nothing more than a "naked ape," it is easy to understand the reluctance of researchers, laboratories, and physicians to wear themselves out seeking ways to prolong its meaningless existence.

Human creativity in all fields depends on the assumption that human life has meaning and that effort is rewarded. Individual artists, scholars, and scientists may still produce occasional bursts of creativity, but as the culture exhausts itself and disintegrates, truly creative works will become rare and will disappear.

8

THE CRISIS IN
DEMOCRATIC THEORY

"L' état, c' est moi." (I am the state.)

Louis XIV

NEITHER PROFESSOR SOROKIN'S SEMINAL WORK nor the present study is a work on politics or political philosophy. Nevertheless, it is essential to deal with politics, because politics has become a central preoccupation of our late sensate culture and a central factor involved in its crisis. Aristotle called man the *"zoon politikon"* (the political animal), referring to the fact that humans always create a society in which to live. In the early days of our history on this planet, politics as we now know it with all its complexities and inherent contradictions did not yet exist. Much of the social order was traditional and customary. Rule was exercised by the monarch and administered by the "ministers," his servants. The crown generally was inherited but sometimes was captured in war or stolen in a coup d'état or palace revolution. The system was simple; there was no campaigning or electioneering.

The term *politics* is derived from the Greek word *polis* (city). Politics came into being on a very small scale with the little city-states of Greece. The tendency towards colossalism (discussed in the preceding chapter as a characteristic of

159

our sensate sociocultural supersystem) is naturally reflected in our politics as well. It is not that modern governments control larger portions of the earth's surface than ancient monarchies—the Roman and Arab empires were larger than most modern states—but that they are far more intrusive and pervasive, reaching into every area of social and personal life.

Consequently politics, like so many other things today, suffers from colossalism. In the nominally or genuinely democratic systems that have been set up throughout Western culture, every adult is potentially involved in the political process by virtue of the right to vote, and absolutely everyone—adult or child, voter or not—is affected by it. Politics has become invasive and all-embracing. This creates what Jacques Ellul called the "political illusion," the idea that every question is a political question and that, therefore, all the answers must come from politics.[1]

In a period of political colossalism, a change in one strategic place or in one key element can have ramifications throughout the entire culture. In the late sensate period that preceded the rise of Christianity, the conversion of one man, the Emperor Constantine, suddenly wiped out obstacles to the sociocultural shift that had begun. In our own sensate period, the destructive triumph of one man, Adolf Hitler, in quite a different way broke down barriers to our sociocultural shift.

Constantine came on the scene as the old sensate order was crumbling, and he removed the barriers to the ideational culture of early Christianity. Hitler also came to power in a period of the "Decline of the West." He admired Spengler (who did not admire him) and dreamt that he could reverse the decline and found a thousand-year Reich. He wanted to overcome what he recognized as a degenerate sensate culture and replace it with a demented kind of idealism, the "Myth of the Twentieth Century." His thousand-year Reich would probably have succumbed to its own internal contradictions even if he had not aroused almost the entire world against him.

Historians in future decades will see Hitler's influence at the end of our sensate era as being as decisive as that of Constantine in his. Constantine facilitated one great sociocultural shift by removing the barriers to the rise of a

---

[1] Jacques Ellul, *The Political Illusion*, trans. Konrad Kellen (New York: Random House, 1972).

new culture; Hitler unwittingly may have facilitated the shift we are now experiencing by smashing the remaining strength of the older system. His accomplishment, if we can call it that, was to create a situation in which the structural defenses of Western civilization were broken beyond repair, in spite of the illusory triumph of the old order represented by the Western Allies.

Hitler would not have had the success that he had if Western culture had not already been in transition, at a watershed where a slight nudge could be sufficient to cause it first to tilt to one side, then to topple. Constantine's nudge accelerated the transition to the Christian culture of the early Middle Ages; Hitler's shove intensified the disorder of the transition period.

THE IMPORTANCE OF POLITICS IN THE LATE SENSATE PHASE

The overwhelming acclaim that Hitler enjoyed during his first years of triumph is evidence of the importance of colossalism in our own transition period. Men and movements such as Hitler and Nazism can succeed only when the foundations of order have eroded. While final success was denied to Hitler and his Nazis, they did much to make the West, and indeed the whole world, ready for a "new order." Like his predecessors Mussolini and Lenin, his contemporary Stalin, and his successor Mao, Hitler created a totalitarian system in which all of the smaller institutions that carry a culture are either *gleichgeschaltet* (brought into line) or eliminated. The individual is separated from vital connections to family, community, church, school, labor union, social club, or any other structure that supports individuality and offers a defense against being submerged into an "atomistic mass."[2] Unfortunately, even without becoming totalitarian in the sense of Nazi or Marxist one-party rule, popular democracy can also fall prey to colossalism. Instead of being a system in which each individual has a voice in determining state policy, it becomes a method

---

[2] This expression, coined by Hannah Arendt, refers to a situation in which individuals become like atoms, distinct from one another and with no ties except to the gigantic mass, in which anonymity prevails. Hannah Arendt, *The Origins of Totalitarianism* (New York: Harcourt Brace, 1968).

for standardizing and homogenizing the populace while maintaining an illusion of liberty and personal independence.

Hitler and his Nazis claimed that their National Socialist Party made politics into a science for the first time in history.[3] This "new science of politics" eroded the remaining foundations of the traditional social order either directly or, in the case of the nations that fought against him, by forcing them to centralize and standardize, to create a "democratic" colossus capable of resisting the Nazi colossus. The political illusion seduces supposedly free people with promises that the right political choices will guarantee prosperity and happiness, exacting only a supposedly small price in the loss of freedom and individual dignity.

Our entire sociocultural supersystem has reached a point of great instability. A transformation is inevitable. It is up to the present generation to decide whether the coming transformation will resound our calling to reflect the "image of God" or will instead relapse into finding meaning and purpose in the accumulation of sensate goods and fleeting satisfactions. The choice is between a fresh appropriation of our dignity and responsibility as creatures made in the divine image or a new and even more catastrophic attempt to show that man has "come of age" and can and should live *etsi Deus non daretur* (as though there were no God).[4] The first would lead us into a renewed ideational or idealistic culture; the second would merely prolong an already moribund sensate phase and make a total cultural collapse inevitable.

THE CRISIS OF LEGITIMACY

The crisis in democratic theory expresses itself in a futile quest for legitimacy in government. Governments in past centuries—primarily monarchical—claimed

---

[3] The official name of the party was *Nationalsozialistische Deutsche Arbeiterpartei*, NSDAP for short, "National Socialist German Workers' Party."

[4] By this phrase, Dietrich Bonhoeffer (1906–45) meant that we humans must assume full responsibility for our world and not expect God or an angel to rescue us from our self-created predicaments. Unfortunately, in practice it often comes to mean that if there is no God to whom we are responsible, we can behave any way we please.

allegiance on the basis of dynastic legitimacy or, as in the Holy Roman Empire, on the basis of election by legitimate electors. If the king or emperor was the lawful heir or properly elected by the proper electors, his rule represented the will of God. The old maxim *salus populi suprema lex* (the welfare of the people is the supreme law) supposedly set the standard by which monarchs ruled and prevented them from becoming tyrannical.

As the ideals and convictions of the idealistic era faded, monarchy came into disrepute. Democracy was put forward as a far better alternative; indeed, in the United States it came to be taken for granted that democracy is the form of government ordained by God. During the revolutionary upheavals that began in England's North American colonies and France, the old principle of legitimacy was replaced by the concept of a sovereign people: *vox populi, vox Dei* (the voice of the people is the voice of God). The difficulty is that while one man (a monarch) or a few can rule, the people as a whole cannot rule or can do so only in small communities where the voice of each citizen can be heard.

Democratic theory insists that the people, if permitted to choose their leaders, will choose wisely and thus obtain better and more gifted rulers than those installed on the older principles of dynastic legitimacy or election by a few noble electors. Unfortunately, in an age of chaotic syncretism and colossalism this simply is not true or is true only in exceptional cases. Realization of this fact is one of the reasons for general and growing dissatisfaction among people in democratically-ruled nations with the consequences of their own democratic choices.

Today the candidate for the highest position in the state may be elected if he or she enjoys popularity and celebrity even for a moment, provided it is the crucial moment. Theoretically, an informed electorate will choose the best men and women to be leaders; in practice, they choose the most celebrated, including sports heroes, actors, and even confidence men and striptease artists. A crisis in legitimacy cannot be resolved by shifting the basis from heredity to the electoral process. When popularity replaces both dynamic legitimacy and personal merit as the criteria for the choice of a head of government, the result is a loss of legitimacy for government itself. Once the influences of undisguised personal and class interest prevail and quantitative colossalism becomes the rule, the democratic process is undermined and with it the legitimacy and integrity of every supposedly "democratic" government. In the era of legitimacy, popular trust in government rested on the theory that the ruler was God's choice. When the people themselves choose, and come to realize that they often choose badly, trust necessarily begins to wane.

At the beginning of the twentieth century, most of the world was ruled by emperors and kings, as indeed it always had been since the beginning of recorded history. Monarchy still seemed the natural form of government for most human societies, but the growing crisis of late sensate culture was soon to shatter it. In the year 1900 there were several smaller monarchies, and the British, Russian, Chinese, Japanese, Turkish, Ethiopian, Spanish, Dutch, Belgian, German, and Austro-Hungarian empires controlled most of the world.

The theory of popular rule is badly out of step with the reality of the way governments now work. Instead of being a principle that helps a culture remain integrated, government is becoming another disruptive force. Earlier, single tyrants could be identified and distrusted, disliked, and even hated. Modern governments, despite efforts to personalize democratic regimes by focusing on the president or prime minister, have become immense, complex, and essentially anonymous even in small countries. People have become mistrustful and hostile, but they lack a visible tyrant to dislike; they are increasingly characterized by an unfocused distrust of unknown, anonymous authorities.

Monarchy had great powers of endurance and survived a number of sociocultural shifts, but changes were coming everywhere. It was taken for granted that the change from monarchy to democracy, or from colonial status to independence, was fundamental and all-transforming. Unfortunately, it is now evident that such changes are frequently only what Sorokin called "facile but shallow artifices." It has always been a mistake to assume that democracy is God-ordained or even the best and most equitable system that humans can work out. The increasing sense of frustration and disillusionment with the results of democracy is leading to a frustration with democracy itself. Yet hardly anyone thinks of monarchy as an alternative, nor would they willingly submit once again to dictatorship. This impasse of government—the growing sense of the failure of what was thought the ideal form of self-government—is not a symptom of the failure of government but of the exhaustion of the sociocultural system. It is one more reason to recognize that a fundamental transformation, much more than the change from monarchy to democracy, is underway.

Such a transformation, if it is to bring about renewal, must be more than a "popular revolution," however "democratic." Popular revolutions may depose tyrants, but they generally cause chaos because they not only overturn the chief of state but also disrupt many of the normal habits of social intercourse and economic interaction. The French Revolution soon became so chaotic that to most people making Napoleon emperor seemed a return to sanity. After the Russians overthrew the autocratic government of the czar, the country soon succumbed to the one-man rule first of Lenin, then of Stalin and his successors, from which it has only recently emerged.

THE WEAKNESS OF DEMOCRACY
IN A SENSATE CULTURE

Although it might seem that democracy, because it seeks to give the majority of the people what they want, might be suited to a sensate culture, in which the satisfaction of personal wants is the *summum bonum,* in fact there is an inherent tension between democracy and sensate culture. The great democracies of the ancient world (e.g., Athens and the Roman republic) arose during an idealistic culture and did not survive the shift to sensate culture. Democracy requires self-discipline and self-control on the part of the masses—qualities that are derided and destroyed by sensate culture. Although democratic theory teaches that the consent and participation of the people in government gives legitimacy to a democratic regime, in fact it does not appear to do so. This is true in part because the theory is not being applied and in part because even if it were applied it would be unworkable under the conditions of late sensate culture.

Our present sensate culture increasingly lacks one of the most important conditions for a vibrant democratic government, namely, moral responsibility and integrity on the part of a majority of the citizens. Democratic institutions necessarily presuppose that people will govern themselves in many areas of life, but this is precisely what is discouraged and impeded by the sensate attitude, "Eat, drink, and be merry." The idea that there are certain eternal or divine principles of justice that most people will respect without compulsion (which is characteristic of both ideational and idealistic cultures) disappears in a sensate culture where people are interested only in things that give pleasure, avert pain, and provide immediate gratification. When people do not have ideals and principles that move them to act without compulsion for the good of all, no government functions smoothly or well—a democratic government perhaps less well than others.

In the sensate phase of society, it is extremely difficult to maintain faith in the moral legitimacy of government, whether monarchical or democratic. Inasmuch as most of the governments of the world today (including the supranational United Nations Organization) are committed, at least formally, to democracy as the only acceptable form of government for people on earth, the crisis in government expresses itself today as a crisis in democratic theory. The failure of democracy will soon be seen as the failure of humanity altogether.

Citizens would like to think that democracy can function justly and efficiently and that it is the most effective agency to promote the general welfare, but it seldom works that way. Democracy presupposes a consensus of values, widespread agreement concerning what constitutes the morally good and desirable life. These are features of an integrated culture, but they become lost as a culture disintegrates in a transition phase. Consequently, one can predict with certainty that the democracy that we in the West profess to value is doomed to die if the sensate phase continues without any fundamental reorientation. When any form of government functions well, without the need to resort to extensive compulsion, it is a sign that the citizens it governs have an adequate degree of personal responsibility and integrity. In an overripe sensate culture, governing a large multitude of people becomes progressively more difficult no matter what the political system, whether monarchy or democracy, oligarchy or dictatorship, because people interested only in that which gratifies their own senses find it next to impossible to act spontaneously and without compulsion for the benefit of the community.

The Founding Fathers of the American republic were perfectly aware of this fundamental fact. When the thirteen British colonies revolted against the King of England and established a republic, its founders repeatedly spoke of relying upon religion and faith in God and invoked divine favor to protect the new nation. Although Western culture as a whole was already well into its sensate phase, the sensate ideology of "Eat, drink, and be merry" was not yet dominant in the backward American colonies living on the edge of an uncharted continent. A large segment of the American population embraced the Christian religion, and many of its prominent members, if they were not Christians, at least adhered to an idealistic philosophy and cherished virtues comparable to those of Christianity.

This idealistic bent, or elements of it, has survived for a surprisingly long time in an increasingly sensate culture, but its death-knell was heard in the United States in the 1960s. President Kennedy thought he could still call upon it, and he did succeed in stirring up the fires of idealism one last time. In his inaugural address in 1961, President Kennedy made an appeal to the remnants of the idealistic mentality among the American people: "Ask not what your country can do for you; ask what you can do for your country."

Unfortunately for Kennedy's hopes, the remnant was not hardy enough to accomplish what he expected of it, for the culture was already too sensate, and the influence of the mass media and mass communication was rapidly exterminating virtually every memory of earlier idealistic attitudes. These trends were exacerbated by Kennedy's assassination in 1963 and by the murders of his brother Robert and of the civil rights hero Martin Luther King Jr. in 1968. Even if the president himself had not been assassinated, it is doubtful that the idealism he sought to utilize would have proved adequate to the challenges he envisaged. These atrocities, combined with the bloody and futile war in Vietnam, did much to destroy the remnants of the older idealistic mentality among the American people—indeed, across much of Western culture as a whole.

Thus, events of recent history—historical accidents so to speak—have all contributed to the increasingly acute crisis of democratic theory in Western society, although its fundamental causes lie in the nature of the sensate culture itself, not in historic incidents, however dramatic.

As a sensate phase progresses and becomes both more pervasive and increasingly degenerate, both autocratic governments and democracies naturally resort to the expedient of bribing the masses in order to remain in power—bread and circuses in the Roman Empire, various forms of entitlements and welfare in the modern democratic welfare states. Subsidies for some of the more exotic elements of society through national endowments for the arts and humanities contribute to chaotic syncretism, which works against the moral consensus needed for democracy to function. The trend toward colossalism (discussed in chapter 7) treats individuals more and more on a collective basis, the modern mob in which no one has deep and abiding ties to anyone else but only to the state through its governmental and welfare organs.

THE CRISIS IN DEMOCRATIC THEORY

Democracy has been consecrated as the ideal and only just form of government on earth. "Making the world safe for democracy" justified America's entry into World War I, and the United States and other powers continue to intervene here and there in an effort to establish democracy where it does not yet exist. The United Nations, officially a peace-keeping organization, readily authorizes military action to restore or preserve democracy. It would never do such a thing to restore a deposed monarch, no matter how legitimate his claim or how ancient his lineage.[5] The few remaining monarchies, with the exception of some Muslim states, all loudly proclaim that they are democratically ruled. Even the failed Communist dictatorships called themselves democracies, as the People's Republic of China still does. But what does the word *democracy* really mean today?

The fundamental axiom of democratic political theory is this: Power comes from the people, and governments must derive their authority from the just consent of the governed. The earliest democracies and republics, Greek and Roman, were small city-states in which the direct participation of a substantial number of citizens in decision-making and government was possible. Of course, even in the small city-states, the franchise was limited; not everyone could participate. The words *democracy, republic, monarchy,* and *empire* do not tell much about the degree of freedom that citizens or subjects enjoy nor the degree of

---

[5] Neither the great democracies nor the United Nations reacted when the oldest royal house in the world, that of Ethiopia, was overthrown and the emperor murdered by what turned out to be one of the bloodthirstiest tyrants of the modern era.

compulsion to which they may be subjected. It is sometimes easier to live under a king than under a parliament, and a monarch sometimes is quicker than a democratically installed bureaucracy to hear the petitions of an ordinary citizen.

Within the democracies of the Western world, the word *democracy* seldom means what it appears to mean. There are various problems and inconsistencies in the way democratic theory is put into practice. Different countries are becoming ungovernable in different ways; some are resorting to tyranny, while others may simply slide into chaos. The United States offers a striking example of the impasse of democratic theory in a late sensate society.

Democracy, as noted earlier, had its origin in relatively small communities. Modern democracies have forebears in the small free towns of medieval Germany and in the towns and rural cantons of Switzerland. Like the ancient Greek city-states, they were small enough to make more or less direct interaction between the citizens and their officials possible. The first modern "republic" on a national scale, France, quickly turned into a dictatorship ruled by terror, then embraced Napoleon as emperor. After many trials, wars, and foreign occupations, France has become a centrally governed state with popular elections, but the average Frenchman today enjoys less personal freedom and endures more interference from the national government than his ancestors did under Louis XIV, the "Sun King," who said, "*L'état, c'est moi*".

Democratic theory holds that the people as a whole—whether thousands, millions, or tens of millions of individuals—each with his or her own ambitions, desires, and disappointments, know enough and are competent enough to choose their rulers wisely. The democratic voting process makes no distinction between the sixty-year-old professor of moral philosophy and the twenty-year-old streetwalker; each one has one vote. The slogan "One man, one vote"—or "One person, one vote," as we say today—is taken as a divine command to be enforced everywhere. One might say "math makes right": Authority and power are supposed to belong by natural right to the greatest number.

It may seem that the principle, "One person, one vote," gives dignity and power to every individual. Unfortunately, the reality is different. In the United States, for example, the theory says that all votes are equal and that the majority rules. This theory itself is not necessarily flawless but, even worse, it is not applied in practice. In the United States, perhaps more than in other Western country, it is not the majority but a minority who rule. This comes about in two ways:

1. So few eligible voters go to the polls that winners are invariably elected by a minority of those eligible, even when they obtain a majority of votes cast.

2. When more than two candidates stand for one office, the winning candidate often does not have a majority of those actually voting but merely a plurality.

When voter participation is low and candidates are elected by a small plurality, it is evident that the democratic system is not functioning as democratic theory prescribes and that "majority rule" is not being implemented. The process does not function in reality because too few people vote, and too few people vote because of disillusionment with the process.

Prior to the twentieth century, voting rights in most countries were limited to particular groups: for example, male citizens, heads of families, male citizens of a particular race, property owners, those able to read, write, and pass a literacy test. There were plausible reasons behind several of these limitations:

- Men were sometimes seen as heads of households, voting on behalf of whole families; in several countries, all men were liable for military service, and the ballot was tied to national defense.

- Property owners were assumed to have an interest in community stability.

- Those who could not read or write were assumed to be less well-informed and perhaps less intelligent on an average than the literate.

Implicit in any limitation of voting rights is the theory that those given the right to vote should be the ones most likely to have the interests of the community at heart and therefore best able to make decisions that will benefit the entire community. Sometimes when the franchise is limited, those eligible to vote actually do feel a sense of responsibility for the general welfare rather than merely for their own interests, but one cannot depend on it.

When the franchise is unlimited, there is no guarantee that either those who actually vote or those they elect will have the best interests of the community at heart. Particularly when the culture is in the process of disintegrating, special interests of the most diverse kind dominate. An attitude of *sauve qui peu* (every man for himself) becomes widespread. When the units of government become larger, the ability of eligible voters to make wise decisions declines. Elections become popularity contests. High offices are won or lost because of a clever slogan, a tasteless joke, or even a slip of the lip, magnified millionfold by the omnipresent media (shown on one hundred million television screens and repeated on millions of printed pages).

Once in office, the officials, whether wise or foolish, unselfish and honest, or venal and corrupt, are bombarded by a mass of advice, petitions, pleas, abuse, insults, and innuendo from morning to evening, all of which is spread around the entire nation by energetic media. The slightest indiscretion is magnified to gigantic dimensions. In the United States, the phenomena of radio and television talk shows and instant opinion polls bombard the most conscientious officials and the general public with information, advice, and insults in such quantities that it becomes difficult or impossible to sift out accurate information and worthwhile advice from misinformation, abuse, and outright slander.

In the United States the power of the national government based in Washington virtually negates the ability of people scattered across a wide continent to rule themselves. Detailed federal regulations fill almost one hundred thousand printed pages. The simplest and most straightforward expressions of the will of the people, given for example in a popular referendum, can immediately be overthrown by state or federal judges allegedly on the basis of the Constitution. In fact, the Constitution means only what the judges want it to mean at any moment, neither more nor less. Popularly voted constitutional amendments can speedily be declared "unconstitutional" by unelected judges. By a series of fictions and subterfuges, the rights of the smaller entities (from states through private corporations to individuals) to set their own standards and to determine what is in their own best interests, are supplanted, abolished, or reversed by nondemocratic central government decisions, frequently by decisions of unelected administrative officials. In their place, the daily affairs of citizens across a vast continent are subject to rules made in the capital, sometimes by elected officials but more often by unelected anonymous administrators, bureaucrats, and judges.

171

Is this system really superior and preferable to the systems in which decisions were made by monarchs and aristocrats, who might actually be more immune from the pressures of the mob and the passions of the moment? If it is superior, it is only because in a democracy the ruling powers, at least some of them, can be put out of office by the people without the revolutionary violence that is often necessary in a monarchy.

Conditions in the United States are paralleled on a smaller scale in other democratic nations. In Europe, which consists of several medium-sized and smaller nations each with its own variety of culture and traditions, the trend is to consolidate everything into a central European bureaucracy that will rival or surpass the bureaucracy of the United States.

The ever-growing size of the effective governmental units makes democracy more and more a fiction. As the United States has been progressively transformed from a federal union of somewhat sovereign states into a centrally-ruled superstate, the ability of individual citizens or even of local communities to manage their own affairs has become more and more limited. If it was a fiction in earlier days to speak of the king as the "father" or "shepherd" of his people, it is a fiction today to speak of "government of the people, by the people." "For the people" may still apply, in that elected and appointed officials usually have the good of the people at heart, but "by the people" has become an illusion.

Modern technology and modern means of communication make it possible to poll the citizens on issues of every sort at a moment's notice. The people, or at least a "scientifically selected sampling" are asked daily what they think about a current issue. Sometimes elected officials use the results of such polls to make decisions; as often as not they disregard them—perhaps wisely, since such poll-taking seldom allows for deliberation and careful answers on the part of those polled. When the number of voices to be heard approaches a quarter-billion, the ability of any individual to be heard on a particular topic is reduced to nearly zero. It is as impossible for the will of an individual citizen to influence the decisions of government as it is for a glass of water spilled from the deck of a riverboat to affect the level of the Mississippi River.

The realm of personal life and conduct where individuals can freely decide what they want to do and how they wish to lead their own lives is constantly shrinking. The ability of parents to direct the education and protect the innocence of their children has virtually been destroyed. Schools increasingly resort to the technology of law enforcement and metal detectors in a futile attempt to replace the lack of moral orientation in the home. The dissatisfaction and frustration of the people with the political process is growing and becoming more evident day by day.

Perhaps Oswald Spengler's prediction of the rise of new Caesars at the end of the millennium will be fulfilled, on the theory that "anything is an improvement on this." It is increasingly apparent that the present democratic structures are no longer functioning as intended and promised, and the suspicion is growing that they are incapable of doing so.

The rise of mass media and rapid communication makes it more possible than ever for momentary swings in the popular mood and sudden shifts of allegiance to overwhelm and transform entire societies. In a late sensate culture, where no values are accepted as permanent and universally valid, it is impossible to predict what kind of changes may lie ahead, but it is easy to see the possibility of transformations as dramatic as that of the breakup of the Soviet Union in 1991 or the end of the Weimar Republic in 1933.

DEMOCRACY AND SENSUAL SELF-INDULGENCE

Unlike ideational and idealistic cultures, which can influence people by moral persuasion and appeal to authority and to ideals, a sensate culture can appeal only by offering sensual gratification. When a sensate culture is wealthy and luxurious, as Western culture now is, it becomes increasingly difficult to motivate people to exert the self-denial and effort necessary to overcome dangers and avoid economic catastrophes. If a charismatic leader such as Alexander the Great, Napoleon, or Winston Churchill should arise in the West now, it is doubtful that he could stir a Western population from its comfortable, self-indulgent lethargy. It is difficult for the population of a democratic society in a late sensate culture to generate its own moral sense or to build the morale necessary to produce endurance under difficult and trying conditions. In such a culture, Jesus' words, "not to be served, but to serve" (Matt. 20:28) strike most people as pure foolishness. Idealistic societies prize service; sensate societies cherish gain.

173

Because an entire culture is not transformed at a uniform rate, nor does transformation take place everywhere at once, even in a sensate culture there will remain pockets and backwaters where moral appeals can have an impact. As the sensate mentality becomes more pervasive, democratic politicians are forced to become nothing but demagogues, flattering the people and offering them easier and easier acquisition of more and more material goods and pleasures, as the Roman emperors provided the plebs with bread and circuses.

This approach must ultimately be self-defeating, however, because material goods can be provided only by the use of resources and the exertion of effort, and these are available only in a society that is prepared to engage in self-discipline and self-denial. This is part of the reason for the extreme emphasis being placed in the West on sexual pleasure and self-gratification by virtually any and every means with any and every person or thing. This is proceeding apace in the West; the implications were evident to the great philosopher of history Arnold Toynbee, who wrote, "Sexual license is an expression of a loss of faith and hope in mankind's future."[6] Professor Toynbee was replying to Daisaku Ikeda, at that time president of the idealistically oriented Buddhist Soka Gakkai organization in Japan, who had just said, "I suspect that the loss of sexual morality and the absence of love in sex is part of the trend to think of life in terms of material values only: sex is being converted into nothing but a means of pleasure completely divorced from spirituality. I am convinced that until we analyze this trend in the light of its fundamental causes we will never arrive at a solution."[7]

The loosening of all moral and ethical restraints on sexual conduct is a logical and almost inevitable consequence of popular democracy in a predominantly sensate culture. Economic realities prevent a government from offering continually more material goods to its people. Opportunities for sexual indulgence, by contrast, seem limitless. Relaxing legal and social restraints on sexual behavior appears to give people hedonistic satisfactions without costing government

---

[6] Arnold Toynbee and Daisaku Ikeda, *Choose Life: A Dialogue*, ed. Richard L. Gage (London: Oxford University Press, 1976), 20.

[7] Ibid., 18.

anything, but once all restraints are gone, people rapidly become jaded and government has nothing more to offer.

Unfortunately, just as a well-fed donkey will not be motivated to pull a wagon by the offer of still another carrot, a sexually satiated voting public soon reaches a condition where there are no further cheap pleasures to be offered. The pursuit of material and sensual gratification will turn to the pursuit of drugs and other technical means of increasing pleasure, but each new gratification reduces motivation and further undermines all sense of altruism and community service—necessary conditions for the functioning of a democratic system.

THE ABOLITION OF DEMOCRACY?

In centuries past, and with increasing completeness in the twentieth century, monarchies have been abolished, ruling houses and noble families liquidated. Monarchy rested on four thousand years of tradition and showed great resilience. Even after kings and emperors were deposed and killed, the idea of monarchy did not die. The Stuarts returned to the English throne, and the Bourbons to the French, at least for a time; France accepted two emperors and another king before becoming definitively republican. In this century, the monarchical idea seems finally to have lost its ability to survive a crisis. The Bolshevik revolutionaries murdered the last czar and wiped out his family; the Chinese imperial line died out with the last Manchu emperor; Britain, Japan, and a few other countries are formally monarchical but in reality are democracies.

The rise of tyrants in present-day democracies is not at all impossible, but the return of kings and emperors seems out of the question. The monarchies were no longer able to keep the loyalty and stir the imagination of the people, so they have passed from the stage of history. The democracies, however, are also entering a phase of impotence and irrelevancy. Must they also be abolished or simply pass from the stage? If so, what can replace them? Within the context of our late sensate culture, no happy solution is possible. For this reason, we must hope for a thoroughgoing sociocultural renewal, on the scale of the conversion of Europe after Constantine. If there is no such renewal, we face a slide into chaos with no idea what may come next.

175

9

THE CRISIS IN
EDUCATION

> . . . *A child who gets his own way*
> *brings shame to his mother.*
>
> *Proverbs 29:15*

AMERICA REPRESENTS AN EXTREME EXAMPLE of a problem that is becoming endemic throughout all of Western civilization—one that threatens to affect other highly developed countries. It can be expressed with three words: equality, authority, and excellence. The quest for *equality* has produced the collapse of a fundamental pillar on which education rested, namely *authority,* and the virtual disappearance of one of the primary goals that education was intended to achieve, *excellence.*

Nowhere is the loss of authority more evident than in the field of education. The very idea of education presupposes that the educator or teacher knows or can do something that the learner does not know or cannot do; it also presupposes a willingness on the part of the learner to be instructed and to learn. These presuppositions are implicit in what we mean by the word *authority.*

It is important to be specific about what this word means in the context of education, for the word itself has become so suspect in our era that an appeal to authority will immediately cause many people to stop their ears. *Authority* is often associated with *authoritarianism* and rejected, or at least looked on with suspicion, as guilty by association with the vices of tyranny and the abuse of power. As the word is commonly used, it is often confused with *power*. The late political philosopher Hannah Arendt has helped us to overcome this misunderstanding by pointing out the important distinction between mere power and true authority:

Power is the ability to force compliance with one's demands.

Authority is the ability to command voluntary obedience.[1]

Naturally an educator needs to be able to secure cooperation from his or her charges or education cannot take place, but it makes a great deal of difference whether the educator possesses authority or must resort to the use of force, whether moral or physical. The crisis in American education began with the loss of authority; its consummation comes when not only is there little or no authority to secure voluntary cooperation from those to be educated, but when power too no longer exists, or those in charge lack the courage or initiative to use it.[2]

When an individual or an organization must resort to force to secure compliance with its requirements or orders, it betrays by this action that true authority no longer exists. Soldiers, workers, and team players understand the tremendous difference between the spirit and performance seen when a commander, foreman, or coach is respected for quality of character and the level that will be attained when a leader can give orders only by virtue of the office. (Under such circumstances, the term *leader* is actually a misnomer, because having to give orders that are obeyed simply because of position rather than power demonstrates neither leadership nor true authority.)

When authority in the true sense declines, institutions and structures become disorderly and disoriented; they cease to perform their intended functions. If

---

[1] Hannah Arendt, *The Crises of the Republic* (New York: Harcourt Brace, 1972).

[2] The title of a book by the well-known educator Dr. James Dobson, *Dare to Discipline* (Wheaton, Ill.: Tyndale House, 1987), suggests what is lacking not merely in many families but throughout the entire educational establishment.

they have enough power, force can be utilized to achieve a measure of compliance and to create the appearance of effectiveness. When insufficient power is present or the use of force is inhibited, disorder and disorientation increase until the structures become totally ineffectual or until some form of tyranny arises to restore function.[3] This principle holds true for society as a whole, not merely in education. Its consequences can be observed throughout history and affect entire sociocultural systems, however the effect of a loss of authority frequently becomes apparent first of all in education, the process by which a culture shapes—or misshapes—the generation whose character and spirit will determine its future. Perhaps this is because education, by contrast with military, business, commerce, and even hierarchically organized religion, depends more heavily on moral authority and is less able than the others to preserve an appearance of effectiveness by the use of force. When force must be applied on a large scale in education, it is a sure indication that the educational process is collapsing, if indeed it has not already failed.

The phenomenon of disorder reaching a point at which it virtually demands the rise of a tyrant has occurred time after time and in country after country through history. It becomes evident to all when it takes place in government. One well-known example of how a decline in authority fosters the rise of tyranny may suffice: The first Roman Emperor, Augustus, was a man of such stature that despite his personal failings and flaws, he possessed true moral authority. Augustus seldom had to use his power to secure obedience; as *princeps*, he cast the first vote in the Roman Senate, and the other senators followed his lead. Cynics may object that the senators, who were not men noted for their civil courage, did this simply out of prudence or even fear. To say this would be to misunderstand the kind of authority that Augustus possessed.

The sorry tale of Augustus's successors in the first imperial dynasty presents a different pattern. They gradually lost dignity and abandoned integrity, in the process forfeiting respect and rapidly losing all true authority. Disorders and disturbances were multiplied, until the last emperor of the Julian house, Nero, was despised by his own Praetorian Guard and finally was assassinated. Nero's

---

[3] The conviction that prolonged disorder will ultimately give place to a tyranny of some kind is a central idea of all political philosophers from Plato to the present.

murder was followed by a brief period of turmoil, after which a hard-bitten, ruthless and efficient military commander, Vespasian, succeeded to the purple,[4] restoring a kind of order but at great cost in freedom and human dignity.

Many great educators, from the Greek philosopher Plato to the late Eric Voegelin (1901–85) have pointed to three stages in the decline of democracies:

1. Political evolution makes it difficult for wise and prudent leaders— the *aristoi* (the best, the true aristocracy)—to direct the people.[5]

2. Changes in the political process make it difficult for wise and prudent leaders to be elected.

3. The deterioration of education makes it difficult or impossible for wise and prudent leaders to be formed.

The ultimate consequence is the rise of tyranny. This is seen as inevitable in Plato's thought; in Voegelin's it can only be averted in our society by a recovery of religious values and orientation.[6] If we look honestly at conditions in North American culture, we will see that we are very close to Plato's third stage if we have not reached it already.

No tyranny has yet arisen, either in American society as a whole or in the educational system. However, unless these trends are reversed, particularly

---

[4] The right to wear "the purple" was a prerogative of the emperor and occasionally of a designated successor or colleague sharing the imperial power.

[5] The terms *aristocrat* and *aristocracy* are obnoxious to our American democratic minds. It is important to note that from Plato onward, philosophers have seen two basic factors as constituting an aristocracy. Most societies—even ours—have a favored class of hereditary noble, magnates, officers, or at least people of inheritied wealth and position. One of the functions of education was to take such privileged aristocrats and train them to be suited for public service. The second factor was education itself, by which people without inherited wealth or position could develop the knowledge, prudence, and virtue necessary for leadership in society. One of the unfortunate features of education today is that it increasingly fails at both tasks: imparting character and moral principles to the offspring of the favored classes, and training the young of the general public in the qualities that would make them deserving of public confidence and trust.

[6] See Glenn N. Schram, *Towards a Response to the American Crisis*, expanded ed. (Front Royal, Va.: Christendom Press, 1993), 149–62. esp. 161.

in education, it is hard to foresee any long-range alternative to increasingly tyrannical control.

The institution of firmer control including force or threats of force offers some hope of temporary improvement in educational performance, but it is no long-range solution. Late in 1995 a retired army general was appointed as superintendent of the Seattle, Washington, public schools. Can it be that on a very small scale segments of the American public are beginning to feel as the Romans apparently did—that a firm, military hand has become the only remedy for growing chaos?

AUTHORITY: WHERE THE PROBLEM BEGINS

A generalized breakdown in authority is easily observed in the loss of the symbols, habits, and traditions that accompanied authority. In classical thought, authority depended directly on *dignitas* (dignity, worth) and *virtus* (virtue). A person with diminished dignity and virtue or none at all could not possess authority. Titles, honors, symbols, and badges of office were not so much intended to create dignity as to indicate that their bearer possessed it and to summon others to respect. The evolution of democracy in the West, particularly in the United States, has resulted in a growing loss of all these symbols of dignity, presumably in the quest for increasing equality among all people.

The United States Constitution prohibits the use of titles and trappings of nobility. It would be a serious misunderstanding to suppose that the Founding Fathers had no place in their thinking for human qualities such as dignity and virtue. What they meant by abolishing titles of nobility was to declare that true dignity and virtue are not inherited but must be developed and displayed by individuals. Respect must be earned, but once earned, may be given public recognition. For this reason, although titles of nobility were abolished, other titles and symbols were retained.

In modern America, with few exceptions, the titles and symbols that survived more or less intact into the twentieth century have now been either discarded altogether or turned into their opposites. The President of the United

States is still addressed as *Mr. President,* but he is also increasingly referred to by his first name or even by a shortened or diminutive form.[7] Titles such as "the Honorable" and "Reverend" still exist but are often uttered in a sarcastic tone, as though their use implied the opposite of their literal meaning.

An even more significant trend is the decline in civil discourse, where insults, and vulgar and obscene speech and gestures have become common in public and private discourse between superiors and inferiors as well as between equals. The conversations of high school girls and boys has become as full of vulgarities and obscenities as the proverbial waterfront saloons of former years, and even a liberal college education does not teach students cultivated speech. The coarsest obscenities appear in the form of spray-painted graffiti.

The loss of the symbols that once were supposed to accompany those persons and institutions whose dignity and virtuous character merited respect and authority is mistakenly seen as evidence of a desirable trend: "progress in democracy." It is definitely a sign of an *evolution* in democracy, but an evolution in deterioration not progress. As Plato wrote, in democracies in decline men become increasingly insolent, disrespectful of authority, and given to extreme sensuality. Each of these phenomena is present in modern, democratic America as well as to a greater or lesser extent in other contemporary democracies, even where they are least to be expected and where their influence may be most harmful, namely, in education.

Education involves imparting knowledge to those who do not at first possess it, teaching virtue to those who are not fully aware of it, and developing moral excellence in those whose characters are still immature and unformed. In order to teach, a teacher must not only have knowledge to impart but must be able to command the attention of pupils and inspire sufficient respect so that they willingly learn. Some lessons can be taught by force—"drummed in," as the Germans put it—but force is a poor and ineffectual substitute for authority where teaching and learning are concerned.

---

[7] This is particularly the case when there is a perception that the man in question does not possess great innate dignity and virtue. Franklin D. Roosevelt was called "F.D.R." but hardly ever "Frank"; Ronald Reagan was seldom if ever called "Ronald" or "Ron," but one hears President Clinton commonly referred to as "Bill" and his Republican antagonist as "Newt."

The decline in authority is traceable to two chief developments: The first is the loss of a generally shared consensus about the common good—a loss manifest in the general adult public and evident to the children and adolescents who are to be educated. Where the systems of truth as well as standards of justice and ethics are in crisis, there can be no general agreement on what constitutes the common good. Under such circumstances, it becomes difficult to recognize particular teachers and institutions as virtuous, as possessing dignity and authority, and to recommend that they are especially worth hearing and following. The second is the perversion of the doctrine of equality. From being a principle designed to recognize the potential dignity and worth of every human individual it has been perverted to the point that it is no longer possible to acknowledge any special dignity, achievement, or authority on the part of anyone at all. Thus a democratic principle that is entirely valid within its proper context becomes destructive when made absolute and universal.

EQUALITY RUNNING AMOK

It is indeed true, as the United States Declaration of Independence affirms, that "All men are created equal," but it is also true that this concept—*equal*—can only be defended in the context of the verb *created* with its reference to a transcendent Author and his purpose.[8] There are great differences among humans with regard to age, experience, abilities, knowledge, and moral excellence. It is on these differences that authority rests, and where they are not recognized and respected, there is no authority and there can be no education other than indoctrination or the kind of obedience training to which dogs and other domestic animals are exposed.

---

[8] It should not be necessary to point out that *men* includes both men and women. This fine principle was unevenly applied, however. Two of the rights named, liberty and the pursuit of happiness, were withheld from slaves. From a theological perspective, all human beings, whatever their race, sex, age, or condition, are equal in the highest and most fundamental sense, in that they are made in the image of God. They are, of course, unequal in physical strength, health, wealth, wisdom, longevity, and many other respects.

A concept of equality that denies all real differences between people is totally hostile to education. "My opinion is as valid as yours" may be acceptable where matters of taste are concerned—*De gustibus non disputandum est* (there is to be no disputing concerning tastes)—although even there it is questionable. It is surely better to be Socrates dissatisfied than a pig satisfied and it is at least arguable that Enrico Caruso was a greater singer than Elvis Presley. Where objectively verifiable facts are concerned, all opinions are definitely not equally valid, and where moral principles are involved, surely important differences exist. "Do unto others as you would have them do unto you," the Golden Rule, has a different function and a greater value in society than its modern perversion, "Do unto others before they do unto you."

If all persons are equal in all significant respects, it becomes logically impossible to suppose that one person can teach others. Of course no one actually believes that all persons are equal, and certainly not children and adolescents in school and young adults in university, but the officially promoted *fiction* of generalized equality is destructive of the authority that is necessary for education to function.

FROM THE TOP DOWN

One reason why authority in education has declined is that individual and institutional authority is based on the acknowledgment that such individuals and institutions exhibit virtue and serve the common good, and contemporary culture has lost its consensus as to what constitutes the common good. This did not originate in disillusionment or rebellion among the common people but as a loss of orientation, abdication, and betrayal precisely where authority, dignity, and virtue should have been best safeguarded—in the institutions of higher and highest learning. According to political scientist Glenn Schram,

> There is little doubt that colleges and universities are central to the crisis in education. They are also central to the society-wide crisis of authority concerned for the common good, owing to their immense impact on American culture—an

impact in the final analysis greater, probably, than that of the mass media, influential though the latter may be.[9]

The prestigious institutions of North America (such as Harvard, Yale, Princeton, Stanford, the University of Chicago) and all their rivals and imitators entered the second half of the twentieth century with their authority, dignity, and virtue still apparently intact. The majority of college students, being less than twenty-one years old, were still legally minors, and the colleges saw themselves as *in loco parentis* (in the place of a parent) and consequently felt both obliged and authorized to teach moral principles and to uphold standards of behavior, civility, and morality, including sexual morality.

Much has been written about the student revolution of the sixties, when college deans and presidents were held hostage, offices were occupied, *free speech* came to mean the coarsest vulgarities and obscenities, and virtually all men's and most women's colleges were made coeducational overnight (with far more emphasis on the *co* than on education). They were followed in due course by the elite private boys' schools and many of the girls' schools. Dropping the age of majority to eighteen meant that most college students were officially if not actually mature and that colleges could no longer claim a quasi-parental authority. *In loco parentis* was thrown out at about the same time that parental authority in general came to be tacitly abolished.

Gender equality meant that women's colleges and dormitories could no longer maintain special rules for the protection of feminine virtue as they had done in the past (with not unintended consequences for the protection of masculine virtue as well). Indeed, dormitories, floors, and sometimes even rooms were made open to both sexes, with absolutely predictable results: generalized sexual activity. Sexual behavior was removed from moral concern, and inasmuch as sex had always constituted a major concern of personal ethics, ethics became increasingly relativized and irrelevant. Since one of the traditional purposes of education has always been to teach ethics, when sexual behavior was removed from ethical scrutiny the teaching of ethics immediately lost much of its substance and

---

[9] Schram, *Towards a Response*, 78.

in fact has more or less been abandoned as a significant part of the educational process.[10]

When heterosexual conduct ceased to be subject to moral restraint, those with homosexual inclinations demanded no less liberty; first gay, then lesbian, and finally bisexual individuals and organizations demanded and received rights, recognition, and subsidies in the name of diversity, pluralism, and multiculturalism. A "medical service" that violates the age-old Hippocratic Oath as well as traditional Jewish and Christian moral principles—abortion—is now regularly provided by college health facilities. Prophylactics, even of the distinctive sort that are used in certain homosexual activities, are not merely made available but are advertised and in some cases generally distributed to students—a practice begun at the college level that is increasingly promoted in secondary schools. The theory that sexual conduct is simply a matter of personal taste, not subject to moral scrutiny, directly contravenes the moral teachings not only of Judaism and Christianity but of many other religions and philosophies as well. To say that sexual conduct is not subject to moral principles is so counterintuitive that removing sexual behavior from moral scrutiny comes close to abolishing moral scrutiny altogether. If morality cannot regulate sexual behavior, it is rendered impotent and can regulate nothing at all.

University administrations that attempted to suppress prejudice and discrimination in the 1950s, dropping requests for photos on applications for admission and withdrawing recognition from undergraduate organizations with racial or religious restrictions such as some fraternities, began to promote and endorse divisiveness, prejudice, and racial preferences and separation into newly segregated dormitories under the misleading rubrics of diversity and multiculturalism. The concept of equal respect and dignity for men and women from every ethnic background triumphed in American higher education only in this century, and it has already been superseded by the legitimization of new varieties of tribalism and theories of racial separatism and superiority. Even more significant than the potentially disruptive effect of such changes is the fact that they represent a dishonest and dishonorable abandonment of some of the very principles that created academic excellence in the past.

---

[10] Exercises in "values clarification" do not teach ethical norms or standards of conduct but merely help students "determine their own values," which is quite a different thing.

THE ABOLITION OF EXCELLENCE

The widespread favoritism to women and racial minorities openly proclaimed in announcements of positions has certainly skewed if not abolished old commitments to academic excellence and impartiality. From having been, in theory at least, "no respecters of persons," university admissions and faculty search committees became obsessed with race, gender, and even sexual preference in their eagerness to fulfill mandated or imagined quotas.

Thus the American educational establishment began to do to itself, almost totally voluntarily, what German science and education had done to themselves under the Nazis. Although German educators had reason to fear retaliation if they resisted government manipulation, it is a sad commentary on the German intellectual world that very few of its representatives offered resistance. By excluding Jews and banning those of less than totally politically correct views, Germany deprived itself of some of its most valuable potential leaders. Something similar is now happening in the United States.

The new, reverse racism, sexism, and diversity are not the basic problem, but their spread is symptomatic of the problem, namely the replacement of the pursuit of truth with what is called "political correctness." The term *politically correct* is derided as misleading, but actually it is quite appropriate. Education in the dictatorships was required by force of law and police power to stay politically correct. In our liberal democracy, there is no secret state police[11] to enforce political correctness, but most of the educational establishment follows it slavishly nonetheless. The willingness to suppress truth in order to be politically acceptable necessarily makes truth less important to the community and is destructive of the whole nature of education.

Traditionally, and indeed logically, one of the primary purposes of education in a democracy is to train leaders in intellectual ability, integrity, and moral excellence to create, in place of the hereditary aristocracies of the monarchies, a true aristocracy of ability and virtue. This task has been increasingly abandoned and even repudiated at the national level. One can speak of the

---

[11] *Gestapo* is the abbreviation for Geheime Staatspolizei—secret state police.

decapitation, or perhaps even of the emasculation, of the educational aristocracy. Moral excellence has been almost totally repudiated; in fact, the concept is dismissed as meaningless. The propagation of knowledge without moral excellence is hardly conducive to the common good; it simply produces better-educated villains.

The loss of integrity at the top is not all-pervasive. In fields where objective control and scientific verification are possible—such as medicine, physics, and engineering, among others—America's colleges and universities still produce impressive results. Across the board, however, the results are not good. The tremendous expansion of higher education that began after World War II has brought millions of uninterested and marginally qualified students into colleges and universities. The fact that such institutions are either partly or largely dependent on student fees to survive creates an incentive to expand enrollment figures even at the cost of awarding degrees and honors to those who have only paid for but not earned them. The demand for equality as well as the desire not to impose arbitrary Western, Eurocentric, or male-oriented standards has led to grade inflation, which means that "high honors," when they are awarded, may mean little more than "satisfactory" did in times past.[12]

What has happened in higher education has also affected, or infected, secondary and even primary education. The usual means of measuring academic accomplishment, such as the scores on nationally administered college entrance examinations (the SAT and ACT tests), have been in gradual but almost uninterrupted decline for over twenty years. The stories of high school graduates who cannot read are legion. Although public schools spend immense sums on buildings, equipment, and highly paid administrators, American schoolchildren attain results that are far inferior not only to those in Asian countries such as Japan and Korea and to prosperous European countries such as Switzerland, but even to the results attained in less favored regions such as Slovenia.

The total loss of authority is symbolized by the increasingly commonplace presence of police officers in high schools and even in lower schools and by

---

[12] In a related development, some primary and secondary schools have abolished grades altogether or replaced them with vague comments such as "cooperates" or "improving" in the effort to prevent pupils from feeling superior or inferior to others.

the introduction of metal detectors to prevent children from bringing guns and knives to school. America may well propose to place computers in every schoolroom by the end of the century, as President Clinton did in his January 1996 State of the Union address, but the costliest and most complex teaching aids will be of little value when teachers possess no authority to teach and students possess no willingness to learn.

10
THE CRISIS IN
MEDICINE

*When the physician can decide who shall
live and who shall die, he becomes the
most dangerous man in the state.*

Christoph Hufeland

MEDICINE HAS COME TO OCCUPY an ever more substantial place in human
life and culture. While medicine used to be relatively ineffectual and rather
cheap, in the past few decades it has become far more effective and incredibly
costly. In the United States, for example, medical costs make up one-sixth of
the gross national product. It is now a more important element in the culture
than education, national defense (at least during peacetime), religion, or the
arts. Once considered an art and a calling, medicine has become both industrialized and commercialized. In the United States, which often serves as the
bellwether for all of Western culture, medical care, surgery, psychiatry, and
hospital care are advertised like automobiles and cosmetics:

"The University of Chicago Hospitals—at the forefront of medicine."

"The only Harvard-trained specialist in male sexuality in Northern
Illinois. . . ."

The origin of medicine was modest. Since the beginning of recorded history, sickness and injury have plagued the human race. Human beings have tried whatever they could to heal the sick and injured, but, unfortunately, sickness and suffering are better attested than healing and cures. In the long-run, everyone dies. Thus there is a natural limit to what medicine can do, but as it succeeds in enabling more and more people to extend their lives beyond the point at which sickness or injury would have ended them in the past, it encounters increasing frustration—the law of diminishing returns. Its therapeutic possibilities become less and less effective, while its cost rises astronomically. The cost of prolonging an individual's life by a few months or even weeks can exceed all that the person spent on health care over a lifetime.

In addition to being industrialized and commercialized, medicine has become politicized, increasingly defined as a right of all citizens (indeed of all residents, citizens or not) in modern Western states. Because medical care prolongs many lives to the point where the cost of that care becomes impossible for most individuals to bear and creates a huge burden on public finances, the right to medical care is being "supplemented" by a "right to die." This strange "right"— for it is odd to define something that everyone *must* do as a right—can be provided by physician-assisted suicide. In the Netherlands, physician-assisted suicide is already being supplemented by involuntary euthanasia.

Such developments could not have been imagined in past centuries; indeed, they were not imagined even half a century ago. Some age-old scourges such as smallpox and poliomyelitis can now be prevented relatively inexpensively, but the triumphs over certain cancers have become incredibly costly, and no amount of money as yet can give victory over AIDS or Alzheimer's disease and other degenerative processes of aging. Medicine began in prehistory as a simple human concern to give relief from pain and distress and to facilitate healing; it has become an incredibly complicated enterprise, the ramifications of which are contributing to the disorientation of ethics and law.

A GLANCE AT THE HISTORY OF MEDICINE

Artifacts from prehistoric civilizations offer evidence that medical procedures existed even before writing was invented. Surgery is older than written history; archaeology has unearthed bones that were broken and set, and even surgically opened skulls, some of which have scarring in the opening indicating that the patient survived the operation at least long enough for scar tissue to form. But such early surgery was crude, painful, and dangerous, and the pharmacopoeia of those early days contained only few and often ineffectual remedies. Religion and magic seemed to many to offer better prospects for healing and relief of suffering. Grossly obese statuettes found on archeological sites, sometimes taken to represent fertility goddesses, may have been votive offerings seeking supernatural help for persons suffering from pathological obesity.

When did medicine actually begin? Did Eve have to dress Adam's wounded side after she was formed from one of his ribs? Was it Adam who tied Cain's umbilical cord after Eve bore her first child? The first pages of Genesis do not speak of medical acts, but they describe situations in which medical acts may have been required. From the earliest times, men and women have suffered sickness, injury, and death, and have drawn upon all their wisdom and experience in the effort to heal the one and postpone the other, linking medicine and religion as they sought to do so. As people are plagued by sickness and infirmity and generally die before they are ready to do so, they find their existence and its meaning mysterious and want to know not only how and why they exist, but what they can expect when this earthly life is over.

Religion seeks to explain the mysteries of life, to come to terms with the unknown, and to obtain help for people from a power or powers greater than themselves. Quite naturally, it seeks to obtain healing for sufferers. This function of religion continues even today. The well-established, more formal religions do not usually make healing services part of their ministry, and in consequence "faith healers" and charismatic healing services are frequented by those whom medicine has failed to satisfy.

Medicine and health care may seem to be among the more tangible and practical aspects of a culture by contrast with its religion, but like religion, medicine attempts to deal with things that cannot be explained scientifically. It too calls upon powers sometimes only dimly understood to bring help with the problems of life, birth, and death. In early cultures, the two disciplines were naturally closely related. Illness was frequently thought to be caused by bad religion—offended deities or demons. Healing could therefore be sought from good religion, with the help of persons wise in the ways of spiritual realities as well as knowledgeable about herbs and other remedies. The witch doctor is often portrayed as an object of ridicule, as someone whom no enlightened, modern person could take seriously, but many a modern physician armed with the most modern medical technology confesses, "I treat; God heals."

The wisest and most learned people in early cultures were often the priests, and medicine frequently began under priestly or religious auspices. Assuming that sickness had a spiritual origin, the priest or medicine man could try to discover what offense brought it on and could examine the nature of the sickness itself. When an offense to the gods was suspected, it was natural to seek healing by religious or magical means as well as by utilizing the limited therapeutic measures available. Therapeutic possibilities were limited; for many serious conditions, little or nothing could be done. Of course, the natural curative powers of the human body permitted even ignorant physicians and priests to claim many apparent successes.

When medicine entered the era of recorded history, it was part of an integrated culture and had an important part to play in many different spheres of life, less because of what it could do—for it could actually do rather little—than because of the importance of health and suffering in human experience. As civilization progressed, medicine progressed, especially since the beginning of the scientific revolution and with increasing rapidity during the past century and a half.

In the first Babylonian empire eighteen centuries before Christ, the celebrated Code of Hammurabi—the world's oldest law code—dealt with medicine. In that unified culture, which centered on the throne with the monarch playing a semidivine priestly role, the physician was trained, examined, and paid by the royal household. Those who did best in their examinations could become physicians to the royal household; those who did less well treated the nobility and wealthy citizens, while the poorest candidates treated the common people. Medical care was available to all classes without cost, reflecting the degree to which it was fully integrated into the culture. An unfortunate aspect of this government-provided care was that the physician was a servant of the state and was expected, among other things, to keep the monarch informed about the affairs of his subjects.

Our records for Egyptian medicine are half a millennium later than those of Babylon; there, too, medicine was an integral part of an early ideational culture. Although the Egyptians did not consider it part of religion or a magic art, the study of medicine was associated with the great temples and the priestly educational system. Egyptian physicians have left detailed and accurate descriptions of particular maladies and a pharmacopoeia of five hundred frequently useful drugs and herbs.

Hippocratic Medicine

Our knowledge of the history of medicine expands tremendously in the idealistic period of Greek culture. The tradition associated with the name of Hippocrates has proved extremely durable. It remained dominant in medicine through the sensate period of the Roman Empire; it was developed and reinforced in both medieval Europe and the Muslim lands of the Near East. Only in the late sensate phase of our own culture has it begun to be seriously challenged.

The Hippocratic tradition, so hallowed by centuries of veneration and observance, came into being in Greece during the fifth century B.C. The ideational culture of the heroic period was becoming idealistic, combining an appreciation of empirical evidence and the real world with its sensitivity to supersensory realities. Medicine became more clearly a science and an art rather than magic, but it was science and art dedicated to the gods—to Apollo, Asclepius, Hygieia, Panacea, and all the other gods and goddesses. There is an extensive corpus of works attributed to Hippocrates and his school that provides excellent descriptions of medical and surgical conditions as well as useful advice of a preventive and a moral nature.

The integrated nature of idealistic culture in this period is reflected in the fact that the physician was expected to take an interest in his patients' moral and spiritual lives as well as in their physical health. The most familiar element of the tradition, the Hippocratic Oath, refers quite naturally to the deities venerated in that era. The oath was adopted in amended versions by Christians as well as by Jews and even Muslims. In whatever country it took root, the Hippocratic tradition taught physicians to consider their work a holy calling and to hold themselves accountable to God (or the gods), to their professional colleagues, and particularly to their patients.

Hippocratic medicine defined the physician's duty to the patient for the first time; the patient was to be seen as made in the image of the divine. Outside of the Hippocratic tradition, physicians frequently worked for the monarch or the state. They had no specific duty to their patients as individual human beings in the same way that a veterinarian has no specific duty to the dogs or horses he treats but rather to the owner who pays him. Hippocrates instructed his students and all who followed in his tradition concerning their duty to the patient first of all. Specifically, the new physician promised not to perform or counsel abortions and not to perform or counsel "assisted suicide."

The widespread acceptance of abortions in the West entailed a devaluation of the Hippocratic Oath; in the United States, the Oath was specifically rejected as a guide to medical ethics by the United States Supreme Court in January 1973. That approval of abortion would soon be followed by approval of euthanasia, as opponents of abortion predicted and abortion supporters denied, is being proved true in several countries.

It may seem to be a digression to look at detailed aspects of early medicine, but these provisions of the Hippocratic Oath are important because they reflect a fundamental understanding of human nature and man's moral responsibility—an understanding that is entirely compatible with idealistic culture but that comes to appear naive and foolish in a sensate culture. The prohibition against providing a deadly drug or counseling anyone to take one would appear to rule out physician participation in execution by lethal injection, which is becoming the "treatment of choice" for condemned criminals in the United States.

Whether a person sentenced to die is killed by a headsman with an ax, a hangman with a noose, a warden pulling the switch on an electric chair, or a white-coated "health care professional" with a syringe may seem a trivial difference to the condemned man or woman, but resorting to capital punishment by lethal injection with its medical aura, even when no physician participates, is a significant clue to the pervasiveness of the cultural shift our society is undergoing today. The serious moral question of capital punishment is reduced to a discussion of technique, and a change in technique suffices to quell the protests of many who are otherwise inclined to oppose the death penalty.

Significantly, the Hippocratic physician worked for the patient. Unlike the Babylonian physician a millennium earlier, he did not work for or report to the monarch but instead had to respect the patient's privacy. Again, this is typical of an idealistic culture, which values the human soul and sees it in a position of personal responsibility to God. A culture that rejects all supersensory realities finds it increasingly difficult to respect the individual as an individual and will come to look on him or her as only organic material, to be cared for and enhanced as long as it is useful and to be discarded in a sanitary manner when its usefulness is over.

Hammurabi's physicians practiced government medicine; Hippocrates gave us human medicine. Today, consistent with a sensate mentality, we are returning to government medicine, in which the treatments afforded a patient will depend on the patient's real or potential value to the state. Various national health service plans in the West today are moving to make the physician the servant of the state, which will ultimately take precedence over all duties to the patient.

Finally, the Hippocratic physician looked for rewards and sanctions from his fellow physicians, from the general public, and not least, from the divine order. His responsibility was not to government but to God and to man.

When a culture loses its awareness of and sense of responsibility toward God or the divine order, in other words, when it is no longer ideational or idealistic but sensate, it becomes increasingly difficult to respect individual human beings as such. They become ciphers in the calculus of societal utility, like the animals in a veterinarian's care, treated and healed when it is possible and economically feasible, but painlessly disposed of when it is not.

MEDICINE IN THE SENSATE CULTURE

Medicine, like the other aspects of an integrated culture, conforms to the basic orientation of the culture, although like religion, it may preserve some distinctive attitudes of its own. In a sensate context, medicine tends to disregard all approaches to healing that do not depend on material means—surgery and drugs in particular. In an ideational society, the tendency will be to disregard medical therapy and to look only to the spiritual realm for healing. Even in our contemporary society, which is predominantly sensate, there are people who prefer a purely spiritual remedy for sickness; this is the attitude of the religious denomination known as Christian Science.

Although in principle one would expect a sensate culture to take only material causes and cures seriously, in our own overripe sensate culture, people are increasingly turning to "alternative" medicine, which is based partly on the wisdom or lore of herbalists and other healers of the past, and partly on various occult and magical influences that only a few decades ago would have been rejected as nonsense and superstition redolent of medicine men or shamans.[1] This too is an example of chaotic syncretism. It reflects the sociocultural shift that we are beginning to experience, leading to a gradual abandonment of the certainties of sensate reality and a search for other sources of truth.

Much of the general public is of two minds concerning the triumphs and achievements of modern medicine. On the one hand, medicine (particularly specialists and great hospitals) is held in almost religious awe. On the other hand, the immense cost of medical services along with what some perceive as avarice and indifference to human suffering on the part of many health care professionals, highly publicized failures of particular therapies, techniques, physicians, and hospitals, and the apparent ease with which the profession is abandoning the Hippocratic Oath and embracing euthanasia and abortion is creating a loss of trust in physicians and a hostile atmosphere toward the profession.

The medical establishment itself is beginning to turn away from the absolute ethical principles (specifically, from the standards of Hippocratic medicine) that enabled it to gain such respect in the past. For centuries, medicine has occupied such a special status in culture that it was able to hold to the absolute standards of Hippocrates, formulated in an idealistic culture, long after most of Western culture had become thoroughly sensate and ceased to think in terms of divine or natural laws being universally valid and binding. Despite outbursts of cynicism and satire, the general public perceived physicians as having higher ideals and a greater sense of dedication than general mankind. Now, however, the full impact of the shift to sensate culture has battered down traditional medical principles, with the United States and the Netherlands leading

---

[1] Our sensate culture does not deny the psychosomatic nature of many illnesses nor exclude the possibility of psychic healing, but it regards the human psyche as part of the material world. The field called "alternative medicine" is immense and includes genuinely wise and helpful procedures and products long ignored by academic medicine as well as many things based on fantasy, superstition, and the occult and totally lacking in experimental verification.

the way in spurning the Hippocratic maxim, *Primum non nocere*—"First of all, do not harm." Medicine here and elsewhere is increasingly accepting the utilitarian approaches of abortion, euthanasia, and physician-assisted suicide. This shift in our approach to medicine is another indication that our overripe sensate culture is in a transition phase. If the sensate sociocultural supersystem is in a crisis, as is plainly the case, we need not be surprised to find medicine also in a special crisis of its own. The crisis of medical costs (the debates in the United States over Medicare and Medicaid) is only the most visible part of the crisis in medicine, which is part of the crisis of culture as a whole.

Modern medicine has an ability to cure diseases that were previously considered death sentences. It can even go so far as to change, or appear to change, one of the most fundamental aspects of nature—an individual's sex. Thus medicine appears to be transforming the human condition and raising man above nature, freeing him from the constraints of biology. In fact, however, it is plunging humanity and medical science into an ever deeper predicament. The effort to indefinitely prolong human life begins to exclude all awareness of man's spiritual nature. People who think of themselves as having an eternal destiny and the prospect of eternal life are less likely to cling frantically to mortal life.

The Hindu teaching that the soul is repeatedly reincarnated is often proposed to explain the fact that the very high culture of India, primarily Hindu, has traditionally viewed human suffering with indifference and life as cheap when contrasted with the Christian West. Christianity emphasized the hope of a future life but denied reincarnation; each person lives on earth only once. This gave an impulse to compassionate concern and care for each individual, but at the same time it made it easier for physicians and patients to accept the inevitable defeat of death, believing as most did that death does not spell the end of an individual's existence.

As Western culture has become fully sensate, and as the sensate mentality has increasingly taken hold in medicine, there is no longer a general conviction of life after death nor of a divine judgment where one must give an account for the deeds done in earthly life. Consequently, when life is no longer attractive, medicine forgets *primum non nocere* and administers deadly drugs, euphemistically called "death with dignity" or "physician-assisted suicide."

199

Medicine in the West, having shucked off its earlier Christian convictions, is becoming increasingly manipulative in dealing with human lives, from the facile abortion of unwanted babies to the increasingly accepted termination of elderly or chronically ill patients, the material value of whose lives seems to have become inadequate. In a purely sensate culture, especially in its degenerate phase, nothing is more natural than for medicine to cease to be a healing art dedicated to the gods and to the dignity of the individual and to become a utilitarian technique for limiting social costs and improving social utility. The achievements of modern medicine are creating virtually insoluble financial problems—a situation made worse by the fact that more and more social and behavioral problems are being treated as medical problems.

Although the situation varies in details from country to country in the West, medical care in the United States is not atypical. Among the many inconsistencies and contradictions of American public policy, there is a determination to increase the care and provisions made for the disabled, the aged, and the medically indigent, contrasted with pressure for the rationing of services and even the promotion of physician-assisted suicide as the appropriate way to deal with long-term human suffering and cut medical costs at the same time.

Medical educators, philosophers and social scientists, whether they hail these developments or deplore them, recognize them as "a break with the humanitarian tradition," and attribute it to "the biologization of ethics under Ernst Haeckel and other Darwinians of his day."[2] This is true, but it is not the whole story and does not express the full nature of the break. The humanitarian tradition in medicine goes back to Hippocrates and was continually reinforced through the idealistic phase of Western culture,[3] particularly by religion—Christianity, Judaism, and Islam. It must necessarily come to an end, however, in the sensate phase of culture, in which culture, having "liberated" man from the "superstitions" of the categorical imperatives, has "taken from

---

[2] See Jürgen Sandmann, *Der Bruch mit der humanitären Tradition,* in *Forschungen zur neuren Medizin- und Biologiegeschichte,* ed. Gunter Mann and Werner F. Kümmel, vol. 2. (Stuttgart and New York: G. Fischer, 1990).

[3] See Ludwig Edelstein, "The Hippocratic Oath," in *Supplements to the History of Medicine,* vol. 1 (Baltimore: Johns Hopkins, 1943).

[man] an invisible armor that unconditionally protected him, his dignity, his sanctity, and his inviolability."[4]

Much of the problem results from a false definition of the physician's task as "ending suffering." Hippocrates himself never spoke of "ending suffering" but only of healing. If human life has no meaning beyond the pleasures and pains of bodily life, if there is nothing to look forward to after death, it is apparent that an excess of suffering will make living seem a burden to be thrown off as speedily as possible. It is self-evident that death ends suffering—at least here on earth. (What happens afterwards in eternity is a matter with which medicine is not prepared to deal.) If Hippocrates had been concerned primarily with ending suffering, he would have prescribed rather than prohibited deadly drugs. He made a categorical distinction between healing and killing, and while he acknowledged that healing is often impossible, he rigorously rejected killing.

The trend to euthanasia is being facilitated by a curious emphasis on "patient autonomy," which permits the liquidation of the useless or suffering under the pretext of affording each individual the maximum range of choice. Our late sensate society no longer even bothers to ask *whether* physicians have the right to kill certain patients but assumes that they do and argues only about how and when.

America's most eminent Surgeon General, C. Everett Koop (served 1981–89), has frequently said, "The corruption of law conspired with the corruption of medicine to produce this situation." A surgeon who has devoted his life to helping handicapped infants and children can only look on the present situation as a total reversal of all the values by which he has lived. Dr. Koop is correct, of course, but even his sweeping criticism only touches the surface of the systemwide cultural crisis. It is not only the professions of law and medicine that are corrupted, but the crisis pervades the entire culture. The ready resort to euthanasia for problem patients is symptomatic of the fact that the culture itself is ripe for euthanasia. One will reject this convenient solution only if one has ethical fixed stars, such as used to be provided by both the Christian faith and the Hippocratic tradition.

---

4 Pitirim A. Sorokin, *The Crisis of Our Age*, 2d. ed. (Oxford: Oneworld, 1992) 134–35.

Medicine, like engineering or industrial production, is often considered a technique rather than a philosophy or worldview. In fact, however, medicine brings its practitioners into touch with a broad range of human existence; changes in the culture sooner or later must affect medicine, and changes in medicine cannot fail to affect the entire culture.

11

THE NEXT
PHASE

Since without civilization and culture,
Christianity cannot live, it lives in
perpetual agony.

Miguel de Unamuno

THROUGHOUT THIS BOOK, we have dealt primarily with Western culture and civilization and have shown that the crisis that currently affects them is neither temporary nor minor but is a systemwide crisis of immense proportions that affects every aspect of our common life. The systemwide crisis of the West inevitably involves the rest of the world, for all the nations of the earth, with their distinctive cultures and patterns of life, are becoming ever more closely interconnected. This means that whatever affects Western culture affects the entire world, and whatever affects other parts of the world affects us. During the past two centuries, many aspects of Western culture, particularly Western technology, have been taken over in other societies. With Western culture, there has been an influence of Western religion (i.e., Christianity), which has altered other cultures and been altered itself in the process. Many important distinctions between cultures still exist. Trends and developments that are well established in the West may be slow in coming or totally rejected elsewhere. In general, however, Western developments, both beneficial and harmful, are imitated around the world.

Characteristics of other cultures are also permeating Western society. Yet despite the evident tendencies to disintegration and syncretism, Western culture as we know it is still enough of an integrated system to be described and dealt with in a distinctive manner. The whole world cannot be treated as a single unit; each culture must be dealt with on the basis of its distinctive capacities for renewal. We may, indeed we must, learn from the other cultures of the world, but the crisis of the West will not be solved by grafting in elements from Indian, Chinese, or African cultures. That would only increase the chaotic syncretism that is one of the symptoms of our own Western malaise.

From the perspective of Christianity, the loss of culture and civilization is agonizing. But from the perspective of civilization and culture, is the loss of Christianity agonizing? There are large segments of the population, even within nominally Christian countries, that take a negative view of the cultural presence of Christianity and, if possible, an even more negative view of any attempts to create a distinctive Christian political presence.

Human beings are human regardless of whether they are cultivated or civilized; one does not need to be "cultured" in any self-conscious sense in order to be human. Human beings are also human regardless of whether they belong to Christianity or any other religion. Being human is a quality that is independent of culture and religion. However, the kind of humans that we are is never independent of the culture and civilization that surrounds us nor of the religion that we embrace or reject.

If humans are creatures of God, made in the divine image, then it is evident that our human dignity depends not on our mental or athletic ability, education, or degree of artistic sensitivity, but upon our God-given nature. No one needs to "become" human, for each of us is human by nature and by divine endowment. One can, however, become *inhuman*. Humanity was called into being by God, but inhumanity is the work of rebellious humans.

Man is God's handiwork; culture is man's handiwork. The Book of Genesis tells us that God created man and woman as the last of his works, and then he pronounced all his works good. Following the creation, according to Genesis, came the Fall into sin, and man has hardly improved since then.

Evolution tells a different story. Man was not made good and then fell afterwards, but the story of life on earth is an upward movement. Living beings improve and advance with time and natural selection. By this reckoning, man is the best product that the earth has yet produced; yet man, evolution's highest achievement, is going sour. Thus the doctrine of evolution gives an ambivalent message with regard to human dignity for it strongly implies that there will be improvements in the future compared to which we present humans shall seem as undeveloped as chimpanzees seem compared to us. Such a view would make eugenic breeding and manipulation plausible. In a primitive form, it was used by Hitler to justify the extermination of "subhumans."

Just as Spengler and others applied the organic model to cultures, in the aftermath of Darwin, today many people apply the evolutionary model to them. Cultures evolve just as species do, and later cultures will almost inevitably be better than earlier ones.[1] Modern civilization was taken for granted to be an improvement on the Middle Ages. Perhaps this is so, but it is no longer at all evident that modern civilization is continuing to improve or even to be stabilized at the best level achieved thus far. Cultures may be healthy or sick, harmonious or discordant, energetic or languid, depending on the way those who make them up live, think, and act. Cultures can be inhuman, in the sense that they reject and violate what we consider human or humane ideals. In order to be able to say what actions and attitudes deserve to be called human, we must know what man is and ought to be, what is worthy of human nature and what is unworthy. This then is the question: "What is man?"

ORIENTATION: MAN THE MEASURE OF ALL THINGS?

One of the earliest Western philosophers, Protagoras, coined the famous maxim, "Man is the measure of all things." In order for this maxim to make sense, one has to know what man is in order to be able to measure other things by him. Protagoras, living in the idealistic phase of Greek culture, assumed that human nature is a given and is intuitively known. Explicit divine revelation—such as the biblical teaching that God has made us in his own image—is unnecessary;

---

[1] Interestingly, Spengler rejected Darwinism and did not apply the concept of evolutionary development to cultures. He did not believe that cultures progress by the "survival of the fittest."

we can know ourselves and our human dignity without having to learn from any divine teacher. To assume that man can really know himself and distinguish between good and evil by the use of his own rational ability apart from any supernatural revelation or guidance contradicts the ideational approach to reality.[2] Needless to say, this assumption was no longer made in the early centuries of Christianity, but it has taken hold again in the sensate era and is now the common presupposition of most modern thought. Unfortunately for our sense of the dignity of man and of the value of humanness, when this assumption remains dominant for too long, it leads to the conclusion that instead of being on the verge of discovering everything, man can know nothing. Thought itself is simply a physical, biochemical phenomenon with no actual meaning.

After several centuries of acting on the assumption that we can think autonomously and be a law unto ourselves, needing no help from God or divine revelation, we have lost our earlier naive confidence in our own dignity and destiny. Man begins to call his life absurd and to describe himself as "a useless passion," "a passionate nothingness," "a naked ape." During the 1930s and 1940s, Hitler wiped out millions of human beings, calling them "subhumans" and "useless eaters." During those years and into the 1950s, Stalin and Mao Zedong liquidated even more. It is self-evident that a useless passion cannot be the measure of anything, much less of all things. Something vital has been lost. No longer do people confidently echo the Psalmist's words to God, "What is man, that Thou dost take thought of him?" or know the answer, "Thou hast made him a little lower than God" (Ps. 8:4–5).

Between being the "measure of all things" and becoming a "useless passion" lie two millennia of Christianity and a complete cycle of cultural shifts, from the idealistic culture in which Protagoras lived through the sensate culture and its degeneration, the ideational and idealistic cultures of early and medieval Christian civilization, and finally Western sensate culture, now in its final, degenerate phase. Protagoras had what we might call a naive understanding of man; Christian doctrine, building on its foundation in the Hebrew

---

[2] From an idealistic as well as an ideational perspective, this is the mistake called "the pretended autonomy of theoretical thought" by Dutch philosopher Herman Dooyeweerd.

Scriptures, had a clear foundation in reality for human dignity—the conviction that man is the creature of an all-wise Creator, made in that Creator's image. Although Christianity teaches that man is flawed through sin and that his nature has become corrupted and his intellect unreliable, it tempers this gloomy awareness with the teaching that man is still significant in himself and in the sight of God. Man is called to a divine purpose here on earth and to companionship with God in the hereafter. The Hebraic and Christian concept of the Fall explains the flaws and corruptions of human nature and conduct by accepting the reality of sin. It does not look to man to repair the damage on his own but rather looks to God to provide a Redeemer. God must extend forgiveness and restoration.

A culture that fails to reckon with God and instead makes autonomous man the center of his own universe at first seems to glorify man and to provide him with great vistas of freedom, but instead it runs into progressively greater disasters. Human nature *is* flawed, and although we are capable of good, we are also prone to evil and to corruption. The great universities of Germany, which at one time led the world, provided the professors of medicine for Hitler's programs of human experimentation and euthanasia; the most eminent American universities have become centers where sexual license and depravity are praised and the only conduct that meets with official rebuke is open disapproval of immorality.

AFTER US, THE DELUGE?

According to the account in Genesis, which has parallels in the myths, legends, and folktales of several cultures, God promised Noah that he would never again destroy the earth by a flood. He did not guarantee, however, that humans would never do something worse to themselves. We are not confronted with literal rising waters as in the deluge but with a rising tide of changes, problems, and trends, any one of which carried to its logical conclusion might engulf us and make human life on earth either altogether impossible or at least no longer worth living.

As we have delineated in the preceding chapters, all of Western civilization is in a systemwide process of disintegration that began slowly, almost imperceptibly, but is now rushing ahead at breakneck speed. It is not simply that some of the finer things of life, such as classical music, haute couture, fine literature, beautiful furniture, and the like may no longer be found, but that human life, if it continues at all, may be forced into a state that is hardly preferable to animal existence. Sociologists, economists, and statisticians can easily point to present trends that, if prolonged, will lead to sweeping disasters.

- death of the human race by the year 2500 (Pierre Chaunu)
- suffocation of the world under a crushing weight of an exponentially exploding population (Paul Ehrlich)
- nuclear disaster (Carl Sagan)
- raging epidemics (Jonathan Mann)
- economic disasters of all kinds (most economists)

Some of the predictions or possibilities—such as a collision with a comet, which would effectively destroy the earth—involve things that we cannot influence at all. Others, however, are of our own making, and for some the likelihood that they will come to pass is much greater than that of a devastating collision with a comet. The systemwide crisis our culture faces today is a human-generated crisis. If it breaks in upon civilization with its full destructive potential, the fact that we caused it will not help us. Before it becomes full-blown, however, the fact that we humans are bringing it about suggests that we also may help to disarm it.

Most present-day futurologists (if they do not happen to be running for public office) see much to dread and little to hope for in the immediate future of humanity. The prospects have changed dramatically since the excitement after World War II, when the victors thought that by eliminating two powers bent on world conquest they could secure a happy and prosperous future for the entire world. People in the second half of the twentieth century have lived under the shadow of intercontinental nuclear war and the annihilation of the entire human race. While that threat seems to have vanished with the breakup of the Soviet Union in 1991, the world has not experienced a surge of optimism and hopefulness anything like that felt by the victorious powers after World War II. It is as though people around the world realize that our entire human society is too far gone to be rescued by a simple redrawing of international boundaries or the reduction in nuclear stockpiles and standing armies. The persistence of a sense of foreboding after the elimination of what was supposed to be the main cause of world anxiety indicates that the world senses the loss of direction and potentially fatal drift of its most dynamic and dangerous culture—Western Christendom.

Like so many futurologists, Sorokin warns of an impending day of wrath if certain trends continue. But unlike many others, Sorokin was not a fatalist or a pessimist. The same data and analysis that enabled him to see the day of wrath lying ahead permitted him to see the possibility, even the likelihood, of avoiding it, *provided* that we correctly recognize our situation and know where and how to look for the way out of the dangers that lie before us. He noted several times in the history of the human race on earth when an apparently irreversible decline and degeneration was turned around and a renewal and rebirth followed. It was evident to him that such positive developments are the consequence of neither new technologies nor better management and social planning, but they come about when societies understand their predicament, receive the grace to see the way out of it, and have the will and the energy to choose that path. Sorokin did not think the solution lay in his analysis (nor do we), but he hoped that his analysis would help society to understand the dangers and recognize the need to discover and take the way of creative resolution.

Sorokin's vision was not limited to the closed circle of earth. He was deeply aware of the fact that our human life is lived *coram Deo*—before God. God indeed allows us great freedom, which we may abuse for ill but we can also use for good, and he does not abandon us entirely to our own expedients but can and does offer "grace to help in time of need." For this reason, we too can believe that the sweeping changes that are inevitable do not necessarily mean degeneration; they can also lead to regeneration and renewal. Indeed, they will do so if we are "vouchsafed the grace of understanding" and act upon it.

Although a Russian Orthodox Christian himself, Sorokin did not call for an explicitly *Christian* revival or reorientation. However, in the cultural context in which he wrote, his appeals would naturally be given a Christian interpretation by many readers. Others, of course, would use the general and at times ambiguous way in which he spoke of spiritual realities and divine grace to plead in favor of a generic religiosity with no specific doctrinal content. Today it is necessary to be more explicit than he was. If we look for spiritual renewal and a recovery of moral values, we need to be able to say *whose* spirit and *what* values. In a civilization formed by Christianity, the logical place to look first is within the Christian heritage itself.[3]

Does such an element in fact exist within the Christian tradition and impulse, or need we look elsewhere? Is there anything sufficiently strong and stable within what remains of our civilization's Christian heritage to enable us to experience a renewal, a "new dawn," as Sorokin put it? Christians may hope so, although many have lost heart. Others may doubt it or even be hostile to the possibility, but in the light of the severity of the current crisis, they should not reject it out of hand.

RECOVERING THE PERMANENT THINGS

Our systemwide crisis needs a systemwide solution. The crisis, due to the disintegration of the form of culture that has dominated the Western world for nearly six centuries, has led to a loss of vision, a loss of a sense of calling and purpose, and, most importantly, to a loss of the three "permanent things" of which Paul spoke: "Faith, hope, love, these three" (1 Cor. 13:13). A popular Beatles song of the 1960s claimed, "All you need is love." But love is singularly lacking in Western civilization. America in particular is facing a crisis of violence in the home, in schools, and on the streets, in fictional form in the entertainment media, and even in sanitary clinics and hospitals where for suffering or unwanted patients, killing represents a solution.

This deficit in love has been accompanied by a loss of hope. Acquisitive love, the desire to possess the person or thing loved, is possible under the worst of conditions, but self-giving love, *agape*, needs to be able to *hope*. Despite the fact that the threat of imminent nuclear devastation has receded,

---

[3] It is customary in many intellectual, media, and political circles today to heap scorn on Christianity as a relic of the past, an obstacle to human progress and improvement. The difficulty with this assumption is that it may deprive the culture of a very important perservative and curative element.

neither Western culture in particular nor the world in general seems to have much hope or to be looking to the future with expectancy. Hope simply is not possible when there is no basis for confidence that things will turn out well.

How can individuals or societies have such a confidence when so much of what they see and hear all about them looks bleak and foreboding? The answer, of course, is *faith*, which has been defined as "being sure of what we hope for and certain of what we do not see (Heb. 11:1 NIV)." In other words, to revert to the specialized language of our sociological analysis, hope depends on confidence in supersensory realities, a confidence that can only be gained by means of faith.

It is generally conceded that Western society has all but abandoned a conscious awareness of and commitment to the faith out of which it grew. This does not mean that all of the individuals in our Western culture lack personal faith, but faith is increasingly banished from the structures of Western societies by supposedly neutral but in reality determinedly hostile and atheistic policies. For example, the government of the United States has never officially espoused atheism or rejected religion in general, and certainly not Christianity in particular. However, in a series of measures—especially in decisions of the Supreme Court—the American government has increasingly pushed all religions, and particularly Christianity, to the margins of society.

The expulsion of traditional religion has been accompanied by the incredible increase in violent crime, moral degradation, and all the elements of cultural chaos of which we have spoken. Too many factors are involved in the massive sociocultural shift of our era to permit one to argue that all is caused by a loss of faith. On the other hand, the signs of deterioration are so closely associated with the loss of faith, the disappearance of hope, and the deficit of love, that it would be absurd to deny the intimate connection of cause and effect.

Chinese society grew up with a highly pervasive orientation based on the philosophy—almost a religion—known as Confucianism. The Communist revolution under Mao sought to throw out Confucianism lock, stock, and barrel. The long-term results are not yet evident, but the whole world now knows the incredible carnage in life and happiness that Mao's revolution has wrought. Its effects are only now being dealt with and partially healed. Throwing out a millennia-old culture has been very costly for China, in part because it was done so violently. But was violence the only reason for the cost? We are throwing away our Christian culture in a nonviolent manner, but who can guarantee that because it is not violent, the loss will not be costly?

Karl Marx derided all religion (including the Christian religion that he had once professed) as an "opiate of the people"—a narcotic enabling them to endure miseries for hope of a better world to come. Marx thought he could eliminate Christianity and yet preserve hope, indeed improve hope, by pointing to a better life, a more perfect society in this world. This was a substitute eschatology, and Marxism was, in Arthur Koestler's expression, "the god that failed"—an opiate far worse than Marx thought the teachings of Christ or Confucius. Without faith in the eventual victory of good over evil in the Kingdom of God and the prospect of eternal life, human societies in the West have progressively lost hope. Like Marx and Hitler, secular Western thinkers and politicians once proclaimed a faith in the future limited to this world, but they have failed disastrously. In the Western nations that succumbed neither to Marxism nor to Hitler, the secular varieties of hope have not been imposed by force, but here too their failure is becoming increasingly undeniable. Here and there political leaders still seek to inspire the masses with promises of a bright future, but there remains a widespread sense that our problems are beyond us, that humanity is already living on borrowed time, and that the clock is running out.

What can we hope for at the end of the second millennium? It is symbolic for the loss of hope that the great medical advances of the late 1990s are not cures for cancer and AIDS but euthanasia and abortion—methods in which "killing represents a solution. " A "solution" of this kind can hardly be a source of hope. As long as the concepts of a loving God and the promise of eternal life were important elements of the consciousness of most people in the West (even if not firmly believed), other lesser promises, such as full employment, peace, or a cure for heart disease, could help to promote a sense of confidence and hope for the future. However, without the undergirding confidence that there is a God with a beneficent purpose for humanity, such lesser promises are insufficient to sustain confidence.

Without faith, both individuals and societies lose hope, and without hope, individuals and societies begin to lose love, both in the sense of disinterested, self-giving love, and in the more familiar sense of strong emotional attraction and commitment. Western society is increasingly becoming a society of love-lessness, with a rising tide of internal violence of all kinds on every side.

If the present systemwide crisis of Western culture involves a loss of these "permanent things" and indeed is largely a consequence of their loss, it is reasonable to assume that the crisis can only be overcome by a recovery of these values, by a renewed access to the source from which they arise. Will such access be gained? The result will depend in part on which of two currently opposing movements eventually comes to prevail:

1. The renewal and revival of a religious vision, especially of a Christian vision, which can be observed in a beginning stage in several Western societies.

2. The increasing hostility to religion in general and to Christianity in particular in governmental, media, and educational circles in many of those same societies.

At the end of the twentieth century the society based on Christendom is in crisis. Many of the world's people may say, "That does not concern us. Our people are not Christian and never have been." That may be true, but while the traditionally Christian powers no longer rule most of the world, their influence permeates it, and any dramatic change within Christendom will affect the entire world. Even within nations that once took it for granted that they were "Christian," the official posture is that they are "secular" or "lay" and that Christianity is but one religion among many—a more or less useful (or dangerous) private hobby. People say, "We are not Christians, and are not going to become Christian. Our society is pluralistic and multicultural. There is no established church; there are no official doctrines. The fate of the religion and of so-called Christian culture is irrelevant to us."

Today, even within nations where more than half of the people formally belong to a church, it is unlikely that many of them think that their own future and that of their society is deeply involved in the crisis of Christendom. In actual fact, however, Western civilization is so permeated by Christianity that the crisis of Christendom is inevitably also the crisis of Western civilization, and the world is so permeated by Western civilization that the crisis of the West becomes the crisis of the world.

Christianity remains more firmly established among the general population in the United States than in any other Western country. (The growth of Christianity in South Korea has been so significant that it may now be stronger in that Asian country than in several nominally Christian European nations.) Despite this—or perhaps for this very reason—Christianity is now being more heavily attacked from within the governmental and social power structures in America than in any other Western country, with the possible exception of Canada. It is at least possible that in the very place where there is the greatest potential for a recovery of a sense of the "permanent things" in the general population, government pressure may be brought in to prevent it.

It is important to remember, therefore, that great cultural shifts such as those we are discussing may sometimes be retarded or advanced by government action, although they cannot be caused or prevented thereby. If the United States government, for example, were to throw itself wholeheartedly behind some form of religious renewal, it could not bring that renewal about. Conversely, if renewal is under way and the government should try to suppress it, it could not be any more successful than the governments of imperial Rome in the past or of Communist China today. Renewal and recovery of whole cultures depends on large numbers of people receiving the "grace of understanding," accepting it, and acting upon it. Governments can foster or hinder the manifestations of this understanding, but they can neither generate nor suppress the grace that produces it.

The sensate culture around us has virtually exhausted itself. There are no forces within it that could permit it to recover the vitality it possessed for several centuries. In fact, the decline of the present sensate culture is becoming so precipitous that a complete social disintegration threatens several societies. This can be prevented only by one of two things: rigorous, intensive governmental controls such as those envisaged by George Orwell in *Nineteen Eighty-Four*, or a fundamental reorientation such as late imperial Roman society experienced in the fourth and fifth centuries of the Christian era.

REORIENTATION

Our Western culture was formed by Christianity, but it now contains many different and discordant elements, some of which actively repudiate whatever they recognize of its Christian base and reject it as false and oppressive. The confident, positive orientation toward man and his destiny, indeed toward truth itself, which Christianity maintained, has been forgotten or explicitly rejected.

The late sensate culture of the Roman world, like ours, was diverse and pluralistic. The innate tendency of a sensate culture to syncretism and colossalism runs counter to the principle of integration; an integrated system exhibits an integrated, coherent world and life view, but as the sensate culture ripens and begins to decay, it also disintegrates and manifests mutually conflicting trends and views. When the sensate society of late Roman paganism was transformed by adopting Christianity, it once again achieved a relatively unified world and life view. Our own late sensate culture manifests an even greater chaotic syncretism than did late Roman culture because it has taken in elements not merely from the Mediterranean, North African, and West Asian spheres, but from the entire world. The mass communications media have the ability to confront communities and individuals any place in the world with cultural and social patterns drawn from other places and societies, to place differing, clashing views and traditions alongside one another, and thus to make it increasingly difficult for an individual or a culture to take any particular set of standards for granted or to know how to evaluate differing standards and determine which ones are best.

Our culture is now at a crucial point. It must either experience a far-reaching reorientation and renewal, or it must disintegrate into chaos. Signs of incipient chaos are already visible in many aspects of North American life; Western Europe appears more stable by contrast, but even in Western Europe forces already present are causing serious strains and potentially can cause total disruption. During the twentieth century, two movements attempted to create a fundamental reorientation:

1. The Nazi movement was based on a narrow theme, potentially appealing to only one racial group among many. Its attempt at self-aggrandizement was crushed in blood and ashes after scarcely a decade.

215

2. Marxism also represented a unified world and life view—one that explicitly repudiated not only Christianity but all religions and all supersensory reality. Marxism has now been banished virtually everywhere in Europe and the Americas, and its doctrines and worldview no longer command popular enthusiasm or allegiance anywhere in Christendom. Nevertheless, the passing of that great, unified system of doctrines and values has not yet meant a return to the older Christian orientation in Russia and elsewhere.

Nazism had a quasi-religious aspect, although it called itself scientific; Marxism claimed to be totally materialistic as well as scientific. Both ideologies represented attempts to set up a unified cultural system in place of the increasingly chaotic syncretism all around them. Neither Nazism nor Marxism could be successfully maintained despite their ruthless use of force. Nazism was defeated by foreign adversaries, but even if this had not taken place, it is likely that its inherent tensions and contradictions would have caused it to fall in fewer than the seven decades required by Soviet Marxism. It seems apparent that attempts to reintegrate the disintegrating sensate culture on a materialistic base, even when imposed by force, cannot succeed for long. The great question is this: What can replace it?

12

END OR
NEW BEGINNING?

*. . . and all our pomp of yesteryear is
one with Nineveh and Tyre.*

Rudyard Kipling

WHAT LIES AHEAD FOR THE HEIRS of Western culture? What lies ahead for world civilization, which is so intimately involved with Western culture? Indeed, what lies ahead for the human race? There are several possible outcomes of our present systemwide crisis; only one of them is hopeful. Sorokin writes of the "sole course of salvation open to us." It is important to identify that course and try to see what each element of our society—individuals, communities, institutions, and structures—can do to steer the development in the right direction, the one that "leads not to death but to the further realization of man's unique creative mission on this planet."[1] This present exhausted, degenerate phase of Western Civilization *need not* foreshadow the end of our culture and civilization, but it inevitably will if certain present trends are prolonged to their logical conclusion and more promising ones are choked off or suppressed before they have a chance to bear fruit.

---

[1] Pitirim A. Sorokin, *The Crisis of Our Age*, 2d ed. (Oxford: Oneworld, 1992), 264.

ECLIPSE

One "solution" to the cultural crisis of Western civilization is eclipse. In view of the tremendous scientific, industrial, and economic potential of the nations of the West, it may not seem the least bit plausible to suggest that Western culture may go into a permanent eclipse and end in the situation predicted by Kipling in his poem "Recessional." It is certainly not impossible that the culture of the West will become one with Nineveh and Tyre, those vanished cities of history and legend.

Is it altogether unlikely that the rich and powerful nations of the West, including the United States (the only remaining superpower at the end of the twentieth century), could suddenly shrivel and disappear from the world stage or at least be reduced to impotence? For a time in the late 1970s, after the humiliation of the United States in Vietnam, it seemed to much of the rest of the world that the USSR was the one remaining superpower. Even during the 1980s many U.S. defense experts feared that the USSR would react to President Reagan's efforts to rearm the West with a devastating first strike against the United States.

As late as 1988 the nations of the West still thought of themselves as confronted by a powerful, united bloc of forces committed to their ultimate defeat if not destruction. Soviet efforts to take over the West by subterfuge or outright aggression provided the material for novelists and filmmakers. Then, almost without warning, the Soviet colossus started to come apart. It began with the mass exodus of population from East Germany—the German Democratic Republic—in 1989 and culminated with the abortive coup d'état in Moscow in the summer of 1991, a last-ditch effort to maintain the "evil empire" in its familiar form. The coup failed, and its failure precipitated the complete breakup of the Soviet Union and its disappearance from the world stage at the end of that year. By the beginning of 1995, the once mighty Russian army found itself embarrassingly frustrated by the resistance of one small group of little more than a million rebellious people in the Caucasus.

Could it happen here? No one expects the United States—rich, powerful, with armed forces scattered around the world and vast economic interests on every continent—suddenly to crumble and collapse. But then no one expected it of the

Soviet Union either. In the great, wealthy nations that form the heartland of Western civilization, there are factors already present that could produce similar debacles on a large scale. *Sic transit gloria mundi* (Thus passes the glory of the world).

DETERIORATING SOCIAL SYSTEMS

Every system needs to be able to recognize what belongs to it and what does not. Ours no longer can. Some systems, especially most machines, cannot repair themselves but must be repaired by an entity outside themselves. Some complex systems (chiefly living organisms) do have an ability to repair themselves, provided they are not disrupted in the process by the introduction of factors that do not belong to them and that they cannot recognize.

- The human body recognizes organs that do not belong to it and will reject even the healthiest organ transplant unless the most precise efforts are made to neutralize the body's natural immune reaction.

- Machines and industrial systems can process only the materials for which they were designed. A plant that processes coal to make synthetic gasoline will not process potatoes or iron ore—at least not without substantial modifications.

- If a family loses the mother through death or divorce, the children will seldom accept another woman, even one of the same age, size, and background, as their mother without a considerable period of adjustment, and perhaps not even then.

- When a football team calls a time out and sends an injured halfback off the field, it will not accept the best baseball pitcher as a replacement. It will not even accept a halfback from the opposing team—at least not without a major reorientation.

- When an infantry unit has suffered losses in combat, those soldiers cannot be replaced with sailors, even sailors from the same nation, nor can they easily be replaced by infantry speaking another language and armed with different weapons.

- If a Roman Catholic bishop is killed in an accident, he cannot readily be replaced by a Methodist bishop, much less a Hindu priest, a Buddhist monk, or a Democratic precinct captain.

These are self-evident facts. Is it reasonable to expect that larger and more complex systems such as cities, states, nations, and national economies have no need and no ability to recognize what belongs to them? May we suppose that such complex social structures will simply and naturally integrate new, alien elements without problems instead of rejecting them outright, or at least demanding that they adjust and adapt before being accepted?

A culture is in some ways like an organism. There is a limit to how much stress it can stand. The most powerful industrial nations of Europe, Germany, France, Great Britain, and Italy are wealthy and apparently sound, yet each one has problems that could cause a sudden crisis. Several of the most serious of these arise because the social systems have become porous and cannot define and identify their own borders, can no longer tell what belongs to them and what does not, and therefore cannot initiate the modifications that are necessary to keep a society integrated and functioning. The states of the newly formed European Union now have no passport controls at their mutual borders. One of them, Italy, cannot watch over its entire long coastline; as a result, immigrants from many countries can land in Italy and then make their way to their preferred destinations anywhere else in the Union.

Several major social problems have been with the Western nations for so long that they are simply accepted as facts of life. Chronic large-scale unemployment, especially of the young, is one of these that can make aliens—and eventually enemies—of citizens. When large numbers of people are out of work, even with unemployment compensation, or, even worse, are altogether without adequate means of support, they cease to function as integral members of society. Broken families, fatherless children, and homeless people lose their function and place in society. Society ceases to "recognize" them; they no longer have a place in society, and it no longer knows how to deal with them. They themselves can no longer tell what their function is or should be. Alienated through no fault of their own, they contribute to the society's disintegration, especially when present in large numbers. Groups and subgroups that do not share an accepted social and moral orientation become hard for the society to identify. As a result, the society has difficulty finding a place for them or giving them valuable tasks to perform and useful and satisfying roles to play. This is not to say that strangers simply cannot be integrated and must inevitably disrupt a society but rather that points of contact must be found or created so that strangers will cease to be "strange" and can participate in a society without causing it to disintegrate.

During the first three-quarters of our national existence, the United States was extraordinarily successful in creating such points of contact. People from various backgrounds and diverse religious traditions were integrated into a common national life. Currently the task in the United States has become much more difficult because of government policy during the past three decades. It preferentially admits immigrants from backgrounds and cultures that are even more diverse than those of the existing population, it has done little to impede the flood of illegal immigrants, and the new social orthodoxy known as multiculturalism discourages immigrants from making an effort to adapt.

In the present state of world development, large-scale open warfare between religions *appears* unthinkable. Yet there were over a thousand years of open warfare between Muslims and Christians that began with the Arab aggressions after A.D. 636, were resumed in the Crusades of the eleventh through the thirteenth centuries, were continued by the Muslim Turks in the East and the Christian Spanish in the West, and were resumed again and again by the different parties. They more or less ended with the defeat of the Turks at Vienna in 1683 (if we do not count wars in Africa, Arabia, and the Crimea). Civil war in the Balkans and genocidal persecution of Christians in the Sudan should remind us that peaceful coexistence between Muslims and Christians is not a thing that can be taken for granted.

Even where violent conflict does not seem at all likely, religious tensions are rising in two of the European nations that traditionally have had integrated cultures and have been the foremost examples of much that is good in Western civilization—Germany and France.[2] The Christian culture of these two leading nations has weakened over the past century. Since World War II, they

---

[2] Germany and France have also given examples of some of the things that are worst in Western culture, namely revolutionary terror, wars of conquest, and Nazism.

have admitted but failed to integrate millions of Muslim Turks and Arabs, who for their part come from old, rich, and proud cultures. These newcomers are not ready to abandon their own traditions and become Frenchmen or Germans, even though their own familiar customs and attitudes are found strange and often received with hostility in their new countries. Can they fit into their new fatherlands?

To admit large numbers of people from another culture into an existing social structure will inevitably cause strains. The situation is aggravated when leading representatives of the host culture—government leaders, intellectuals, and media pundits—are in effect ashamed of it and make no effort to introduce the newcomers to it. When the two cultures have a history of mutual rejection and hostility, as do Christians and Muslims or France and its former North African colonies, problems are inevitable.

The task of harmonious integration is a challenging one, certainly not impossible, but one that will require tact, patience, time, and tolerance. In modern industrial nations, employers are generally interested only in getting the work they want at the lowest possible cost, not in helping immigrants relate to the surrounding culture. In many cases the cultural leaders, influenced by pluralism and multiculturalism, encourage the newcomers to create and maintain alien enclaves in the larger society. This is one of the unintended effects of the well-intentioned program of bilingual education in the United States.

Consider what havoc cultural diversity can reap when these four factors—tact, patience, time, and tolerance—are lacking and when the diversity is pushed to its extreme limits, sometimes with arrogance on the part of the newcomers. A frightening example of what the future may bring is presented by the civil war in Bosnia-Herzegovina. As long as the sultan or the Hapsburgs ruled, or even the Communist dictatorship of Yugoslavia, the tensions in Bosnia-Herzegovina were subdued and did not result in open warfare. The ethnic differences are not great, and all of the people speak the same language, but without unity and a shared sense of common purpose, Roman Catholic Croats, Orthodox Serbs, and Muslims drawn from both nationalities have brought disaster to what was once a moderately stable and socially viable society.

When formerly integrated nations are Balkanized—France becoming perhaps one-quarter Algerian, Germany one-fifth Turkish, or Italy one-sixth Albanian—will they be immune to the kind of disruption that wracks Bosnia?

It may be objected that developments in the Balkans hardly threaten the rest of Europe, and certainly not the world. Nevertheless, the factors that have caused immense disruption and suffering in Yugoslavia are present and growing in other larger and strategically more important places where they have not yet caused generalized conflict and violence.

In every nation of Western Europe there are persistent structural problems of unemployment, agricultural overproduction, abandonment of the family farm, aging, and population decline, to name but a few. There is dislocation, disruption, uprootedness, and a sense of purposelessness even among the people who are ethnically, linguistically, and religiously part of the same culture. Certainly those who are still strangers must feel these tensions even more strongly.

Europe has gradually learned how to live with the religious tensions between the major Christian confessions. Will its still nominally Christian majority be able to live peaceably and productively with an increasingly assertive Muslim minority? Now that Communism has lost its great Soviet power base, it seems that many once frightened nations are slipping into a tranquil slumber, as though no further life-threatening challenges need to be feared. Religious tensions could well become more dangerous than ideological differences both within individual nations and between nations.

The tension between Islam and Christianity is potentially the most dangerous for Western culture. The Muslims have created a number of high cultures over the centuries, but they are hardly in a position to duplicate this accomplishment where they are in the minority. What they can do is to dilute and ultimately destroy the remnants of the Christian foundations of Western culture, with results that are impossible to predict but that are hardly likely to include social stability.[3] Since World War II, millions of Muslims have entered Western Europe as guest workers and refugees, and smaller numbers have entered the United States, where their influence is to some extent augmented by the Black Muslim movement. They now constitute substantial, undigested minorities in countries that until recently were uniformly Christian.

---

[3] It is important to keep in mind that the problem is caused not so much by an influx of immigrants from diverse backgrounds as by the failure of the leading elements in the receiving society to integrate them into the host culture.

Many Muslim and non-Muslim scholars dismiss as unfounded the suspicion that the Muslims in general or the immigrants in particular have any plan or program to subvert or remake the culture of their host countries. That at least *some* Muslims would like to reduce both Christianity and Judaism to submission seems undeniable. On the other side, there are energetic if modest efforts on the part of some Christians not to actually subjugate Muslims but to make Christians of them. (The majority of Christians, however, seem content to leave the Muslims in peace, unmolested by missionary efforts.)

The possibility of Muslims contributing to the destabilization of Western culture is our concern here, because it relates to the crisis of *Western* culture. The West has now been moderately infiltrated with Muslim minorities, while some of the majority Muslim areas that once had substantial Christian minorities, such as Algeria and Turkey, now no longer do. Thus the likelihood of internal religious tensions causing major social problems is greater in the West than elsewhere. Many people in government and intellectual circles in the nominally Christian West view this development with surprising indifference. Perhaps because they do not take their own inherited religion seriously, it does not occur to them that others may do so, and that in the case of Muslims, many do.

In several countries, nativist and racist movements have arisen. They are not yet strong enough to cause major disruptions of social harmony, and because of the indifference of the upper classes and intellectuals to the problem, they are based largely in the lower and lower middle classes and do not enjoy much social prestige. These are precisely the classes that are most affected by economic problems. When jobs are threatened, the economy is deteriorating, medical costs are soaring, and government instead of having solutions seems interested chiefly in expanding its own power, there is a possibility that unstable elements in the population will unleash chaotic violence.

Historically, revolutions usually occur not when a population is suffering the worst privation, hardship, and oppression but when a relatively prosperous and somewhat free people thinks that its freedom and prosperity are being taken away. Unfortunately, most of the great revolutions of modern times have reduced the people to a far worse situation than they had before. This happened dramatically in France, Russia, and Iran as well as in a number of other places.

In each case, the disorder and confusion brought on by the revolution invited attacks by foreign powers. If any great nation of the West undergoes real disruption, it is likely other powers will be prepared to intervene and take charge. If a generalized chaos and confusion should arise, it is even more likely that the debilitated nations of the West will find themselves at best placed under some kind of a mandate, at worst totally subjugated by powers they recently disdained.

If this prospect seems unrealistic, consider the fact that Russia, the successor state to the once mighty Soviet Union, which only a short time ago was in a position to threaten the entire world with nuclear annihilation, has found it difficult to master the rebellion of a republic of 1.2 million people. The pressure of poor and starving populations and the temptation that rich, self-indulgent, and smug Western societies offer them make violent conflict not merely conceivable but probable.

In short, one possible outcome of the current systemwide crisis of Western civilization is the catastrophic collapse and subsequent subordination of the proud peoples of the West to other peoples—stronger, more numerous, and more determined, if perhaps less "civilized" in our sense of the word. If one were able to contemplate this from God's perspective, it might seem merely one further step in the march of humanity. From the perspective of those who belong to Western civilization, the possibility of the collapse of our culture, even if it does not entail the extermination of our peoples, is hardly one to regard with tranquillity. Eclipse is a real possibility.

A SECULAR AWAKENING: WOULD IT HELP? COULD IT HAPPEN?

The nations of the Western world have grown rich and strong thanks to individual freedom and the right and ability of individuals to work for themselves and develop their creative and productive potential to the fullest. Individualism and regionalism have been crucial to the development of Western culture. The current worldwide tendency to create ever larger structures runs absolutely contrary to the fundamental principle of Western culture since the advent of Christianity, which is to allow the greatest possible variety of national, ethnic, linguistic, and even religious expression within a broad but common and shared framework.[4]

Each of the major Western nations consisted at one time of many small communities where people knew each other and where at least a measure of public interest, community spirit, and mutual solidarity was a matter of course. Within the West, although neither charity nor welfare in the modern sense was organized by the rulers or governments, the Christian churches preached charity and compassion, and the state expected and honored such attitudes. Laissez-faire capitalism—every man for himself and the devil take the hindmost—was tempered and made more bearable, even in the absence of government welfare programs, by the religious doctrines and practice of charity and compassion.[5]

As long as the traditional religious and other nongovernmental bodies in the West promoting charity and compassion were effective, they greatly mitigated the lot of the poor and underprivileged. Traditional providers of charity—not yet redefined as "welfare"—were weakened and eventually made irrelevant by two developments during the last century:

1. *Darwinism.* Darwin proclaimed the principle of the "survival of the fittest" as a biological axiom; social Darwinism elevated it to a moral imperative and thus justified letting the less fit suffer and disappear. This helped capitalists to rationalize the rapacity of their laissez-faire system and, before the monstrous horrors of world war sobered even the militarists, Darwin's theories were cited to prove that war is necessary for the advancement of civilization.

2. *Government welfare programs.* During the nineteenth century, governments began to supplant the churches and private agencies, including the family, in providing a measure of assistance and

---

[4] Organizations such as the United Nations, with its ill-fated "peacekeeping" forces dispatched here and there around the globe, NATO (the North Atlantic Treaty Organization), NAFTA (the North American Free Trade Association), and WTO (World Trade Organization) reflect an eagerness to creat a "new world order" (a term used by then U.S. President George Bush, borrowed unwittingly from the late German Führer Adolf Hitler).

[5] See Marvin Olasky, *The Tragedy of Christian Compassion* (Downers Grove, Ill.: Crossway, 1993).

relief to those falling by the wayside in the economic race. The existence of growing government assistance programs gave to many a sense that private agencies and individual charity were no longer necessary and salved the consciences of the selfish and greedy. Extreme individualism has come to characterize Western culture since the Enlightenment, a movement that weakened both the Christian churches and Christian faith. Extreme individualism is not compatible with Christianity—nor with most other religious systems—but unfortunately, at the end of the second millennium, Christianity in the West appears too weak, too fragmented, and too confused to challenge it effectively.

Religion—or Hero Worship—Can Contribute

There are several examples in history where smaller or larger societies that appeared to be headed for disaster have taken stock of their situation, undergone a fundamental reorientation of values, and reversed what seemed like an irreversible slide into decadence and decline. Two such popular revivals were the resurgence of East Roman or Byzantine civilization after a series of catastrophic defeats by the Arabs. The religious movement known as Iconoclasm was a factor in this resurgence. (Iconoclasm was later rejected by Eastern Orthodoxy.) The revitalization of English society and power in the eighteenth century owed much to the religious revival sparked by John and Charles Wesley and George Whitfield. In both cases, the renewals spread across the whole culture and achieved long-lasting results. In neither case, of course, did it involve the kind of fundamental change of an entire supersystem that was represented by the transformation of the late Roman sensate culture into the early Christian ideational culture, but the changes they brought were substantial and the results they achieved were impressive.

Hero Worship and Pseudoreligion

Closer to our own day, we have witnessed national renewals that were not based on familiar religious values. Instead they involved a spiritual appeal to

227

ancient or Nordic ideals: the Italian and German "renewals" under Mussolini and Hitler. In both of these cases, charismatic "heroes" were able to rouse a demoralized Italian and a defeated German people and spur them on to great accomplishments and terrible deeds. Neither Mussolini nor Hitler built upon what remained of Christian conviction and commitment among their peoples, but at times they pirated Christian terminology and concepts for their own purposes. Their appeals for national and ethnic renewal pointed instead to the real or imagined glories of ancient Rome or the Germanic race, sometimes in messianic language.

These examples of forcible, ideologically based efforts at the renewal of culture are not such as inspire optimism. The Soviet effort, which lasted from 1917 until 1991, was hardly better, although it scored greater successes. Even at the point when it was breaking down, there were still enthusiasts and propagandists outside the Soviet bloc praising it for trying to create a "new Soviet man" and to bring in a beautiful future for the human race. It is apparent that this tremendous effort, which cost tens of millions of human beings their lives and additional millions every shred of decency and dignity, has been an abysmal failure and has left a social and moral chaos behind it.[6] The ongoing efforts to create a Marxist society are now located chiefly outside the Western world; with the exception of Cuba, by the early 1990s Communism had vanished from the West. It would seem that it has totally failed. Pseudoreligions are dangerous remedies for cultural decline, but they keep cropping up.

In several countries, leaders have promised renewal, often using pretentious and even messianic-sounding language:

"my New Order" and "the Thousand-Year Reich"—Hitler

"the New Deal"—Roosevelt

"the New Frontier"—Kennedy

"the Great Society"—Johnson

---

[6] The new Russian government has opened its arms and its borders to spiritual influences of all kinds, and traditional and nontraditional Christian bodies as well as representatives of other religions and old and new spiritual movements are taking advantage of this receptivity. If a new ideational or idealistic culture does in fact lie before us, it might begin in Russia.

"the Cultural Revolution"—Mao

"the New American Revolution"—Nixon

"the New Covenant"—Clinton

A variant that was not sent down from the top was "the revolution of the sixties," a sort of Rousseauist hope that by destroying the "hypocrisy" of petty bourgeois, Christian-tinged morality and conventions, a new "Age of Aquarius" would drop down out of somewhere.

Of course the picture is not entirely bleak. In addition to these efforts to impose renewal and cultural change on a people, usually by force, there have been lesser but still significant examples of partial renewals—examples that reveal that societal degeneration can be checked even if they are not broad enough or sufficiently enduring to provide a pattern for the renewal of the entire culture of the West. Following the Second World War, liberated France and defeated West Germany developed fresh energies and enjoyed a substantial renewal, again under the leadership of charismatic figures—Charles de Gaulle and Konrad Adenauer—but without religious overtones. These brief national renewals, not yet a full half-century in the past, have already largely spent themselves. They did not involve a fundamental reorientation but only temporary and partial changes of values and emphasis. Nevertheless, they show that downward trends are not absolutely irreversible. Although they were limited and of short duration, they offer hope that a more thorough renewal may lie in our future.

Most of these efforts and programs—good and evil—relied on the kind of "facile but shallow artifices" of which Sorokin writes. The two that came closest to involving fundamental reorientations were the worst, namely those of Hitler and Mao. Hitler's ended with much of the world in ashes. After causing an immense but often hidden holocaust among his own people, Mao's renewal also seems to be in decline and is retreating from some of its most ambitious ideals without actually renouncing them or admitting they are unattainable. The "Age of Aquarius"—the nonpolitical "revolution of the sixties"—also involved a fundamental reorientation but, unlike Hitler and Mao, it had no power structures to enforce its vision, and it remained a melancholy tribute to wishful thinking.

The efforts and temporary successes of these recent leaders were possible because the peoples whom they addressed and sought to renew were in distress and looking for ways out. Unfortunately, the popular mind did not grasp the fundamental nature of the problem but attributed it to foreign enemies, evil individuals, selfish corporations, greedy minorities, oppressive structures, and the like and thus deluded themselves that a convulsive effort against the perceived enemies and structural abuses would open a wonderful future for their nations. As the wonderful futures have vanished, some buried in blood and ashes like Hitler's, others simply evaporating in the midst of faltering economic structures and collapsing social orders, the people of several countries have become progressively more disillusioned and less willing to anticipate that changes of any kind will be truly beneficial.

Sorokin's Spiritual Vision

Sorokin, although formally a Christian himself, did not emphasize a specifically Christian element in the renewal for which he hoped. He anticipated that renewal might come by means of a reorientation that would in effect adopt most of the moral and ethical principles of Jesus but without the label. These principles are essentially Jewish in origin and are largely compatible with the ethical teachings of the other higher religions. They come without the necessity of conversion or dogmatic commitment. Sorokin called for "creative altruism" and established a short-lived university center to foster it.

Sorokin's hope for what may be called a nondogmatic spiritual renewal was not unique. His idea resembles another nondogmatic attempt to introduce many Christian principles into public consciousness and public life: the "Oxford Group" movement founded by Frank Buchman. There have been other efforts at such a nondogmatic moral renewal, particularly during the period of hopeful anticipation at the close of World War II. However, no real change has resulted from them; indeed, the crisis has continued to intensify. They reveal the weakness of moral uplift without a firm foundation in faith.

There is a widespread awareness that moral reorientation is necessary. It is reemphasized in every American political campaign, but very little of a concrete nature is done to bring it about. The failure of the efforts for renewal by force and the impotence of the attempts to bring it about by pious wishes reveals the urgency of Sorokin's repeated contention that divine help is necessary. If we human beings are confined entirely to our own resources, the difficulties will remain insurmountable. The difficulty is that appeals for grace are generally couched in terms of a specific kind of religious renewal and, therefore, immediately run into opposition from the cultural forces that reject religious institutions and specific doctrinal commitments. Even rather broad appeals for moral reorientation and renewal are widely rejected if they bear a specific religious coloration.[7] Spiritual renewal is seen by many to be necessary, but "generic" spirituality is not possible. Hence, proposals for renewal must be offered from an identifiable religious perspective, and as soon as that happens, it immediately runs into opposition that threatens to stifle it before it begins.

INDIVIDUAL RENEWAL: BEGINNING WITH ME

Some leaders see individual change as the key. Among them, the best known of our era is the great evangelist of the twentieth century, Billy Graham, of whom it is said that he has preached to more people than any other man in history. Graham sees personal conversion to Christ as the starting point. Consequently, his efforts and those of others who agree with him can hardly have a great impact on people who are not ready to accept Christianity, for in effect they must accept the Christian message of personal regeneration before turning their attention to societal renewal. The message of Graham and other Christian evangelists is specific, clear, and if widely accepted, certainly would change society. Yet precisely because of their religious specificity, messages such as Graham's are dismissed out of hand by some segments of society and actively opposed by others.

Mild forms of a generally Christian or Judeo-Christian renewal program have been offered by Pitirim Sorokin, Frank Buchman, Martin Luther King Jr., and others who came out of a Christian milieu themselves but hoped to appeal across

---

[7] In the United States, the formation of the Christian Coalition has aroused vehement opposition from the media and much of the political and intellectual establishment, despite the fact that the Coalition's goals are not so different from what would formerly have been considered ordinary human decency.

religious and confessional boundaries to people in general. All these saw their appeals for a fresh understanding of our crisis and a fresh determination to find and follow the altruistic way out of it fall on deaf ears. Perhaps Sorokin, although disappointed, should not have been surprised, for he warned that we need the "grace of understanding." Even if this grace is granted—and all those who think that God exists and has a purpose for humanity hopefully expect that it will be granted—understanding and obedience on our part are also required.

THE CONVERSION OF A CULTURE

Can an entire culture "be converted"—i.e., turn away from entrenched patterns of selfishness and self-indulgence and replace them with patterns of altruism? Can an entire society begin to act in accordance with the Second Great Commandment, "Thou shalt love thy neighbour as thyself" (Matt. 22:39 KJV)? So fundamental a change in orientation cannot be commanded by dictators, however sincerely and earnestly they may try, as the disastrous failures of Communism show. Neither can it be organized by social engineers nor be effectively promoted by moral preaching. The spirit that Sorokin, Buchman, King, and others like them wanted to see permeate society can come only in the wake of a massive cultural shift. Our analysis suggests that such a shift is beginning to take place. Such a spirit accompanied the rise of Christianity; perhaps it would accompany a renewal of Christianity—not of ecclesiastical power or theocratic structures but of the spirit of its Founder, as expressed in the Beatitudes of the Sermon on the Mount (see Matt. 5:3–11).

The late Roman Empire was so jaded and disillusioned that it was ripe for transformation by the new religion of Christianity. Is our sociocultural supersystem similarly ready? It surely is jaded and disillusioned. Virtues, ideals, and heroism are regularly derided in the media and the arts. It is inevitably taken for granted that anyone who espouses firm ethical principles, praises virtue, or dares to express criticism of anything that classical Judeo-Christian morality condemns will be derided as judgmental, puritanical, and in all likelihood hypocritical.

Every society needs a moral core, a shared consensus on principles and ideals in order to remain viable. The progressive dismantling of the principles and ideals that have created Western culture has reached a point where the society will soon cease to be self-sustaining. If that happens, either the social fabric will unravel, plunging the culture into chaos, or a complex system of controls will have to be instituted to preserve order at the expense of freedom. Such a system could be either harshly totalitarian, like that of the former Soviet Empire, or milder and outwardly benevolent. An example is the sort of state paternalism exhibited in Swedish socialism, which is repressive not only toward all local traditions and voluntary associations, but of the family structure and of individuality. The only alternative to the disintegration of the social fabric is a widespread and general reawakening of the public to the kinds of truths, principles, and ideals that characterize ideational and idealistic cultures.

If we take the short-term view and look no farther back in history than the early days of our sensate culture, we will see only deterioration and disintegration and can only expect things to grow worse at an accelerating rate unless a benevolent or malevolent despot appears to establish a semblance of order and cohesiveness. If instead we look farther and observe how sensate cultures have been renewed, especially in the shift that transformed pagan Rome into Christian Europe, we have good reason to hope for something better. What will be required is a fundamental reorientation, a fresh appropriation of transcendent beliefs and values. This is something that no government can require by law or impose by reeducation; it must come from above human heads and be taken into human hearts.

If it is to happen, it certainly must happen before and instead of the desperate resort to total state control and total planning that characterized the former Soviet Union and is still being attempted in Communist China. When the unstable but still Christian and Western culture of imperial Russia collapsed under the German pounding and the internal misery and disorder of World War I, an intense effort was made to replace traditional values with a state-imposed Communist morality and to create new Socialist man. This immense effort suddenly collapsed in 1991, and it has become clear that the abolition of the moral and altruistic base of Russian Christianity, with all its faults and inconsistencies, was not replaced by something better but by a moral vacuum. The

Russians and the other nationalities that people the vast territory of the former USSR are finding it very difficult to put something in its place, and plaintive voices asking for a return to tyranny are already being raised across that vast territory.

PROSPECTS IN THE "NARROWER WEST"

Unlike the Soviet Union and several of its successor states—which belong to Western culture in the broader sense—the narrower West, Western Europe and North America, has not suffered the moral and spiritual privation of decades of monolithic, materialistic dictatorship. More remnants of the ideational and idealistic foundations of Christianity have survived in the narrower West, but the cultural fatigue and disillusionment of Western Europe and North America is profound. Are the wealthy nations of the West in any sense ready to receive the "grace of understanding," if it is given, and to act upon it? That is the great question. The answer will determine whether the spiritual twilight that we now experience is the darkness before the dawn or the dark before the deepest night.

The sense that moral renewal is needed is widespread in the West, but there is also widespread fear and apprehension about the spiritual and moral choices, decisions, and sacrifices that must be made in order to bring it about. Awareness of the fact that the entire national welfare system must die within a few years if corrective measures are not taken is not sufficient to persuade the American public to make *any* sacrifices today, even if it is pointed out that the "sacrifices" do not involve *reduction* of benefits but simply a slowing down of *increases* in government largesse. One may well wonder whether a population that is so unwilling to sacrifice any of its comforts today in order not to lose them all tomorrow is morally and spiritually capable of receiving and acting upon the grace of understanding if a gracious Deity should grant it. Is it capable of choosing any virtue, no matter how noble and edifying, if to do so it must pay even a small price in comfort and ease?

If we conclude that the people do not have that capability, then there is little that can be done other than to attempt to make America's slide into chaos

234

or totalitarianism as slow and agreeable as possible. Is there no alternative then, no hope to get off the "broad road that leads to destruction"?

There is a spot of bright light on this pessimistic landscape; indeed, it could be the glow that marks the sun shining through clouds that are beginning to break up and scatter. If human beings are made in the image of the divine, then man and human society cannot indefinitely be deaf to the voice of conscience and blind to the vision of virtue. Individuals here and there have listened and looked up, and voices—for the moment voices *clamantes in deserto* (crying in the desert), few and scattered—are beginning to sound calls for reorientation and renewal. Much more widespread and pervasive than the challenges to renewal is the growing sense of uneasiness with the deepening crisis of culture and of longing for answers of a spiritual and idealistic nature. Can anything be offered, will anything be offered, to fill this longing and bring about a transformation before our "pomp of yesteryear" becomes "one with Nineveh and Tyre"?

The militant secularism and religious indifference of the last decades have made our society suspicious of and hostile to any movement and every proposal that bears the label of traditional religion, especially Christianity. Now there are some indications—only hints for the moment, but growing—that disillusionment with the fading favors of a rotting sensate culture is causing people to abandon that suspicion and to become receptive to solutions that are identifiably Christian, not merely idealistic or spiritual in the vaguest sense of the term. Where conditions are most desperate (for example, in the prisons and the drug culture), specifically Christian enterprises have been first tolerated, then accepted, and finally enthusiastically endorsed.[8] As people become more aware that our overripe sensate culture is nearing disaster, it is not unreasonable to hope that large numbers of them will be willing to listen once more to the counsel and principles that brought about the great shift from moribund paganism to early Christianity sixteen hundred years ago.

---

[8] Two outstanding examples are Prison Fellowship founded by Charles Colson and the Teen Challenge ministry of David Wilkerson, both of which are now active in many different nations.

CONFUSION OR CONSENSUS?

It may be objected that the Christian world itself is in a state of deterioration and decay hardly less pronounced than that of the sensate society that we decry. Viewed superficially, this is true. Great interdenominational and interconfessional organizations such as the National and World Councils of Churches have degenerated into ineffectual promoters of tepid moral platitudes mixed with occasional efforts to endorse revolutionary and anti-Western movements here and there. It is hard to imagine society being galvanized or renewal ignited by the pronouncements of a Ralph Potter or Emilio Castro[9] or the machinations of COCU.[10]

That there is much confusion within the churches and defection from them cannot be doubted. However, it should be remembered that the early church not only suffered government persecution but had to battle and defeat several movements that would have totally changed its character, among them Gnosticism, Marcionism, and Arianism[11] (the latter being defeated only after the Emperor Constantine himself turned to Christianity). Christianity did not draw on the support of the state to defeat these challenges, for the first two were repelled while the emperors were still pagan and frequently persecuted the church; Arianism actually had the support of the emperors for a time and was put down by more vigorous theology, not by government force.

Christianity did not become the state religion until several decades later under another emperor.[12] Many historians and sociologists, Christians and non-Christians, look on the official establishment of Christianity as having hampered

---

[9] General Secretaries of the World Council of Churches.

[10] The "Church of Christ Uniting," a stalled effort to merge several American Protestant denominations.

[11] Gnosticism and Marcionism, two important second-century rivals to Christianity, taught among other things that the present world was not created by God but by a malevolent demiurge. Arianism was closer to orthodoxy but denied the deity of Jesus Christ, seeing in him instead an angelic being who had taken on humanity. See the treatment in my book, *Heresies. The Image of Christ in the Mirror of Heresy and Orthodoxy from the Apostles to the Present* (Garden City: Doubleday, 1984, and paperback, Grand Rapids: Baker, 1988).

[12] Gelasius I in A.D. 381.

rather than promoted the beneficial influence of Christianity's altruistic moral and social teachings on society at large, for as the church gained in wealth and prestige, it lost some of its early moral vigor. It was not the establishment of Christianity that made the sociocultural shift possible, for it was already in progress before Constantine; freeing the church from persecution accelerated the shift but did not cause it. Official establishment increased the political power of the church but probably diminished its moral influence. The ongoing transformation of the culture came through the teachers, preachers, and theologians, through the schools, universities, and hospitals.

It was under these circumstances that the deep conviction of the Christians—that the highest and indeed only real truth is the truth of God, who made us in his image and placed us here for a purpose—took hold and transformed society. Establishment is not necessary; indeed, it may be harmful. Even toleration, while preferable to persecution, is not altogether necessary. What is necessary is the shared conviction of large numbers of people that "it is He who has made us, and not we ourselves" (Ps. 100:3). What is necessary is to remember or to learn for the first time that we are not the blind products of time plus space plus chance, but we have a dignity that comes from God, a dignity that obliges us to respect and serve one another, to guard and protect human life and the earth that God has entrusted to us. What is necessary is to remember that we have been given a creative mission here on earth and that we must stand "in the judgment" when our tasks on earth are ended.

13

CRISIS AND RESOLUTION

From all that terror teaches, from lies of tongue and pen,
From all the easy speeches that comfort cruel men,
From sale and profanation of honor and the sword,
From sleep and from damnation, deliver us, good Lord.

G. K. Chesterton

WESTERN CIVILIZATION, including Russia and Eastern Europe, is a vastly complex structure of interrelated systems. At present, virtually every one of these systems is in crisis. People tend to be aware of the crisis in areas with which they are familiar. Physicians, nurses, hospital administrators, and patients are all painfully aware of the crisis in health care. Teachers and school administrators are very familiar with the crisis in education. Economists know of the economic crisis. Bishops, ministers, and denominational leaders know of the religious crisis. But not many people are properly aware of the full picture; these are not isolated problems that can be dealt with one by one. It is not merely a question of avoiding "facile but shallow artifices" in dealing with individual problems. Even sweeping and long-term measures that touch only one area at a time will not solve the problem, because it is a sickness diffused throughout the whole society, affecting every one of its aspects. Like a battleship with its hull pierced by several torpedoes, Western culture must inevitably sink unless not merely one or two holes but all of the holes are closed in time.

Among all of the systems that make up a sociocultural supersystem, the ones that do the most to shape and direct the others are the systems of truth. What does a society think is true, fundamental, irrefutable?

Western civilization was inspired by and built upon the Christian world and life view. Christian understanding of truth and of values created the ideational culture that replaced the declining sensate culture of the pagan Roman Empire. This culture was modified through the centuries, becoming first idealistic, then sensate, finally fully and degenerately sensate. At first the Christian value structure was totally dominant. Subsequently, its influence remained strong, despite the fact that other values came to be recognized alongside it. In the present phase of our culture, the sensate values have all but destroyed the idealistic remnants of the Christian system of truth. In the course of their triumph, the sensate values, which once appeared so magnificent and attractive when contrasted with the austerity of the ideational and idealistic phases, have become progressively more decadent. As increasingly larger segments of Western culture have sought after only those goods and pleasures that appeal to the senses, the consumption of consumer goods and luxuries has risen astronomically, but these things cannot fill the human heart with meaning, no matter how abundantly available or how avidly consumed.

The general level of satisfaction and human happiness did indeed rise with the transformation from the harsh world of early industrial capitalism to the compassionate society of the welfare states, but in the last analysis, the people in the welfare states become sated, bored, and unhappy. A sense of foreboding and impending doom affects ever broader segments of culture. The heritage of the Enlightenment, with its emphasis on individual freedom, has reached such an extreme that the normal conventions that enable people to relate to one another in a confident and trusting way are breaking down everywhere. Crime both calculated and gratuitous, fraud, deceit, and bribery in business, industry, and politics are becoming so common they attract the notice of almost no one but the victims themselves. This deterioration has proceeded faster in the United States than in Europe, and some of the extreme phenomena described here have not yet taken hold in Europe, but they are beginning to appear there as well. In Europe as well as in North America, art no longer creates beauty but is meant to shock. Horror, violence, sexual behavior of all kinds, and even bowel and bladder functions are presented on stage and screen and hailed by critics as brilliant and original. These phenomena undermine people's confidence in life and in the future.

In the United States there are special problems, for as a younger culture it is approaching the end of the sensate phase more rapidly than Europe. Education, from the grandest halls of ivy to the humblest preschools, has become preoccupied with teaching about variations and perversions of sexual conduct and providing the opportunities to practice them. The teaching of actual subject matter and intellectual and occupational skills is in decline. The Western intellectual and spiritual tradition, out of which the culture grew and which has sustained it until now, is at best ignored and more often derided and condemned.

Physicians, formerly respected as healers, are becoming suspicious and even menacing figures as members of the profession increasingly demand the freedom to solve difficult cases by interpreting the "full range of medical services" to include such life-ending measures as abortion and physician-assisted suicide. The news and entertainment media have perfected the technique of exposing each real and imagined flaw in public officials as soon as they take office, destroying every vestige of the moral authority that makes it possible for rulers to govern by persuasion rather than to rule by force and compulsion. With few exceptions, the leaders of the most prominent churches devote themselves not to telling people what to believe and how to live in order to know and serve God but to telling them what they do not need to believe and what rules of conduct they may break with impunity in order to fulfill themselves and serve their own base desires and lusts.

Under these circumstances, it might seem that Western civilization is on a downward spiral that cannot be checked. This is what *may* be the case, but it is not what *must* happen. What can prevent it from happening? Two factors are vital: grace and prudence. Grace comes only from God; it is not something that can we we can command, but it is something for which we can ask. Prudence, in the sense in which we need it, means the ability and the will to choose wisely when we have understood the situation and discerned the alternatives and their implications.

By saying that *grace* of a particular kind is the first necessary condition that must be fulfilled, we bring God into the situation. It is evident that a society that emphasizes the supersensory truths of faith will have a different orientation and make different choices from those made by a society that sees only those things that can be measured by the senses. C. P. Snow expressed it this way: "Jam today, or jam tomorrow." A sensate culture operates on the motto, "Eat, drink, and be merry, for tomorrow we die," and for that reason is unwilling to defer gratification even for a brief period of this life and certainly is not prepared to wait for its "jam" in a life to come.

The distressing symptoms evident in Western culture are visible on every hand and are impossible to deny. It is easy to dismiss an analysis of this sort as more doomsaying, which is gloomy and generally unpopular. This would be a mistake, for it is only by understanding the gravity and all-pervasiveness of the crisis that we can avert its worst consequences. We not only need an awareness of which roads lead to an abyss; we also need signposts pointing to "the sole course of salvation open to us."[1] Serious thinkers as well as broad masses of people were willing to think seriously about systems such as Marxism, even when efforts to implement them had failed; even as patently evil a system as Nazism could find its apologists among the intellectuals, at least initially. Is it too much to expect that the ideas and values that have actually created Western culture be given as fair a hearing as the alternative visions that have proved so destructive?

It is easy enough to describe the impact of the shift from supersensory to sensate values. The predicament of our society is evident on every hand; no one can deny the seriousness of our problems and of the dangers that lie ahead. Regardless of the reader's personal convictions regarding systems of truth, any reader ought to find much that makes sense in Sorokin's descriptions of our contemporary crisis, as well as in our sequel in the present work. We can neither create nor command the "grace of understanding." However, if there is any purpose and meaning in the existence of humanity on earth, then it is not unreasonable to hope for help in understanding it from the divine Mind that formed the purpose.

Basic orientations toward truth will inevitably influence the behavior of individuals and of societies. Skeptics and cynics may become heroes, but only

---

[1] Pitirim A. Sorokin, *The Crisis of Our Age*, 2d ed. (Oxford: Oneworld, 1992), 264.

serious believers become martyrs. Frequently, religious teachings and the practices based on them have beneficial effects on society in general, regardless of whether the teachings are accepted by all the members of society. It is not necessary to be a Muslim to recognize that Islamic fervor can make men fight more courageously and take more risks than would be likely if their highest values were those of utilitarian hedonism. It is not necessary to be a Roman Catholic to recognize that a Catholic is more likely to take and keep a vow of celibacy than a Jew or a Lutheran. It is not necessary to be an Orthodox Jew to recognize the benefits that kosher dietary and health regulations can bring to those who follow them. It is not necessary to be a traditional Christian believer to recognize that such a Christian will be more likely to interpret this analysis of cultural change as a call to spiritual revival than a skeptic or secularist will be.

The situation with respect to the entire culture resembles that of the value of Jewish dietary laws and Hippocratic maxims for good health. Very few people actually will follow them unless they belong to the community of belief. When there is no community of shared conviction, governments can seek to impose standards of behavior by law, but it is frequently a lost cause from the start. The governments of the United States and of several other countries wage vigorous war on cigarette smoking and other uses of tobacco. This has reduced smoking but has not prevented adolescents and adults from continuing to take it up. While this partially successful campaign is being waged, drug use, alcohol abuse, family breakup, and sexual practices that lead to the spread of syphilis, gonorrhea, AIDS, and a variety of other diseases go unchecked.[2]

A CAUTIONARY WORD

Pitirim Sorokin wrote as a Christian of Russian Orthodox background. He was extremely open and hospitable to the insights and ideals of all great world

---

[2] An illustration of both the impotence and idiocy of governments is the futile effort to promote the use of prophylactic condoms as though the availability of bits of latex could solve the medical, moral, social, and spiritual problems of disease and illegitimacy.

religions. His analysis and his hopes were not stated in terms of one tradition but appealed to all who are open to spiritual reality, who are aware of God. He has great appreciation for the ideational and idealistic aspects of all religions, and often sounds as though he might accept or even advocate a mixing of religions, rather as Arnold Toynbee did in his later years. The Christian bias and coloration of his thinking is not concealed, but it is not particularly intrusive. Indeed, more than once he refers to God by the unorthodox expression, the Infinite Manifold, suggestive both of pantheism as well as of the chaotic syncretism he condemns. If we recall Sorokin's criticism of chaotic syncretism, we will recognize that he was fully aware of the futile and destructive consequences of mixing mutually incompatible systems. It was apparent in a later work, *The Reconstruction of Humanity*,[3] that he looked forward to a religious renewal to resolve the crisis. He spoke of this renewal in general terms, at times writing as though he were unaware of the contradictions and clashes between the great religions of the world.

Sorokin's failure to come to terms with significant differences between the great religions is understandable. At the time he wrote, Christianity in its various forms was still the quasi-established religion of Western culture. To address the West in terms of religious awakening implied Christianity. It was not necessary to provide alternate versions of his vision adapted to the other religions nor to propose a scheme for reconciling their differences and encouraging mutual assistance. He seems hardly to have reckoned with the hostility of the secular mind (especially in the circles of government, learning, and the media) to traditional religion and its values.

Today the situation has changed throughout Western culture. In 1941 the West was aware of the other great traditions, but only one, Judaism, was well installed in Western lands. In the late 1990s there are two important differences: The first is that Western culture now is not only aware of Hinduism, Islam, and Buddhism but actually has many representatives of each living within its borders. There are immigrants from cultures where those religions reign as well as converts from Christianity or Western secularism. In addition

---

[3] Pitirim A. Sorokin, *The Reconstruction of Humanity* (Boston: Beacon Press, 1948).

to the traditional higher religions, there are many new religious movements, several of them gathered under the name of New Age.[4] These usually have less in common with Christianity than with ancient paganism or with one of the great Eastern religions. Thus it is no longer so easy to presuppose that when people hear the words *religious* or *spiritual renewal* today they will understand them in a Christian or even a Judeo-Christian sense.

The second major difference lies in the degree to which religion in general and Christianity in particular have been driven from their old positions of intellectual and social respectability in Western culture. It has become standard practice with most of the intellectual and entertainment elite to greet the pronouncements of the Pope or conservative Catholic bishops (even more so those of the so-called Religious Right and fundamentalists) with hostility and contempt; even politicians have become prudent about expressing religious faith in identifiably orthodox terms. Under these circumstances, it may be futile even to suggest that the culture in general, and not just its Christian component, ought to take a serious look at the possibility that it may be precisely a recovery of certain fundamental Christian principles—those that stimulated the renewal of late sensate Roman culture—that will enable our culture to experience a new dawn rather than a day of wrath.

The facts of the situation, the reality and pervasiveness of the crisis as described here, are undeniable. Whatever terminology one wishes to use, it is evident that all of Western culture has reached a critical juncture. There are no administrative, scientific, or technological innovations that could enable society to emerge from crisis without suffering systemwide catastrophes. "Facile but shallow artifices" can at best postpone a collapse, thereby making it all the worse when it finally arrives.

What conclusions can and should be drawn from these facts? If one takes the attitude of the late Michel Foucault, the philosopher who detested reason, God, society, and all that society calls knowledge, one might welcome the crisis in the expectation that it will destroy the repressive structures that we

---

4 Two useful books on this subject are Douglas Groothuis, *Understanding the New Age* (Downers Grove, Ill.: InterVarsity Press, 1986) and Peter Jones, *The Gnostic Empire Strikes Back: An Old Heresy for the New Age* (Phillipsburg, N.J.: P & R Publishers, 1992).

mistakenly think of as reason, culture, and justice.[5] Of course an attitude like Foucault's is not universal or even widespread among the common people of the various Western cultures, but, unfortunately, confronted with confusion, vacillation, doubt, and cowardice on the part of those who should be their intellectual and spiritual leaders, the common people are proving increasingly receptive to demagogues and the appeal of nationalism, xenophobia, and even racism.

This creates a difficulty that must finally be faced. Not only the committed Christian, but anyone who is willing to take biblical and Christian foundations of Western civilization seriously ought to be willing to consider proposals to make them once again an effective force for cultural healing and renewal. In the United States, one survey after another reveals that the majority of the American people generally remains favorable to religion and approves of the Christian principles that underlie American society and culture. The problem is that certain antireligious and anti-Christian biases among people in strategic positions effectively check this widespread sympathy for Christian civilization and frustrate every effort to help society preserve the Christian moral and cultural heritage, from the regulation of pornography to the presence of Christmas trees in public places.

In every nation of Western society, there are many who are hostile to Western culture and its traditions, even though few are as wildly destructive as

---

[5] Michel Foucault (1926–84) held one of the most prestigious chairs in philosophy in the world, at the Collége de France. An active homosexual who knew he had AIDS, he deliberately infected many other partners. The astonishingly radical nature of his rejection of virtually every standard that human beings have erected to separate themselves from barbarism and chaos is reflected in these lines: "We can't defeat the system through isolated actions; we must engage it on all fronts— the university, the prisons, and the domain of psychiatry—one after another, since our forces are not strong enough for a simultaneous attack. We strike and knock against the most solid obstacles; the system cracks at another point, we persist. It seems that we're winning, but then the institution is rebuilt; we must start again. It is a long struggle; it is repetitive and seemingly incoherent. But the system it opposes, as well as the power exercised through the system, supplies its unity." Michel Foucault, *Language, Counter-Memory, Practice*, ed. Donald F. Bouchard (Ithaca, N.Y.: Cornell University Press, 1977), 230.

It is characteristic of the end phase of Western sensate culture that the univeristy system attacked by Foucault gave him its most prestigious honors. He attacked all the distinctions on which civilization is based—the distinction between truth and falsehood, knowledge and ignorance, good and evil, sanity and madness—both in theory and in practice.

Foucault. They react critically or even angrily to serious mention of Christianity and automatically reject every measure or proposal to reintroduce practices, principles, or values that smack of that formerly dominant religion. Nevertheless, Christianity, although in a weakened and adulterated form, still continues to supply many of the values and decencies that are yet to be found among the peoples of the West.

For the reader who does not believe in the God of the Bible and who, therefore, does not expect any grace of understanding from that quarter, the analysis in this book may appear totally melancholy, pessimistic, and useless. Nevertheless, our analysis of current conditions and trends is based on actual data, on observations that anyone can repeat. This evaluation is no different from what a large percentage of mankind simply considers common sense, to the extent that they are not so intimidated by the opinion-makers and media elites that they dare not express even criticism, much less condemnation and disgust.

The present analysis will have value for the reader who sees the facts described here and is aware of where they are likely to lead us. It will have value for one who does not look to God or divine grace only if it can be supplemented by a proposal that does not depend on a specific Christian or other religious commitment. We frankly admit that it is not possible to make a serious proposal to those who think that the universe, this earth, the human race, and they themselves are but the accidental products, in the words of Jacques Monod, of chance and necessity, and that the human person is—to quote Oliver Wendell Holmes Jr.—of no more significance in the universe than a grain of sand or a baboon.[6] Is it necessary to be a believing Christian or an observant Jew or to embrace a similar religious view of man in order to think that we human beings possess a certain dignity that makes us deserving of protection and mutual respect? Can people agree that we share a creative mission and mutual duties here on earth even though not all see that mission and those duties in terms of a Creator who has made us in his image?

---

[6] It is another symptom of the crisis of our age to note that there are many among animal rights activists who think that baboons, who are few in number, are of more significance than humans, who are so many, and who pollute and degrade the environment with industrial development unknown among baboons.

Readers who reject religion in general or Christianity in particular as a foolish or dangerous superstition and are unwilling to think in terms of transcendent spiritual principles or values are mired in the sensate mentality and will have difficulty even understanding these proposals, much less accepting them, but they should be challenged to make the effort. The human mind, while hardly infallible, is capable of learning. It has taken Christian society centuries, but much of it has finally learned to reject intolerance toward other religions and to practice tolerance and charity. Surely it is not expecting too much to ask the sensate mind, which so glibly accuses religious people of narrowness and intolerance, to examine itself and ask whether it is not overlooking some significant benefits of ideational and idealistic thinking.

There is more to the ideational and idealistic outlook than mere opinion, fantasy, and prejudice. Everyone, not merely religious people, will be impoverished if the agony of our late sensate culture is allowed to run its course without any fundamental change of direction. Perceptive thinkers such as the late Allan Bloom, author of *The Closing of the American Mind*,[7] briefly awakened hundreds of thousands of readers to the problem, but virtually no one has suggested a way out of the impasse, for the simple reason that the way out depends on divine grace (as well as on human understanding), and divine grace is precisely the thing that our late sensate culture refuses to take into account.

Professional polls as well as everyday experience indicate that most of the people in the United States believe in God, although fewer think that the Bible really is God's Word to us. Is it possible to get from this vague, habitual assent to the convictions that once produced a vigorous idealistic culture back to the kind of commitments and decisions that can revive a degenerate sensate one?

No human society has ever been perfect, and none is likely to be given our understanding of human nature. While neither the bleak prospects of Aldous Huxley's *Brave New World* nor those of George Orwell's *Nineteen Eighty-Four* have yet befallen us, most readers will recognize that the possibility of mankind enslaving itself to political tyranny, technology, drugs, or some other

---

[7] Allan Bloom, *The Closing of the American Mind: How Higher Education Has Failed Democracy and Impoverished the Souls of Today's Students* (New York: Simon and Schuster, 1987).

freedom-destroying power is certainly not remote. If we ever thought that the solution to our problems must come from man alone, the experience of the secular Messiahs—Mussolini, Lenin, Hitler, Stalin, Mao, to name but five— teaches that unaided we are more likely to create a dystopia than anything resembling heaven on earth.

Whether or not one believes in the God of Scripture, it is undeniable that several systems that have systematically repudiated faith in him have made shipwrecks of themselves, destroying tens of millions of lives and immeasurable human happiness in the process. Against this background, it is not unreasonable to argue that even if faith in God cannot be proved, certain presuppositions that derive from that faith have permitted us to create and maintain a society worth having and to expect that they may still do so in the future.

It is an observable fact that there are people who are honest, idealistic, charitable, and altruistic although they do not subscribe to a definite religious faith nor even believe in God and immortality in a general way.[8] There always seem to be some people who possess a kind of natural nobility, just as there seem to be some who spontaneously adopt selfish, vile, cowardly, or debased patterns of behavior. Many people do seem to be able to live for nothing higher than the satisfaction of their own physical and emotional desires, but many cannot. Through all of the centuries of human experience, countless people, women and men, children as well as adults, have produced great effort, overcome great obstacles, sacrificed their goods and even their lives for the sake of others or for perceived ideals.

There are people who can live only for themselves and their own self-gratification. Nevertheless, many, many individuals have people, things, or ideals for which they willingly make great sacrifices, sometimes even giving their lives. As a general rule, most people exhibit the truth of the words of

---

[8] Immanuel Kant denied the possibility of proving the existence of God by the traditional rational arguments, but he then spoke of the existence of God, the immortality of the soul, and of the freedom of the will as "necessary presuppositions of practical reason." He contended that we humans are by nature moral beings and in order to be true to our nature must engage in moral reasoning. Moral reasoning in turn is possible only if we make these three assumptions about final realities. Rejecting these assumptions, as late sensate culture does, soon destroys our capacity for moral reasoning.

Moses, repeated by Jesus, "Man does not live on bread alone" (Deut. 8:3; Matt. 4:4 NIV). Man cannot live without bread, but bread alone, no matter how delicious or how plentiful, cannot satisfy the aspirations and longings of the human heart. When a society reaches the point of repudiating the concept of spiritual truths and ideal values, then all of its people are more or less forced to try to fill their spiritual needs with physical bread, and the result is increasing frustration and distress. Finally, when a sufficient number of people have suffered enough frustration and distress long enough, a prophet or prophets of one kind or another are sure to arise to point to higher values and worthier goals. It is important to ask ourselves what kind of prophet we are listening for and what values and goals we are willing to embrace.

FIRST GLEAMS OF DAWN

Sorokin predicted in 1941 that Western society would shortly begin to turn away from its preoccupation with material goods and physical pleasures and look again to the spiritual world. In the 1960s, the visionary Christian thinker Francis Schaeffer predicted that the closing decades of this century would be a time of "contentless mysticism." It is apparent that such a trend has begun. To some extent their predictions are being validated, for Western society is turning away from the greedy pursuit of the goods it consumes in such abundance and is beginning to cast about for spiritual guidance. The decisive question, at this stage of our cultural history, is not whether we shall become more spiritual, but what kind of spirituality we shall embrace. George Orwell and Aldous Huxley predicted "brave new worlds" of faceless, spiritless totalitarian tyranny. Paul Ehrlich predicted worldwide hunger and mass starvation. Hal Lindsay foresaw Armageddon, giving or at least hinting at dates for those catastrophes. So far, not one has proved right. Oswald Spengler, operating with a much broader perspective and viewing the entire sweep of human history, thought the demise of our culture unavoidable. Only Sorokin hoped that we are at the beginning of a transition to a new ideational or idealistic phase of civilization. The others have all proved wrong, at least so far. Will the few who hope turn out to be right?

Perhaps even a refreshed, sensitive, and confident Christianity cannot renew this sensate culture, but if it cannot, it is not easy to imagine what might do so. In the words of the Austrian sociologist Hans Millendorfer, "The future will be Christian, or it will not take place." To those who have suffered intolerance, discrimination, and abuse at the hands of hard Christians and their nominally Christian institutions, those words may sound menacing, but if the word *Christian* can be understood as pertaining to Christ, and if Christians in their majority can show that they know what that expression really means, then they will not be threatening but hopeful. Our culture is close to the end of a road but not necessarily at the end of the road. There is a way that leads to destruction, as Jesus said, but there is also a way that leads to life. The *dies irae* is a real possibility but not the only one; indeed, not even the most probable one, if indeed there is a God and he has a purpose for his human creatures. *Benedictus qui venit in nomine Domini.*[9]

---

[9] "Blessed is he who comes in the name of the Lord," a biblical text (Matt. 21:9) and the final words of Pitirim Sorokin's *The Crisis of Our Age.*

BIBLIOGRAPHY

Anderson, Olive. *Suicide in Victorian and Edwardian England*. Oxford: Clarendon, 1987.

Arendt, Hannah, *The Crises of the Republic*. New York: Harcourt Brace, 1972.

———. *The Origins of Totalitarianism*. New York: Harcourt Brace, 1968.

———. *The Human Condition*. Chicago: University of Chicago Press, 1958.

Benedict, Ruth. *Patterns of Culture*. Boston and New York: Houghton Mifflin Company, 1934.

Bennett, William John. *The Index of Leading Cultural Indicators*. Vol. 1. Washington, D.C.: Heritage Foundation and Empower America, 1993.

Bloom, Allan, *The Closing of the American Mind: How Higher Education Has Failed Democracy and Impoverished the Souls of Today's Students*. New York: Simon and Schuster, 1987.

Bruckberger, R. L. *La Révélation de Jésus Christ*. Paris: Grasset, 1983.

Carcopino, Jérôme. *Daily Life in Ancient Rome: The People and the City at the Height of the Empire*. Trans. E. O. Lorimer. New Haven, Conn: Yale University Press, 1940.

Coudenhove-Kalergi, Richard N. von. *Ethik und Hyperethik*. Leipzig, Germany: Der Neue Geist/ Peter Reinhold, 1922.

Darwin, Charles. *The Origin of the Species*. New York: Collier & Son, 1909.

Dobson, James. *Dare to Discipline*. Wheaton, Ill.: Tyndale House, 1987.

Edelstein, Ludwig, "The Hippocratic Oath" in *Supplements to the History of Medicine*. Vol. 1. Baltimore: Johns Hopkins, 1943.

Ehrlich, Paul. *The Population Bomb*. New York: Ballantine Books, 1968.

Ellul, Jacques. *The Political Illusion*. Trans. Konrad Kellen. New York: Random House, 1972.

Foucault, Michel. *Language, Counter-Memory, Practice*. Ed. Donald F. Bouchard. Ithaca, N.Y.: Cornell University Press, 1977.

Fromm, Eric. *Escape from Freedom*. New York.: Farrar & Rinehart, 1941.

Gates, Barbara T. *Victorian Suicide: Mad Crimes and Sad Histories*. Princeton, N.J.: Princeton University Press, 1988.

Glover, Terrot Reaveley. *The Conflict of Religions in the Early Roman Empire*. 10th ed., London: Methuen, 1923.

Groothuis, Douglas. *Unmasking the New Age*. Downers Grove, Ill.: InterVarsity Press, 1986.

Hertwig, Oskar. *Zur Abwehr des ethischen, des sozialen, des politischen Darwinismus*. Jena, Germany: Gustav Fischer, 1918.

Huxley, Aldous. *Brave New World*. New York: Harper & Brothers, 1950.

Jones, E. Michael. *Degenerate Moderns*. San Francisco: Ignatius, 1993.

Jones, Peter. *The Gnostic Empire Strikes Back: An Old Heresy for the New Age*. Phillipsburg, N.J.: P&R Publishers, 1992.

Lewis, C. S. *The Abolition of Man*. New York: Macmillan, 1953.

Lindsay, Hal. *The Late, Great Planet Earth*. Grand Rapids, Mich.: Zondervan, 1971.

Mead, Margaret. *Coming of Age in Samoa*. New York: Blue Ribbon Books, 1928.

Medved, Michael. *Hollywood vs. America*. New York: HarperCollins, 1992.

Olasky, Marvin. *The Tragedy of Christian Compassion*. Downers Grove, Ill.: Crossway, 1993.

Reich, Charles. *The Greening of America: How the Youth Revolution Is Trying to Make America Livable*. New York: Random House, 1970.

Rookmaaker, H. R. *Modern Art and the Death of a Culture*. Downers Grove, Ill.: InterVarsity Press, 1970.

Rostovtzeff, Michael. *Social and Economic History of the Roman Empire*. 2 ed. rev. Oxford: Clarendon Press, 1957.

Sandmann, Jürgen. *Der Bruch mit der humanitären Tradition* in *Forschungen zur neueren Medizin- und Biologiegeschichle*. Ed. Gunter Mann and Wener F. Kümmel. Stuttgart and New York: G. Fischer, 1990.

Schaeffer, Francis A. *The Collected Works of Francis Schaeffer*. 5 vols. Wheaton, Ill.: Crossway, 1982.

Schram, Glenn N. *Towards a Response to the American Crisis*. Fort Royal, Va.: Christendom Press, 1993.

Skinner, Burrhus Frederic. *Walden 2*. New York: Macmillan, 1976.

———. *Beyond Freedom and Dignity*. New York: Knopf, 1971.

Sorokin, Pitirim A. *The Crisis of Our Age*. 2d ed. Oxford: Oneworld, 1992; 1 ed., 1941.

———. *The American Sex Revolution*. Boston: Peter Sargent, 1956.

———. *Social and Cultural Dynamics: A Study of Change in Major Systems of Art, Truth, Ethics, Law, and Social Relationships*. 4 vols. New York: American Book Company, 1937–41.

Spengler, Oswald. *The Decline of the West*. Trans. Francis Atkinson. New York: A. A. Knopf, 1926–28.

Tocqueville, Alexis de. *Democracy in America*. Trans Henry Reeve. New Rochelle, N.Y.: Arlington House, 1966.

Toffler, Alvin. *The Third Wave*. New York: Morrow, 1980.

———. *Future Shock*. New York: Random House, 1970.

Toynbee, Arnold. *A Study of History*. New York: American Heritage Press, 1972.

Toynbee, Arnold, and Daisaku Ikeda. *Choose Life: A Dialogue*. Ed. Richard C. Gage. London: Oxford University Press, 1976.

INDEX